The Bush Theatre Book

Edited and introduced by Mike Bradwell

Methuen Drama

Published by Methuen 1997

Volume copyright © 1997 by Methuen
Mackerel Sky copyright © 1997 by Hilary Fannin
Caravan copyright © 1997 by Helen Blakeman
Introduction copyright © 1997 by Mike Bradwell
Contributors: copyright © Bush Theatre 1997;
copyright © Simon Callow 1997

The rights of the authors, editor and contributors to be identified as the authors of this work has been asserted by them in accordance with the Copyright, Designs and Patents Act, 1988

First published in Great Britain in 1997
by Methuen
Random House, 20 Vauxhall Bridge Road, London SW1V 2SA
and Australia, New Zealand and South Africa

Random House UK Limited Reg. No. 954009

A CIP catalogue for this book
is available from the British Library

Papers used by Random House UK Limited are natural, recyclable products made from wood grown in sustainable forests. The manufacturing processes conform to the environmental regulations of the country of origin.

ISBN 0 413 71320 2

Typeset by Deltatype Ltd, Birkenhead, Merseyside
Printed and bound in Great Britain by
Cox & Wyman Ltd, Reading, Berkshire

Caution

All rights whatsoever in these plays are strictly reserved and application for performance etc. should be made before rehearsals begin to: for *Mackerel Sky*: Casarotto Ramsay Ltd, National House, 60–66 Wardour Street, London W1V 4ND; for *Caravan*: Leah Schmidt, The Agency (London) Ltd, 24 Pottery Lane, London W11 4LZ. No performance may be given unless a licence has been obtained.

Contents

For Jim Hitchmough and Roy MacGregor

Introduction – The Bush Theatre, A Personal History

In June 1974 my touring company from up north, Hull Truck, were playing the Wythenshawe Forum Theatre, Manchester, with a show I devised called *The Knowledge*, which wasn't about what London taxi drivers have to have, but rather what you got when you became a devotee of the fat fourteen-year-old guru Mahara Ji.

I played a biker called Dooley who had seen a thing or two in the Merchant Navy. The plot, such as it was, revolved around the teleportation of a Stonehenge paperweight and a man who lived in a wardrobe. Howard Gibbins, then artistic director of the Bush, was coming to see the second night with a view to booking the show for a London run.

There wasn't a second night.

The show, which had been billed as 'a hippy whodunnit' proved too much for pre-'mad-for-it' Manchester – something to do with a line about a cunt in a bottle – and we were kicked out, despite a rave review from Robin Thornber in the *Guardian*, the only audience member left after the interval.

I phoned Gibbins. If he couldn't come to us perhaps we could come to him?

I arranged to perform the show as an audition for one Sunday night only. *Time Out* printed a short article. The theatre was packed and we got a standing ovation and a three-week booking for November.

I don't think it could happen today.

The Bush booking was a turning point in the history of Hull Truck. The show went very well. We were invited to devise a piece for BBC television but more importantly my twenty-three year love affair with the Bush had begun.

Between 1972 and 1974 the Bush produced or hosted seventy-seven productions. In those days the theatre was like a full-time Edinburgh fringe venue with morning shows, lunch-time shows, evening shows, late-night shows, cabarets, kids' shows, mime shows, nudity, fire eating, puppetry and perform-ing rats. So it was that, in the anything-goes spirit of the times, John Arden's political and allegedly libellous *Ballygombeen*

Bequest happily rubbed shoulders with Lindsay Kemp's *Pantomime Turquoise* and the undergraduate Tina Brown metaphorically went to bed with Mike Leigh (see chronology).

Writer in residence Andy Smith wrote everything from socialist cabaret to Punch and Judy kids' shows for Ken Morley. Sal's Meat Market, a comedy improvisation duo with Ray Hassett and John Ratzenberger (later of *Cheers*) shared a bill with the darkly impressionist *Travestie Aus Liebe* from Munich.

The only real discernible pattern that emerged over the early years was an undoubted commitment to the best of new writing including early works by Howard Barker, David Edgar, Franz Xaver Kroetz and Stephen Poliakoff.

Michael Wearing (now an executive at the BBC) was an early director; Antonia Bird (film director), an early stage manager; and Oscar-nominated Mike Figgis, a sound technician.

When Hull Truck arrived with *The Knowledge* we had been on the road for three years and had met largely with bafflement, apathy or downright aggression. Manchester was not the first time we had been run out of town. We knew instinctively that at the Bush we were among friends and the theatre became our London home for the next eight years.

In the summer of 1975 Peter Wilson and Howard Gibbins pitched a circus tent on the Green and produced Brecht's *Edward II* as part of the soggily titled 'Shepherd's Pie Festival'. I played Sid the Spiv in something called *Granny Calls the Tune*. Peter Nicholson, playing someone called Waldo Wheeze, was bitten by a dog. I imagine it served him right.

Stephen Poliakoff was rehearsing *City Sugar* with Lynn Miller and the incomparable John Shrapnel, sadly replaced when the show transferred to the West End. Hull Truck returned with both *Oh What* and *Bridget's House*.

Howard, Peter and Tim Albery left to be replaced by Simon Stokes, Dusty Hughes and Jenny Topper but not before Peter and I had plotted Alan Plater's stage adaptation of Bill Tidy's *Daily Mirror* cartoon strip *The Fosdyke Saga*.

If you're really lucky a show like *The Fosdyke Saga* comes round once or maybe twice in your career. There's some kind of special chemistry between the actors, the script and the audience which takes everybody elsewhere. Perhaps it was the sheer silliness of the whole thing that did it – Penny Nice inflating herself with a conspicuous foot pump while singing 'I'm a disenchanted maiden whom a rotter did besmirch . . .' Roger Sloman crushing Philip Jackson's bollocks in a slow-motion fight sequence played to the theme from *Shaft*. Jane Wood as Emeline Paulhurst whacking Milton Shulman with a rolled-up copy of the *Socialist Worker* . . . It doesn't sound like much, but believe me every night the audience cried with laughter and went home humming the tripe . . . you had to be there.

Life on the road with Hull Truck meant that there were large tour-shaped gaps in my Bush theatre-going, but highlights for me were Howard Barker's *Wax*, Sarah Pia Anderson and Sheila Kelly's meticulously devised pieces *Gin Trap* and *Blisters*, Robert Holman's *German Skerries* and Snoo Wilson's *Everest Hotel*, *The Soul of the White Ant*, *Vampire* and the fabulously ambitious *England, England*, a musical written with Kevin Coyne about the Kray twins.

By the end of the seventies, Jenny, Simon and Dusty, shortly to be followed by Nicky Pallot, established the new writing policy that the theatre maintains today.

Hull Truck toured in with *A Bed of Roses* and transferred to the Royal Court.

Kevin Elyot played a chair in Erik Brogger's *The Paranormal Review* and the Bush launched the careers of Jonathan Gems with *The Tax Exile* and Terry Johnson with *Amabel*.

But it was with Tom Kempinski's *Duet for One* that the Bush had its first major international success. The two-hander, with Frances de la Tour as a wheelchair-bound cellist and David de Keyser as her psychoanalyst, went on to win twenty-seven major awards including three for Best Actress for Frances de la Tour. The production went to the West End and Broadway and was eventually both televised and made into a feature film.

In 1980 Richard Wilson directed Alan Rickman in Dusty Hughes's *Commitments*, a wonderfully funny social satire about the Workers Revolutionary Party and firmly expressed everything I had ever felt about the Trotskyite Left. The WRP had been stalking Hull Truck for years and never forgave us for turning up at a 'Nationalisation without Compensation' rally dressed as the Tolpuddle Martyrs and singing 'I've got a brand new combine harvester'.

Still Crazy After All These Years was my last show with Hull Truck and a co-production with the Bush. Devised over twelve weeks, in stage manager Rick Carmichael's flat in Hammersmith Grove, the play was about four thirtysomething media types finding their sixties idealism headbutted by the Thatcher Revolution – or at least that's what it seems to be about in retrospect.

At the time it nearly killed us. Everyone got ill, previews were cancelled and I finally dictated the last scene to Nicky Pallot at five a.m. on the morning of the first performance before we crashed out on the dressing-room floor.

I directed three shows at the Bush in the eighties: – Doug Lucie's *Hard Feelings* – a mordant comedy about a bunch of ex-Oxford yuppies trying to ignore the Brixton riots with a terrific cast including my favourite actor Frances Barber and ex-Hull Trucker Chris Jury; Terry Johnson's *Unsuitable for Adults*, set in the world of alternative comedy and with a Geoff Rose set so lifelike that punters actually believed that we had converted the theatre into a pub and tried to buy drinks during the action; and *The Oven Glove Murders*, Nick Darke's acerbic take on the *Chariots of Fire* British cinema revival. For this show we opened the windows facing Goldhawk Road and built a set on the roof so it seemed as though Mark Wing-Davey fondling his Oscar was actually on the opposite side of the street. This stunt was entirely justified by the audience's terrified reaction as Tim Roth in mid-sentence nightly appeared to fall out of the window and plunge to his death below.

Sebastian Born had joined Simon, Jenny and Nicky as literary manager and they maintained an enviable record for discovering new talent with *Coming Clean* by Kevin Elyot, *Kate* by Danny Mornin, *Topokana Martyr's Day* by Jonathan Falla, *When I was a Girl I used to Scream and Shout* by Sharman Macdonald, *The Garden Girls* by Jacqueline Holborough, *Raping the Gold* by Lucy Gannon, *A Bright Room Called Day* by Tony

Kushner, and what was to become the first play in *The Wexford Trilogy*, *A Handful of Stars* by Billy Roche.

The gang of four also produced Beth Henley for the first time in this country with both *The Miss Firecracker Contest* and *Crimes of the Heart* and continued to work with the anarchic People Show. It was the People Show's *Whistle Stop* – a train journey with jazz and Trosky – that was playing at the time of the Great Bush Fire of 1987.

I remember hearing the seven o'clock news on the radio and dashing down to the theatre, shocked to see firemen and hoses and torrents of water spilling out of the blackened stage door.

In a remarkable show of solidarity the theatre community rallied round to support the Bush and the Tricycle Theatre in Kilburn which had burnt down a month earlier. Benefit performances were organised by the Lyric Theatre in Hammersmith, Hampstead Theatre, the Royal Shakespeare Company, the Regent's Park Theatre, and the West End cast of *When I was a Girl I used to Scream and Shout*.

Dallas Smith, Chris Jury, Laurence Bowen and I organised 'Raising the Roof', a fund-raising gala at the Royal Court and the Bush was back in business within six months.

Simon and Jenny departed, Jenny to run Hampstead Theatre and Simon to produce for Turnstyle Productions; and Nicky Pallot was joined by Brian Stirner.

In 1989 the Bush produced *The Fatherland* by Murray Watts, and Sally Nemeth's *Millfire* at the Riverside Studios in an experiment with larger spaces, but the real triumphs were at the Bush itself with Billy Roche's *Poor Beast in the Rain* and *Boys Mean Business*, the first play by Catherine Johnson.

Dominic Dromgoole became artistic director in 1990 and soon hit his stride with *The Evil Doers* by Chris Hannan and the weirdly wonderful *The Pitchfork Disney* by Philip Ridley and by directing the award-winning *Our Own Kind* by Roy MacGregor.

I directed Catherine Johnson's *Dead Sheep* with Gwen Taylor, Gary Love, Katrin Cartlidge, Kate Hardie, and the vertically challenged John Key. Geoff Rose's set included real turf, a running stream and a hydraulic mountain that appeared in a cloud of dry ice to the dwarfs' chorus from *Das Rheingold*.

Richard Cameron's *Pond Life* was the beginning of an

association that included *Not Fade Away*, *The Mortal Ash* and *All of You Mine*.

David Ashton was represented by *A Bright Light Shining*, *The Chinese Wolf* and *Buried Treasure*.

And in 1992 the Bush staged the full Wexford Trilogy of Billy Roche's *Handful of Stars*, *Poor Beast in the Rain* and *Belfry*, playing in repertory and touring Britain and Ireland, and culminating in performances in Billy's home town of Wexford.

Those who were there still speak in hushed whispers . . .

Jonathan Harvey's *Beautiful Thing* packed out the Bush, went on tour, and to the Donmar Warehouse before transferring to the Duke of York's and being made into a feature film.

Snoo Wilson's *Darwin's Flood*, declared unstageable by the National, proved to be no obstacle for designer Robin Don and the stage crew as the entire theatre appeared to sail down the Goldhawk Road every night.

Rough Magic and Bickerstaffe toured in from Ireland and Hired Gun arrived with Tracy Letts's remarkable white trash trailer park drama *Killer Joe* which transferred to the Vaudeville Theatre.

Dominic's six years as artistic director also introduced new writers Lucinda Coxon, Sebastian Barry, Jane Coles, Lesley Bruce, Naomi Wallace, Richard Zajdlic, Tamsin Oglesby, and Conor McPherson to Bush audiences and his final 'London Fragments' season of Simon Bent's *Goldhawk Road*. David Eldridge's *Serving it Up*, and Samuel Adamson's *Clocks and Whistles* was celebrated with a *Time Out* award.

And so now I'm artistic director of the Bush and it's the only job I've ever really wanted and it's also the best job in the world.

It's three o'clock in the morning and I'm trying to find a way to finish this piece in a way that accurately sums up, I suppose, my entire life in theatre and what I feel about the place and of course it's impossible . . .

Enda Walsh's *Disco Pigs* sold out tonight and is about to sell out its entire run and I started rehearsing today with a magic cast for Hilary Fannin's *Mackerel Sky* – and Helen Blakeman is casting *Caravan* – and I feel enormously privileged.

I said earlier that when Hull Truck played the Bush we felt

for the first time that we had come home, and editing this book
has confirmed for me how much a home the Bush is for so
many people.

And I mean Home . . .

Because we do New Writing and New Writers move on, it's
easy to think that the Bush is some kind of halfway house or
stepping stone to greater glories in the more obviously
commercial or more conspicuously subsidised sector, but it's
simply not true.

Everybody who has ever worked here over the years has
done so because they believe totally in what we do . . . This is
it. This is where we want to be and this is why we are as
important to the cultural health of the nation as the *Royal*
National Theatre, the *Royal* Shakespeare Company or the
Royal Court.

I don't think there will ever be a *Royal* Bush Theatre and
quite frankly thank fuck for that . . .

It may sound disingenuous, but we have no agenda
whatsoever apart from a profound belief in what we do.

New Writing is perceived as being at best difficult and at
worst unmarketable but this is palpably untrue.

Our audiences have a hunger for new stories and new ways
of telling them and I believe that the words of new writers and
the challenge of new plays hold in safe keeping the soul of the
nation.

We are necessary and we are here to stay.

I've missed hundreds of people out of the story and to them
I apologise. If they come to the Bush I'll buy them a drink – or
more likely they'll have to buy me a drink because, as usual,
we're skint.

The Bush is twenty-five years old – 'What a long strange trip
it's been.'

Mike Bradwell

1972

THE COLLECTOR by JOHN FOWLES

The Bush Theatre opened on Thursday 6 April 1972 in the upstairs dining-room of the Bush Hotel, Shepherds Bush Green. The room has previously served as Lionel Blair's dance studio.

The inaugural production was an adaptation of John Fowles's *The Collector* directed by and starring Bush Theatre founder Brian McDermott. The show was billed as 'prior to West End presentation'.

'Surely this remarkable, off-beat thriller must soon move to a West End Theatre . . . This could be a big hit.' *People*

'Mr McDermott often gets foreign parties coming to the Theatre by publicising it at Speakers' Corner . . . He has been warned by the police.' *Shepherds Bush Gazette*

'A German student leader yelling "filthy and disgusting" led his party of 40 out of a performance of *The Collector* at the Bush last week' *West London Observer*

The show toured to Bastian's Restaurant – Hampton Court.

THE BALLYGOMBEEN BEQUEST by JOHN ARDEN and MARGARETTA D'ARCY, presented by 7:84 Theatre Company

The Ballygombeen Bequest opened at the Bush Theatre on Monday. But at five p.m. on Wednesday the presenting company, the 7:84 Theatre Company, received a letter from Goodman, Derrick and Co., the firm of solicitors headed by Lord Goodman, acting for a Sussex estate agent and landlord Commander Richard Burges which threatened legal proceedings if the performance continued.

After taking legal advice the 7:84 company decided to agree with the request and the production was taken off.

A spokesman for Goodman, Derrick and Co. confirmed that proceedings for libel were being started against John Arden and his wife, Margaretta D'Arcy.

'*The Ballygombeen Bequest* is about a Connemara family threatened with eviction by an English landlord whose name is given as "Lt.-Col Holliday-Cheype". 7:84 administrator John McGrath stated: "The character was not intended to be Commander Burges, but he thinks it is ..."' *Daily Telegraph*

THE RELIEF OF MARTHA KING by DAVID PARKER

'Transsexual Play May Be Next At Bush. Artistic director, Brian McDermott, feels very strongly about the problems facing transsexuals and is thinking of going into Parliament to get the laws changed. One of his friends is probably the most well-known transsexual of them all, April Ashley, with whom he lived before she married the Hon. Arthur Corbett who is the future Lord Rowallan.' *Shepherds Bush Gazette*

'Arts Council Refuse Theatre Grant. So far the Arts Council has given no reason for its refusal. "It's a slap in the face for West London" says Bush spokesman Brian McDermott who stood as the unsuccessful "Actors Anti-Heath's Union-Bashing Act Candidate" in the recent Southall by-election.' *Chelsea Post*

FOR THE LOVE OF PIAF by MAGDALENA BUZNEA

'She stands a pitiful little figure on stage, unkempt and unbeautiful. Then she opens her mouth and sings – and all the sufferings of the poor vibrate in her powerful voice. She is Magdalena Buznea, daughter of a Romanian intellectual whose startling voice is known to thousands of London commuters, for until now her chosen "stage" has been the underground stations where she busks for a living.

Says Magdalena, whose life and loves closely reflect those of the little sparrow of the Paris streets:

'The theatre is in my blood and I have to sing and act until I die. I have to love too. Life without love is meaningless. I have had many loves in the search for the real love in life.'

Nick Newton, co-director of the experimental Bush Theatre, takes up Magdalena's story:

"She kept pestering us time and time again. In the end I gave her an audition."' *Daily Express*

CHRISTMAS CAROL by FRANK MARCUS

'Santa And The Call Girl. Leading advocate against stage nudity Mr D. Maxwell-Stimson has called for the play to be called off because the cast wore see-through costumes – "West Londoners are bored with nudity." The last play he opposed was *The Relief of Martha King* in which the cast wore plastic garments. "These days they have to introduce this sort of thing just to get a zip into the proceedings."' *Shepherds Bush Gazette*

'Actress Walks Out Over Nudity. Controversy over the Bush Theatre production in which an actress appears in the nude thickened this week – the actress got cold feet.' *West London Observer*

1973

'The Bush Hotel is now not so much a pub as an entertainment centre for the area. One established attraction within is, of course, the "Bush Theatre". But just to prove that "all the pub's a stage", the Variety Bar presents an Irish Showband Night (Thursdays) plus an additional "get 'em orff" female artiste on Sunday noons.' *Stage*

TEDDERELLA by DAVID EDGAR

'A welcome antidote to the present craze for Europhilia' *Guardian*

'The show casts Edward Heath as Cinderella left in the cold at the hour of the first European Ball and features drag artiste Jean Fredericks as Harold Wilson. David Edgar has written more than 20 plays . . . or "cartoon documentaries" as he prefers to call them.' *Evening Standard*

MY SISTER AND I by HOWARD BARKER

'. . . impudent social lampoon . . .' Jack Tinker, *Daily Mail*

'Liberating, no doubt, for those still in awe of the nob class'
West London Observer

IN TWO MINDS by DAVID MERCER

Became the basis for Ken Loach's film *Family Life*.

THE POPE'S WEDDING by EDWARD BOND

'. . . opens at the Bush Theatre for its second night in London
tonight. The first was eleven years ago when it had one Sunday
night performance at the Royal Court. Since then it has been
professionally neglected until John Dove revived it for the
Northcott in Exeter and it is his production that is transferring
to the Bush tomorrow with Alison Steadman and Bob Peck.'
Evening Standard

LIMBO by RICHARD DRAIN

'Personally I believe this is nonsense' Harold Hobson, *Sunday
Times*

THE MAGIC OF PANTALONE directed and devised by MARIA SENTIVANY

'There is an half hour interval when we adjourned to the bar to
see England held to a draw by Poland'. *City Press*

UNDER THE BAMBOO TREE by TINA BROWN

'Miss Brown (20) is definitely a name to watch'. M. Billington,
Guardian

'She is in London at weekends watching it take shape and back
at Oxford for the rest of the time working on her finals in
English Literature.' *Shepherds Bush Gazette*

'Above an Irish pub with all the horrors that entails, ladies
would be well advised to go there in a warm pair of trousers'.
Evening Standard

GOOD TIMES by ROY MINTON, directed by MARTY FELDMAN

'Marty Feldman worked for nothing.' *Stage*

1974

'The Bush Theatre is probably the best theatre on the London Fringe at the moment.' *Plays and Players*

OPERATION ISKRA by DAVID EDGAR

'Mr Edgar sets out to discover the causes of revolutionary violence. There are many better plays in London at the moment, but none that deals quite so cogently with our present discontents.' *Guardian*

FLOWERS by LINDSAY KEMP after JEAN GENET

'The demand for seats has been so high that the show's run has been extended by one week already and there are two performances every night.' *Time Out*

'The young hippy-style audience loved it' *City Press*

'Four Object to Nude Mime' *Evening News*

'In the tiny Bush Theatre in 1974 where I first saw *Flowers* sitting more or less next to David Bowie the show seemed to herald a new era; I timorously ventured on this page that this sort of thing might catch on.' Michael Coveney, *Financial Times*

Flowers transferred to the West End and Broadway.

DICK DETERRED by DAVID EDGAR, directed by MICHAEL WEARING

'While others moan the dearth of lively new plays, young David Edgar is spinning them out with varying success.' *Sunday Telegraph*

'In the first five minutes of the show we gather that Mr Edgar does not like Watergate; beyond that he has nothing to say.' Harold Hobson, *Sunday Times*

'Feliks Topolski – the great Polish artist whose Coronation mural hangs in Buckingham Palace – is to redecorate the Bush Theatre. "He is painting the whole of the Theatre for nothing – because he loves it" said Bush director Brian McDermott, whose future plans include a circus and a discotheque.' *West London Observer*

STALLERHOF by FRANZ XAVER KROETZ

Toured Britain and Germany, played at Edinburgh Festival, televised by Thames TV.

'Boorish Bavarians At The Bush . . . Kroetz is reckoned to be one of West Germany's leading playwrights. If it were true his theatre-going compatriots would surely be queuing up to defect to the East.' *Chiswick Times*

'It is difficult to refer to the work as a play – the word has connotations of entertainment.' *Spectator*

'*Stallerhof* presents defecation, masturbation, sexual intercourse, an attempted abortion and other acts calculated to rot the nation's moral fibre.' *Evening Standard*

Programme note:

'The Bush hopes to cushion the entire theatre – however at present can only afford one – The Square Black Cushion: These cushions cost £7 to make and another £1 to fireproof. If anyone would like to donate a cushion to the theatre we would be very grateful.'

THE TEMPORARY THEATRE COMPANY SEASON
JOHN AMIEL/JOHN CHAPMAN/STEPHEN POLIAKOFF/BRUCE ROBINSON/NIGEL WILLIAMS/ADRIAN SHERGOLD/TIM FYWELL/MIKE LEIGH present

4 NEW PLAYS BY 4 NEW PLAYWRIGHTS
THE CARNATION GANG by STEPHEN POLIAKOFF
ASIDES by ALAN DRURY
MARBLES by CHAPMAN/FYWELL/WILLIAMS
THE SILENT MAJORITY by MIKE LEIGH

'Mike Leigh could be described as a theatrical miniaturist; but he is a superb one, nevertheless, and a true artist, albeit in a minor key.' *Plays and Players*

THE KNOWLEDGE presented by HULL TRUCK THEATRE CO., devised and directed by MIKE BRADWELL

'*The Knowledge* takes an utterly frank look at contemporary life and spurts it into the theatre rich and raw.' *Guardian*

SAWDUST CAESAR by ANDY SMITH (writer in residence)

'Ken Morley as Widow Twanky – once seen never forgotten . . .' *Willesden Chronicle*

'Some very small children started wailing at the funnier moments.' *Stage*

1975

HITTING TOWN by STEPHEN POLIAKOFF

Toured to the Edinburgh Festival and later televised by Thames Television.

'Stephen Poliakoff has only just evolved from peascod into apple, but it is already apparent that he's a dramatist of talent and promise.' *New Statesman*

'It is without doubt the most exciting voice in the theatre since the equally honest, precocious birthcry of Christopher Hampton.' Frank Marcus, *Sunday Telegraph*

Director Tim Fywell won the Binkie Beaumont Award for this production.

'Cash Crisis Could Close Theatre. The Bush is £7000 in the red and may have to close early in the new year unless further funding is found . . .' *Shepherds Bush Gazette*

WHITE MEN DANCING by DAVID GALE and HILARY WESTLAKE, performed by LUMIERE AND SON

'White rats scurry around the ears trapped in a miniature network of tunnels tricked out with tiny coloured lights. The plague is coming, a spaceman hoves into view and opens his veins with a chunk of bread. The Black Death enters and ravishes a very attractive naked young girl. She gives birth to a box. The rats nibble at her breasts . . . An old lady old enough to be my aunt laughed herself silly in front of me.' M. Coveney, *Financial Times*

OH WHAT presented by HULL TRUCK THEATRE CO., directed and devised by MIKE BRADWELL

'I predict Hull Truck will proceed on a triumphant journey. Leaving the theatre, the customers in the Irish pub downstairs stood around the television watching the big match. They looked less real than the actors upstairs'. Frank Marcus, *Sunday Telegraph*

SHEPHERD'S PIE 'A Festival Hot Pot' on Shepherds Bush Green included EDWARD II by BERTOLT BRECHT performed in a circus tent

'King Edward battles juggernauts and wins.' *Acton Gazette*

The production toured to Oxford and Lincoln.

CITY SUGAR by STEPHEN POLIAKOFF

Transferred in 1976 to the West End.

'Without pretensions or glib solutions, Stephen Poliakoff shouts a warning at us that is both loud and clear. We ignore it at our peril.' *Sunday Telegraph*

'Human dignity (it seems) can survive, in spite of everything, even in Leicester' *Daily Telegraph*

Lynn Miller won the Most Promising Actress Award in *Plays and Players* magazine for her performance in *City Sugar*.

MR PUGH'S PUPPETS

'Mr Pugh has toured his one-man puppet show throughout Europe and is supposedly one of the best exponents of glove theatre – I should hate to have to sit through the worst!' *Time Out*

'Critics have acclaimed the Bush Theatre as the finest fringe venue in town' *Shepherds Bush Gazette*

1976

EVEREST HOTEL by SNOO WILSON

'A free-wheeling bash at every creed that has ever aimed to improve the human condition from Christianity to Communism, omitting, as far as I can see, only the provision of fluoride in drinking water.' *Jewish Chronicle*

GEISTERBAHN by FRANZ XAVER KROETZ

'*Wozzeck* without the jokes . . .' John Peter, *Sunday Times*

THE SOUL OF THE WHITE ANT by SNOO WILSON

'Snoo Wilson is as good a 100% antidote to Athol Fugard as you're ever likely to get . . . He can shift more themes and characters at one move than most playwrights, and when the Fringe is as good as this it is as good as anything.' *Time Out*

LADYBIRD, LADYBIRD by DAVID POWNALL, a PAINES PLOUGH PRODUCTION

'One of the finest, most moving and poignant productions ever staged at the Bush.' *Acton Gazette*

'I can only indicate the quality of the evening by suggesting that it is like reading Tennessee Williams under water.' Michael Coveney, *Financial Times*

JUVENALIA adapted by RICHARD QUICK from the satires of Juvenal – recorded for *Omnibus*, BBC TV

'Simon Callow – a foul-tempered Woody Allen – is one of the most imposing new talents on the British Stage.' Ned Chaillet, *The Times*

THE NAKED OBSESSIONS OF JOHN DOWIE AND THE BIG GIRL'S BLOUSE

'They make the New York Dolls look like Kloset Kweans who've lost the key.' *Sounds*

BRIDGET'S HOUSE presented by HULL TRUCK THEATRE CO., devised by MIKE BRADWELL

'In its devastatingly sharp social comments it gives one of the most withering and accurate ideas of a lost generation I have seen.' Nicholas De Jongh, *Guardian*

THE FOSDYKE SAGA by ALAN PLATER and BILL TIDY

'Recalls Joan Littlewood in her heyday' John Barber, *Daily Telegraph*

'A show that restores faith in the British Theatre' Albert Hunt, *New Society*

'*The Fosdyke Saga* has set British political theatre back by 20 years' David Edgar

The Fosdyke Saga transferred to the ICA theatre and was subsequently televised by BBC TV.

1977

GERMAN SKERRIES by ROBERT HOLMAN

'Once again the Bush has found a small gem and polished it to perfection.' *Plays and Players*

Winner of the George Devine Award

VAMPIRE by SNOO WILSON

'I gladly offer £10 for the most convincing explanation of why

Vampire is so entertaining and what it is about. Answers on a postcard please. Friends of Snoo Wilson and Bush employees need not apply.' John Ashford, *Time Out*

HAPPY YELLOW by TINA BROWN

'English girl goes to New York and is forced rather quickly to come to terms with American life' *Shepherds Bush Gazette*

PSYCHOSIS UNCLASSIFIED adapted by KEN CAMPBELL from *SOME OF YOUR BLOOD* by THEODORE STURGEON, presented by the Science Fiction Theatre of Liverpool

'If anyone tries to tell you what the play is about, stop them or they will spoil the most startling eight words ever spoken at the conclusion of the first act.' *Time Out*

PILLION by PAUL COPLEY

'All involved are responsible for a beautiful heartwarming piece of work.' Michael Coveney, *Financial Times*

'Paul Copley's *Pillion* . . . shows the writer's in-depth knowledge of the motorcycling fraternity in the West Riding of Yorkshire.' *Brentford and Chiswick Times*

ENGLAND, ENGLAND – a musical by SNOO WILSON and KEVIN COYNE about the Kray Twins, starring BOB HOSKINS and BRIAN HALL and presented at the Jeanetta Cochrane Theatre

'If these villains are England – then I'm Commander Daphne Skinner.' Nicholas De Jongh, *Guardian*

WRITER'S CRAMP by JOHN BYRNE

The Life and Times of Francis Seneca McDade
produced in conjunction with the Nitshill Writing Circle

'The evening is a solid heap of laughter that I can't recommend too highly.' Michael Coveney, *Financial Times*

'This is called a rave review and you should all form an orderly

queue around Shepherds Bush Green and tell the management
that Steve Grant sent you.' *Time Out*

Originally produced at Edinburgh Festival, toured Holland
and remounted at Hampstead Theatre in 1980.

FOSDYKE TWO by ALAN PLATER and BILL TIDY

'The most enjoyable single experience you are likely to find
this side of the Salford Rat Museum.' *Time Out*

Both *The Fosdyke Saga* and *Fosdyke Two* toured major Tripe
Centres in Britain and Holland.

1978

A BED OF ROSES presented by HULL TRUCK THEATRE CO., devised by MIKE BRADWELL

'Moving, hilarious, shocking and acted by a cast who are as
talented as any cast in London. This show must be seen,
especially by all non-believers in theatre.' *Time Out*

Transferred to the Royal Court Theatre.

IN AT THE DEATH, a revue by RON HUTCHINSON, KEN CAMPBELL, SNOO WILSON, DUSTY HUGHES and VICTORIA WOOD

'One of the funniest shows at present in London . . . Miss
Wood is a real discovery of whom more is certain to be heard
both as a writer and performer . . . Director Dusty Hughes, the
Diaghilev of Goldhawk Road' Robert Cushman, *Observer*

'Victoria Wood – a major talent in a minor area.'
Elkan Allan, *Sunday Times*

THE TRANSFIGURATION OF BENNO BLIMPIE by ALBERT INNAURATO

'A terrific performance from Robbie Coltrane as the weighty
hero' Michael Billington, *Guardian*

'Fat play stinks' headline in *Richmond & Twickenham Times*

A GREENISH MAN by SNOO WILSON

'One of the best constructed pieces I have seen for a long time. I recommend the evening warmly.' B.A. Young, *Financial Times*

Televised by BBC TV.

THE DALKEY ARCHIVE adapted by ALAN McLELLAND from the novel by FLANN O'BRIEN

'As Mr Joyce might have said, turn again, away, along, run for the golden speckled show, to the Bushrun.' Aine Ni Ferran, *Time Out*

Toured to Long Wharf Theatre, USA.

1979

THE PARANORMAL REVUE by ERIK BROGGER

'The best joke against the Great Beyond since Noel Coward's *Blithe Spirit*' John Barber, *Daily Telegraph*

THE TAX EXILE by JONATHAN GEMS

'. . . is one of the best new plays the fringe has produced in a long time . . . An unfashionably fashionable play which should on no account be missed.' Steve Grant, *Time Out*

'It is very funny, sparklingly performed and should prove to be an instant hit with bourgeois audiences.' *Jewish Chronicle*

Winner of the George Devine award

AMABEL by TERRY JOHNSON

'A new and very young writer, Mr Johnson, has provided a fascinating embryonic text.' Nicholas De Jongh, *Guardian*

'Mr Johnson has a lively sense of dialogue and some good theatrical ideas.' *Daily Telegraph*

THE PEOPLE SHOW No. 82 – *JIM'S GYM*

'An impressionist's portrait of seedy humanity as dotty and elusive as any Seurat.' *Guardian*

1980

DUET FOR ONE by TOM KEMPINSKI

'. . . is one of the most deeply satisfying plays that I have ever seen. It's a bit early I suppose to compare Kempinski with Pinter and Stoppard but in this play he shows a maturity and insight so rare as to be nearly miraculous . . . *Duet for One* is a major play that deserves to be played for months if not years in the West End.' Sheridan Morley, *Punch*

'The Bush only seats a few more people than a London Bus but with plays like *Duet for One* it ought to be clear that this theatre has picked up the ball long since dropped by fumbling commercial managements.' Ned Chaillet, *The Times*

Winner of twenty-seven Drama Awards including Best New Play. Frances de la Tour won three awards for best actress.

The production transferred to the West End and Broadway (with Max von Sydow and Anne Bancroft)
Feature Film (with Alan Bates and Julie Andrews)

THE ESTUARY by ROBERT HOLMAN

'It's as if the entire works of Eugene O'Neill were being inscribed on the back of a postage stamp.' *Guardian*

COMMITMENTS by DUSTY HUGHES

'Dusty Hughes in his first full-length play has provided one of the most literate and intriguing meditations on the British Left since Trevor Griffiths's *The Party* . . . magnificently acted, particularly by Alan Rickman as Hugh, this is a really superior writing debut.' Steve Grant, *Time Out*

Commitments was subsequently televised by BBC TV as a 'Play for Today'.

LONE STAR and *PRIVATE WARS*, two one-act plays by JAMES McLURE

'The scale of the accomplishment by West End standards could be counted heroic. For a Pub Theatre in Shepherds Bush it is stupendous. I do not exaggerate, James McLure is kin to Joe Orton and Tennessee Williams.' Stan Gebler Davis, *Evening Standard*

'Mr McLure's dialogue is the funniest, sharpest and zingiest currently to be heard in any London theatre.' Michael Billington, *Guardian*

Lone Star and *Private Wars* returned by popular demand in January 1981.

MEAN STREAKS by ALAN WILLIAMS produced by HULL TRUCK THEATRE CO.

'Ruthless, honest, thought-provoking and sad' *Guardian*

'A shambling recital of puerile, unreal and totally vulgar scenes not even linked by the palest shadow of a plot' *Scunthorpe Star*

SHE WAS ONLY A GROCER'S DAUGHTER BUT SHE TAUGHT SIR GEOFFREY HOWE by ANDY HAMILTON and ALISTAIR BEATON

'BUSH SATIRE SHELVED. Mystery surrounds the shelving of a new production by top London Fringe venue the Bush Theatre, abandoned just nine days before the scheduled month's run . . . The difficulty seems to have been getting Art to prove funnier than Life.' *Shepherds Bush Gazette*

1981

THESE MEN by MAYO SIMON

'The best thing this week was undoubtedly *These Men* by the American writer Mayo Simon at the Bush Theatre. It would go well in a small West End theatre. Unfortunately there seems to be a rule that such theatres are only allowed to purvey tripe. The fact that this piece is not tripe may tell against it.' James Fenton, *Sunday Times*

'One of the great contributions to Civilisation of the Women's Movement is that girls are now as vulgar and undiscriminating in their sexual tastes as men.' Milton Shulman, *Evening Standard*

THE LAST ELEPHANT by STEPHEN DAVIS

'I fear that if I go on describing the plot of Stephen Davis' *The Last Elephant* I shall probably be carted away by strange men in white coats.' Michael Billington, *Guardian*

STILL CRAZY AFTER ALL THESE YEARS devised by MIKE BRADWELL – a co-production with HULL TRUCK THEATRE CO.

'It is a model for how a small play designed for a small stage can be a great deal bigger than most in the West End.' Chris Hudson, *Evening Standard*

1982

THE NUMBER OF THE BEAST by SNOO WILSON

'Where is now the master? cry the little crazy boys. He is dead! He is shamed! He is wedded! and their mockery shall ring round the world' *Liber Cordis Cinci Serpente* 11.35

'Disturbingly ugly' *City Limits*

'A shining advert for the quality and commitment to be found on the so-called Fringe' *What's On*

AMERICA–AMERICA season

DEVOUR THE SNOW by ABE POLSKY

'On the first night it was received in the pin-drop silence almost never heard in playhouses now. *Devour the Snow* is unmissable.' *Herald Tribune*

THE MISS FIRECRACKER CONTEST by BETH HENLEY

'It is a fascinating and unusual play, dense with grotesque and bizarre detail, but conveyed with a deep compassion as each character unfolds their dreams and nightmares. I loved it.' Suzie Mackenzie, *Time Out*

COMING CLEAN by KEVIN ELYOT

'An impressive debut ... I expect that in time, it will be recognised as the first mature play about homosexuality.' *Mail On Sunday*

'Male Nudes Bring Blush to the Bush' headline in *West London Observer*

Kevin Elyot won the Samuel Beckett Award.

1983

HARD FEELINGS by DOUG LUCIE, in conjunction with OXFORD PLAYHOUSE

'At the Bush *Hard Feelings* is a marvellous social comedy by Doug Lucie that will make you twitch and wriggle with discomfort at every horrible moment of recognition ... It leaves you quite literally panting for more.' *Time Out*

'Frances Barber – the Catherine the Great of Acre Lane.' *The Times*

'Lucie is a writer to watch and *Hard Feelings* is a play to see NOW.' *Herald Tribune*

Hard Feelings was televised as a BBC 'Play for Today'.

KATE by DANIEL MORNIN

'Daniel Mornin's first full-length play has considerable promise of a writer with originality and impressive purpose.' R.B. Marriott, *Stage*

CRIMES OF THE HEART by BETH HENLEY

'It may not sound like a comedy, but *Crimes of the Heart* is one of the most delightful in London. This prize-winning hit from Broadway has an un-Broadway freshness which would and should grace a West End theatre.' John Barber, *Daily Telegraph*

'A scoop for the tiny Bush which won the British rights against strong competition from the Royal Shakespeare Company.' *The Times*

TOPOKANA MARTYR'S DAY by JONATHAN FALLA

'Both frightening and funny . . . the most interesting piece of new writing for months.' *Sunday Times*

'A first rate first play' *Time Out*

'Feathers were ruffled at the Bush Theatre when the company's star chicken swallowed a large elastic band. The chicken, who played the starring role of Wanka in the Shepherds Bush Green-based company's production of *Topokana Martyr's Day*, swallowed the band shortly before one of her evening performances. In the event nothing happened. Wanka appeared on stage as usual and, as far as anyone knows, the elastic band went through her system without discomfort or disturbance.' *Shepherds Bush Gazette*

Jonathan Falla won the Most Promising Playwright award in *Plays and Players*.

Topakana Martyr's Day was subsequently staged at the Los Angeles Actors Theater starring Herman's Hermit's Peter Noone.

TURNING OVER by BRIAN THOMPSON

'This is a play for anyone who has ever thought that India was the answer to anything. It deserves a vastly longer run than its current month at the Bush.' *Time Out*

'I can only recommend a visit to this hilarious and brilliantly performed show.' Irving Wardle, *The Times*

1984

UNSUITABLE FOR ADULTS by TERRY JOHNSON

'The Bush strikes lucky more often than any fringe theatre has a right to.' Martin Hoyle, *Financial Times*

'A superb and unmissable evening's theatre.' Steve Grant, *Time Out*

PROGRESS by DOUG LUCIE

'. . . what must be one of the best plays produced at the Bush. A small, anguished, hilarious masterpiece.' Chris Hudson, *Evening Standard*

'A vicious satirical comedy, as appallingly funny as anything Mr Lucie has written.' *The Times*

WHEN I WAS A GIRL I USED TO SCREAM AND SHOUT by SHARMAN MACDONALD

'This is a gem of a play, funny, truthful and skilfully crafted' *Evening Standard*

'This remarkable first . . . a beautifully acted document of a daughter's relationship with her mother.' *Financial Times*

'One of the freshest things of its kind since *A Taste of Honey*' *Observer*

Sharman MacDonald won the *Evening Standard* Most Promising Playwright Award and the Thames Television Playwright Award. The play was subsequently performed at the Edinburgh International Festival and in the West End.

1985

'If you had to choose one London theatre for which to buy a season ticket, the Bush would be it.' *Cosmopolitan*

CALIFORNIA DOG FIGHT by MARK LEE

'One of those experiences that renew one's faith in theatre.' Carole Woddis, *City Limits*

RUMBLINGS by PETER GIBBS

'Makes the debut of yet another highly promising writer at the indispensable Bush Theatre' *Guardian*

KISS OF THE SPIDER WOMAN by MANUEL PUIG

'Simon Callow – a Pagliacci of the Pampas' *Observer*

'. . . is one of the best plays I've seen for a long time' *What's On*

THROUGH THE LEAVES by FRANZ XAVER KROETZ

'I came out, as so often from London's most consistently enterprising theatre, knowing a little more about humankind.' *Punch*

A PRAYER FOR WINGS by SEAN MATHIAS

'Intriguing to see Prince and Princess Michael of Kent squatting in the back row of the Bush Theatre.' Michael Billington, *Guardian*

'There can be no better play in the City . . . a magnificent tale of female heroism.' *Daily Mail*

1986

WATCHING by JIM HITCHMOUGH, a Liverpool Playhouse production

'Entertaining, witty, perfectly played, it comes at a time when too many West End comedies seem old and tired.' *The Times*

Watching subsequently became a long-running television comedy series.

MAKING NOISE QUIETLY by ROBERT HOLMAN

'There is a small miracle happening each evening at the Bush . . . one of the most devastating, heart-rending moments I've witnessed on stage. The lives of the characters – and those of the audience – will never be quite the same again.' *Punch*

Nominated for the Kenneth Tynan Award for Outstanding Achievement – Olivier Awards

THE GARDEN GIRLS by JACQUELINE HOLBOROUGH

'The Bush never lets its audience or its writers down, and on this occasion, dealing with the shocking and much misinterpreted area of criminal women, it opens up the whole prison issue for more informed, and compassionate debate.' *Tribune*

Thames TV Writers Award
Time Out Best Play Award
Time Out Best Actress Award to Maggie McCarthy
Time Out Award for Creative Use Of Design

1987

MORE LIGHT by SNOO WILSON

'Confirms his position as the *enfant terrible* of the British Theatre.' *Observer*

'Laced with wit and bizarre invention *More Light* is a dazzling theatrical puzzle that amuses by the profligacy of its ideas and the irreverence of its theories.' *Evening Standard*

PEOPLE SHOW No. 92 – *WHISTLE STOP*

'People who need the People Show are the luckiest people in the world' *City Limits*

In the early hours of 2 June, during the run of *Whistle Stop*, the theatre was gutted by fire.

Manager Saves Staff As Blaze Wrecks Theatre' headline in *Shepherds Bush Gazette*

The next show scheduled was *Effie's Burning* by Val Windsor.

The previous month the Tricycle Theatre in Kilburn had burnt down. The show playing at the time was called *Burning Point*.

A Public Appeal for £50,000 was launched and the theatrical community rallied round. Benefit performances were organised by the Lyric Theatre, Hammersmith, Hampstead Theatre, the Royal Shakespeare Company, the Regent's Park Open Air Theatre and the West End company of *When I was a Girl I Used to Scream and Shout*. A fund-raising Gala at the Royal Court Theatre raised over £10,000 for the joint Bush/Tricycle Rebuilding Fund. Artists taking part included Robbie Coltrane, Emma Thompson, John Fortune, Alan Bennett, Griff Rhys-Jones, Simon Callow, Prunella Scales, Timothy West and the casts of *Serious Money*, *The Amen Corner* and *Bouncers*.

EFFIE'S BURNING by VALERIE WINDSOR was presented at the Offstage Downstairs.

MYSTERY OF THE ROSE BOUQUET by MANUEL PUIG was presented at the Donmar Warehouse.

TATTOO THEATRE by MLADEN MATERIC was presented by the Open Stage 'Obala' Company from Sarajevo at the Almeida Theatre in conjunction with the ICA and the Richard Demarco Gallery.

'One of the most beautiful, heart-twisting pieces that I have ever seen.' *Time Out*

The theatre reopened again on 27 October 1987 with *It's A Girl* by JOHN HARDING and JOHN BURROWS.

'The Wet Paint signs were hastily removed even as press and public milled at the door. London's Best Loved Pub Theatre is back in business.' *Financial Times*

DREAMS OF SAN FRANCISCO by JACQUELINE HOLBO-ROUGH

'Genuine feminist theatre. It has the rare grace and wit to see the pitfalls of segregation in art – or anything else – and both to

make fun and delve deep – fresh and illuminating.' Michael
Coveney, *Financial Times*

Thames TV Best Play Award
Thames TV Best Production Award
Drama Magazine Award to the Bush Theatre for Special
Achievement

'Jenny Topper, Nicky Pallot and the recently departed Simon
Stokes, the three musketeers who for a decade have been
producing work to the highest level . . .' Michael Billington,
Vogue

1988

A HANDFUL OF STARS by BILLY ROCHE

'. . . a first-class debut and yet another find for the management of the Bush.' *Spectator*

'Billy Roche's *A Handful of Stars* is a highly promising first play
. . . I have a hunch that Mr Roche is a stayer.' Michael
Billington, *Guardian*

Plays and Players Award for Most Promising Playwright
Thames TV Award for Best Play
The John Whiting Award

RAPING THE GOLD by LUCY GANNON

'This is a work of outstanding talent.' *Sunday Times*

'In the past two years new work at this theatre has been of so
consistently high a standard that a critic considers himself lucky
when his turn comes to review the latest play here.' *The Times*

Plays and Players Award for Most Promising Playwright
London Fringe Awards to Paterson Joseph for Best Actor

A BRIGHT ROOM CALLED DAY by TONY KUSHNER

'The Bush's sizzling production of Tony Kushner's highly
theatrical play' *Stage*

HEART THROB by CAROLINE HUTCHINSON

'The Bush is back on form with *Heart Throb*, a smashing, funny, well-written and painfully sad play.' *Observer*

1989

THE FATHERLAND by MURRAY WATTS, presented at the Riverside Studios

'There are several moments when, as in the finest Chekhov productions, one finds oneself laughing at the characters through a haze of sympathetic tears.' *Daily Telegraph*

LWT Plays on Stage Award

UTOPIA by CLAIRE MACDONALD and PETE BROOKS

'Something of great interest is happening here. You can actually see new theatre writing pushing out the boundaries and testing itself against physical form. The future beckons. I expect great things.' *Financial Times*

THE MARSHALLING YARD by TED MOORE

'Theatres that are producing work like Ted Moore's need to be championed and succoured; if not we will wake up one morning and discover that there is no longer a theatre to be proud of, merely a museum piece that might as well be covered in concrete along with the Rose.' *Time Out*

BOYS MEAN BUSINESS by CATHERINE JOHNSON

'This is blisteringly well written stuff, with smashing performances all round.' *City Limits*

Thames TV Award

POOR BEAST IN THE RAIN by BILLY ROCHE

'The piece conveys the quality of a legend and its comic dialogue is brilliant.' *The Times*

'Pulsing with both force and pathos of thwarted energies this betting shop drama is a winner of a play.' *Independent*

Winner of the George Devine Award
Thames TV Award for Best Play
Thames TV Award for Best Production

1990

MILL FIRE by SALLY NEMETH, presented at the Riverside Studios

'Nemeth's subject is pain, whose precise causes may never be known, and she draws its map like a cartographer of Hell.' *Sunday Times*

THE EVIL DOERS by CHRIS HANNAN

'Chris Hannan's beautifully written excursion into the back streets of Glasgow life ... Gut tugging comedy.' *Time Out*

Winner of *Time Out* Best Play Award
Winner of Charrington Best Play Award

DANCING ATTENDANCE by LUCY GANNON

'Lucy Gannon is undoubtably one of Britain's most promising playwrights. In her new play, performed at the venue which has nurtured her talent, she reveals an even stronger ability to draw convincing human drama with a poignant message.' *This Is London*

'This excellent bitter and funny play brings out the best in the Bush.' *Independent*

1991

THE PITCHFORK DISNEY by PHILIP RIDLEY, presented by TRYSTERO PRODUCTIONS

'. . . studded with dark jokes and images of shocking beauty *The*

Pitchfork Disney is a modern day version of *Babes in the Wood* seen through an East End gothic lens.' *TNT Magazine*

'. . . tingles with nightmares and obsessional fungi and seems to catch some garish spirit of the age' *Observer*

OUR OWN KIND by ROY MacGREGOR

'A fine debut for MacGregor and Dominic Dromgoole, new artistic director at the Bush.' *Observer*

'It is the kind of first play with sharp enough social antennae to make you keen to see what MacGregor does next.' Michael Billington, *Guardian*

'An impressive debut for a writer of wit, eloquence and a considerable political intelligence.' Claire Armitstead, *Financial Times*

Winner of the first Meyer-Whitworth Award

DEAD SHEEP by CATHERINE JOHNSON

'The Bush has come up with a right cracker in the shape of Catherine Johnson's *Dead Sheep*. It is biliously funny, very well observed and above all communicates a genuine pleasure in writing.' *Guardian*

Winner of Best Play and Best Production Awards, Thames TV

A BRIGHT LIGHT SHINING by DAVID ASHTON

'He possesses that most elusive gift which cannot be taught – an original and arresting vision.' *City Limits*

BELFRY by BILLY ROCHE

'It is rare to witness the complexities of human nature so expertly dramatised.' *Independent on Sunday*

'A delicate, hard, haunting and hilarious play.' John Peter, *Sunday Times*

Winner of *Time Out* Best Play Award
Winner of Carling Best Play Award

1992

The Bush celebrated twenty years at the frontier of new writing.

'What has held the Bush together for twenty years? Blind faith, youthful commitment and a tenacious belief in new writing: above all, perhaps, the conviction that new work deserves the highest standards in acting, direction and design.' *Guardian*

The Theatre won the Empty Space Award for the year's work.

DIGGING FOR FIRE by DECLAN HUGHES, presented by ROUGH MAGIC THEATRE COMPANY

'This is the most fresh, alive and contemporary play I have seen in ages.' *City Limits*

Time Out Best Play Award

WHITE WOMAN STREET by SEBASTIAN BARRY

'The Bush and the Irish have done it again . . . *White Woman Street* is a wonderful experience . . . see it and believe.' *Irish Press*

White Woman Street transferred to the Peacock Stage at the Abbey Theatre, Dublin.

PONDLIFE by RICHARD CAMERON, produced in association with the Royal National Theatre Studio

'London break for Scunthorpe Talent.' *Scunthorpe Evening Telegraph*

'Hook, line and sinker success.' *Financial Times*

'Cameron is plainly a man to watch.' *Mail On Sunday*

Simon Usher won the London Fringe Best Director Award

PHOENIX by ROY MacGREGOR

'one of the most potent and thought-provoking plays to have resulted from the fall of the West Berlin Wall.' *Independent*

THE WEXFORD TRILOGY by BILLY ROCHE

The Bush presented *A Handful of Stars, Poor Beast in the Rain* and *Belfry* in repertory, touring to Wexford Opera House and the Peacock Stage at the Abbey Theatre in Dublin. The productions were subsequently filmed by Initial and broadcast on BBC2.

Laurence Olivier Award Nomination: *Observer* Kenneth Tynan Award for Outstanding Achievement

'The Wexford Trilogy is undoubtedly one of the year's great theatre events. The Bush has discovered a magnificent writer and, in these outstanding productions, it has done him proud.' *Daily Telegraph*

1993

WAITING AT THE WATER'S EDGE by LUCINDA COXON

'A heady combination of intellectual insight and poetic power . . . it is a pleasure to welcome such an integrated production of an exceptional new play.' *Evening Standard*

NOT FADE AWAY by RICHARD CAMERON

'There can be no doubting the skill of the writing: its verbal power, psychological insight and moral vigour. Mr Cameron is a playwright not only to watch, but to hear and heed.' *Evening Standard*

THE CHINESE WOLF by DAVID ASHTON

'I don't know what the dramatist David Ashton is saying, but it is clearly strong and wonderful stuff.' *Daily Telegraph*

BEAUTIFUL THING by JONATHAN HARVEY

'Seldom has there been a play which so exquisitely and joyously depicts what it's like to be 16, in the first flash of love and full of optimism. Truly a most unusual and beautiful thing.' Lyn Gardner, *Guardian*

The Bush subsequently took *Beautiful Thing* on a National Tour, followed by a season at the Donmar Warehouse, transferred to the Duke of York's Theatre in the West End and was filmed for 'Film On Four'.

Joint winner of the John Whiting Award
London Fringe Best Production Award
Nomination for Olivier Award for Best Comedy

THE CLEARING by HELEN EDMUNDSON

'Trenchantly, often movingly blunt about the power of love over moral cowardice' *Evening Standard*

'Highly watchable . . . an evocative product of a well-constructed, moving play whose subject matter is tragically topical' *Mail On Sunday*

Time Out Best Play Award
Joint winner of the John Whiting Award
London Fringe Best Actor Award to Stephen Boxer

1994

THE CUT by MIKE CULLEN, presented by WISEGUISE PRODUCTIONS

'If 1994 brings another writing debut of this quality we shall be in luck.' *Independent On Sunday*

'The best first full-length work by a British dramatist for some considerable time.' *Financial Times*

BAD COMPANY by SIMON BENT, presented by LONDON STAGE COMPANY

'Blissfully, effortlessly funny . . . with more casual, innately funny dialogue in one play than most writers usually manage in three.' *Evening Standard*

'Scarborough's Chamber of Commerce won't find much to laugh at here; anybody else will have a fine time.' *Independent*

DARWIN'S FLOOD by SNOO WILSON

'. . . will remind the world at large that our theatre has been shamefully negligent in failing to sustain the career of so talented and ingenious a playwright . . . smuttier and less high-falutin' than Stoppard's *Arcadia, Darwin's Flood* is the most spectacular intellectual force of the last ten years.' *Observer*

IN THE HEART OF AMERICA by NAOMI WALLACE

'It has the driving political anger and entwining of the personal and the political that marked some of the best British writing of the early Seventies, the vigour and mystical overtones of raw Sam Shepard, and the grace and sensuality of a poet.' *Guardian*

Winner Susan Smith Blackburn Prize
Winner *Time out* Best Design Award

THE MORTAL ASH by RICHARD CAMERON

'His best play yet. This painfully funny, compassionate comedy goes right to the heart of contemporary Britain.' *Independent*

1995

KILLER JOE by TRACY LETTS, a co-production with HIRED GUN THEATER CO.

'If, like so many third-rate "cultural commentators", you think theatre is "dying" then go and look at this dramatic equivalent of an intensive care unit.' *Time Out*

'This is art of the highest order . . . Letts's grim, mordant humour is the work of a master writer.' Jack Tinker, *Daily Mail*

Transferred to Vaudeville Theatre
Winner *Time Out* Award

THE PRESENT by NICK WARD

'What the play captures superbly is the wonder and mystery of adolescence . . . There's no mistaking its atmospheric power, its sinister sexuality and its bracing black comedy . . . The Bush Theatre is on a roll.' *Daily Telegraph*

TRAINSPOTTING by IRVINE WELSH adapted by HARRY GIBSON

'This is a brilliant, bad motherfucka of a play that you are urged to catch while you can.' *Time Out*

TRUE LINES presented by BICKERSTAFFE THEATRE COMPANY

'This stunning new play is the sound of a new generation of Irish drama . . . one of the most appealing plays to hit London for a long time.' *Guardian*

BOOM BANG-A-BANG by JONATHAN HARVEY

'. . . has success written all over it. The first night audience was rhapsodic.' *Guardian*

'Still ridiculously young and talented, Jonathan Harvey is now becoming seriously good.' *Independent*

ONE FLEA SPARE by NAOMI WALLACE

'An inspired piece of theatre.' *Guardian*

'An exquisite revelation of the longings of the human heart . . .' *Time Out*

Winner Susan Smith Blackburn Prize

KNIVES IN HENS by DAVID HARROWER, in the Traverse Theatre production

'David Harrower's tender and tough tale of love and language is the undoubted debut of the year.' *Independent*

1996

LONDON FRAGMENTS SEASON

GOLDHAWK ROAD by SIMON BENT

'The Bush was on an amazing roll throughout last year. It is good to report that 1996 has got off to an equally impressive start.' *Daily Telegraph*

'A wonderfully filthy and funny exploration of life . . . They all squabble, wisecrack, booze and belch for a couple of very entertaining hours' *Observer*

SERVING IT UP by DAVID ELDRIDGE

'Well, it simply isn't fair. 22 years old. A first play produced. And all the verbal swagger, all the fine-tuned insight, all the confident theatricality of an established writer.' Jack Tinker, *Daily Mail*

'A promising debut from a new young writer shows that *Trainspotting* isn't the last word on Britain's disaffected youth . . . Rancidly funny . . . deeply chilling.' Michael Billington, *Guardian*

CLOCKS AND WHISTLES by SAMUEL ADAMSON

'They keep on coming. This week's astonishingly assured first play by an unknown 26-year-old is *Clocks and Whistles* by Samuel Adamson and it leads me to believe that the theatre may be on the threshold of a golden age.' Michael Billington, *Guardian*

'A fitting close to Dominic Dromgoole's rich and memorable period as Artistic Director' *Independent*

Samuel Adamson won the Pearson Television Writer in Residence Award

The 'London Fragments' season won the *Time Out* Award for Special Achievement

THIS TIME TREE BOWER by CONOR McPHERSON

'. . . a touching, marvellously entertaining play which tells a gripping tale with assured panache' Charles Spencer, *Daily Telegraph*

'. . . proves that McPherson – at just 26 – is already heir to the great Irish tradition of absorbing tale telling.' Michael Billington, *Guardian*

Winner of the Guinness Ingenuity Award
Winner of the Pearson Television Writer In Residence Award
Winner of the Meyer-Whitworth Award

In August 1996, the Bush Hotel closed for six months for refurbishment. The theatre went into temporary exile, producing *KISS THE SKY* – a psychedelic musical by JIM CARTWRIGHT – at the Shepherds Bush Empire and *BURIED TREASURE* by DAVID ASHTON at the Lyric Theatre, Hammersmith.

'Hell's Angels are tearing their beards out over a psychedelic musical which opens this month. They have threatened legal action to ensure that *Kiss the Sky* doesn't show them in a bad light.' *The Times*

The pub changed its name to The Fringe And Firkin and reopened in December 1996.

'Luvvies At First Sight For Fringe Opening. Bush Theatre actors, patrons and local dignitaries were among famous faces taking their cue at the bar when the Fringe and Firkin drew back its curtains. To go with the name, the Fringe and Firkin is serving a range of aptly names beers including Fringe, Luvvie, Thespian's Revenge and Shakes-beer.' *The Licensee and Morning Advertiser*

The theatre reopened on 8 January 1997 with:

ALL OF YOU MINE by RICHARD CAMERON

'Explosive . . . It's wonderful to have the Bush Theatre and its impressive, searching new-writing policy back again.' *Independent*

'A direct hit with Richard Cameron's eloquent lament for an eclipsed mining community' Nicholas De Jongh, *Evening Standard*

ST NICHOLAS by CONOR McPHERSON

'This is an immensely sophisticated drama which plays tantalising games with the relationship between writer, actor and spectator while constantly beguiling the audience into suspending its disbelief . . .' Charles Spencer, *Daily Telegraph*

'This gripping tale of one man's self-destruction, compellingly performed by Brian Cox, proves Conor McPherson as an exciting theatrical voice . . . A hugely entertaining and mature work.' *Evening Standard*

LOVE AND UNDERSTANDING by JOE PENHALL

'This is one of the best plays I've seen, ever, at this powerhouse of new writing.' John Peter, *Sunday Times*

'Anyone who cares about contemporary English drama is urged to beat a hasty path to the Bush.' Matt Wolf, *Variety*

WISHBONES by LUCINDA COXON

'Coxon is excellent on the grand passions and crazy longings that lie behind provincial ordinariness.' *Guardian*

GOLIATH by BRYONY LAVERY from the book by BEATRIX CAMPBELL, produced by THE SPHINX THEATRE COMPANY

'A dazzling clear vision of a country divided.' *Guardian*

DISCO PIGS by ENDA WALSH, produced by CORCA-DORCA THEATRE COMPANY

'Enda Walsh's stunning seventy-minute play erupts like a volcano. I use the word "stunning" as near its literal meaning as possible: the play leaves you shaken, uprooted, buffeted by a sense of shock and exhilaration.' *Sunday Times*

Joint winner George Devine Award
Joint winner Stewart Parker Award

MB 1997

Looking Back

Acting, like begging in India, is an honourable but humbling profession. The general conception that all actors are born exhibitionists is far from the truth. We are quite the opposite. Deep down we are shy, frightened people hiding from ourselves – people who have found a way of concealing our secret by stage lights, make-up and the parts we play. Our own self-rejection is what has made us actors. What better way to solve the problem than to be someone else? Even if it's Adolf Hitler . . .

Mary Duff, one of the great drama teachers at RADA, used to ask each of the rather self-satisfied students on their first day: 'Why do you want to act?' She got a variety of answers, but the one she wanted was: 'I don't want to act, I *have* to act!' Unlike other artists, writers, painters and so on, we cannot function on our own. We need an audience. Times are changing. It is the era of the showy musical, where people marvel at the mechanics and come out humming the scenery. Theatres all over the country are chook-a-block with musicals. The days when you could tour a play for fifty-two weeks of the year are gone. Ninety per cent of the actors leaving drama school this year will have given up in despair by the time they are thirty. What a terrible waste. If you can't sing and tap dance as well as act you will get nowhere. How terrible! No wonder the Business is dying. Can Sir John Gielgud tap dance? There is a theory that talent will out. In some miraculous way the best actors will rise to the surface and be discovered. Don't you believe it. Talent is a rare and fragile thing. In a cut-throat business which is all about survival it can, sadly, wither and die – sometimes literally . . .

What is the answer to the problem?

Go back to basics. What did the greatest actor of them all do? He learned how to write, produce, direct and started his own theatre.

Twenty-five years ago people asked: 'Why pub-theatre?' Because it's where it all started. Will Shakespeare and his mates doing their thing at the Ale House. Think about it. We have the most talented actors in the world and most of them are unemployed. Why? Because they have nowhere to work. Theatres are closing down. Cutting back all the time. So. Open new ones. I think it's time drama schools ran courses on how to start fringe theatres. I am very proud and pleased that my baby, the Bush, is celebrating it's first quarter century but what about the forty thousand out of work actors? I would like to see another hundred Bushes. The Bush puts on marvellous shows. They run for a few weeks. Some transfer to the West End, but wouldn't it be great if they could go on tour for a year? God knows they can't say I don't try to start new theatres.

Not just in London either. I look forward to the time when they're writing books about the Tollbooth Tavern, Edinburgh, the Club Foot, Adelaide, and the Temperance Hall, Burgau.

Do you know what is the world's most successful pressure group? CAMRA: The Campaign For Real Ale. A couple of blokes in St Albans realised in the nick of time that the great British public was about to be drowned in Beauty and the Beast (sorry – slight slip of the tongue there) drowned in ersatz rubbish; and turned the whole thing around. Perhaps we should launch CART: The Campaign for Real Theatre? Do you think we'd get any support?

You'd think I'd be sick of fringe theatre by now. I started in 1951 as assistant stage manager at the long since defunct New Lindsey Theatre in Notting Hill Gate. My predecessor had written over the doorway to the stage management's rat-infested glory hole: ABANDON HOPE ALL YE WHO ENTER HERE! He signed his heartfelt message too . . . Dirk Bogarde.

I've never been able to take his advice. And I never will. There is a vast and growing demand for real theatre. It is fascinating to witness the stunned reaction of first-time real theatregoers. When I was starting the Bush (and it wasn't an overnight success like the King's Head, it took two years of hard slog) some bright spark informed me that ninety-seven per cent of the population don't go to the theatre. If you're a pessimist you give up. If you're a fringe impresario you think what a terrific potential audience!

One of the biggest problems when you are launching a new

project is the cost of publicity. Advertising equals bums on seats. But it doesn't matter how good you are if nobody knows. We had the same problem in the early days at the King's Head and the Bush – we couldn't afford to advertise. I had invited the Mayor of Hammersmith to the Grand Gala Opening Night and promised to give all the proceeds from our first ever night to charity. The press was invited, of course, and there were to be pictures after the performance as the Mayor was presented with a sizeable cheque for local charities. I was so busy what with one thing and another – I'd written the opening play as well as playing the lead – that I hadn't had time to check how things were going at the box office until the first night was almost upon us. I asked my partner how many people we had booked in for the Gala First Night. He studied the booking-in book and counted . . . 'Three,' he said. 'The Mayor, his wife and a photographer from the *Shepherd's Bush Gazette*.' Disaster. I explained to the cast that we were taking a break in rehearsals in order to secure some paying customers. I got hold of some electrical wire and went down to the cellar. There I lashed together some beer crates before setting off for Speakers' Corner in Hyde Park, where I explained our dilemma to crowds of fascinated tourists while my partner trawled through the audience. After about an hour I'd lost sight of him and I called out his name. 'Keep talking,' he shouted 'we're half full!' The *Daily Mail* ran a story headlined 'Soapbox plea saves a play'. I can't imagine how they got hold of the story. After that I became a regular at Speakers' Corner every Sunday afternoon. The police were very tolerant and I developed quite a fan club – talking for up to four hours non-stop. On about my fourth appearance a man in the crowd put his hand up and proclaimed: 'I can testify that what that man says is true. I have visited his little theatre and it does have the finest actors and actresses in the best plays in London at very reasonable prices – you can get a good seat for as little as 30p!' I couldn't believe it. I'd never seen him in my life before and suddenly it felt like a revivalist meeting as a woman shouted 'And I can testify that what he says is true because I've been to his little theatre too!' I would recommend Speakers' Corner to any frustrated actor. I very rarely got heckled and was on nodding terms with Lord Soper. People always ask what I talked about. It was basically one big commercial for the Bush while my partner sold tickets, but you have to try to keep it entertaining. You'd get lots of rich American tourists who'd wandered across from the Dorchester. I'd slag off all the hit shows in the West End. Tell them not to believe the old saying: 'A bird in the Strand is worth two in Shepherds Bush.' Oh, I was a right little radical in my leather jacket and shoulder-length hair, but we got hundreds of paying customers as a result. One thing about performing al fresco; you don't need a critic to tell you if you're any good. You either have a crowd or you don't. As far as I can make out there are only two things you must not do at the Home of Free Speech – criticise the Queen or sell theatre tickets. Twenty-five years ago the police were very good about it. They called me down from my beer crates and whispered, 'Could we have a little less of the "seats in all parts" sir. It is illegal to sell things in Speakers' Corner. May I suggest your man sells the tickets from the other side of those railings over there.'

Erstwhile Bush artistic director, Dominic Dromgoole – now working with Sir Peter Hall at the Old Vic – was quoted in the papers as saying the Bush was started by a genius who now goes around dressed as Adolf Hitler wearing stockings, suspenders and high-heeled shoes. He's talking about my one-man play/cabaret but people might take this the wrong way. Worse still, it might put off would-be fringe producers when we need all we can get to create more opportunities for new writers and actors. Somebody worked out that the little theatres I have started over the years have given employment to the equivalent of the entire membership of Equity so I don't care if people do sometimes mock and call me 'Britain's most small-time Impresario' – how many jobs have *they* created?

C. Brian McDermott

*   *   *

Ah well it's good experience, I suppose, was my father's analysis having seen me in *Wilfred* playing a role in which I was never offstage and had a ten-minute monologue at the end.

No, Dad, this is *it*. This is about as good as it gets: playing a big part in a small theatre to an audience receptive to your every nuance. Later, in the bar downstairs, the landlord dealt with a drunk by concealing his keys between his knuckles and punching him hard in the face, drawing blood and knocking him to the ground right under my mother's nose. Not what my parents expected to see at the post theatrical drinks session, but it made me think my dad was right: it *was* good experience. And this was not Shaftesbury Avenue, thank the Lord. It was around this time that I started mentally dividing people in our profession into the Bush types, and I suppose, the luvvies: us and them, the real people and the twerps. Sadly we are still outnumbered, but the fight goes on.

Until recently I held the record for most appearances at the Bush (five plays), but I think someone else has it now, maybe Paul Copley or Simon Callow. I first mounted the back stairs in 1973 with *Dick Deterred*. Actor freaked after one week, was replaced by someone who couldn't sing; actor split with girlfriend on morning of technical, got drunk, technical cancelled. Later the producer (did we have such things?) sacked the director. I walked out in support of the director (now a high-powered BBC executive producer), but none of the other actors joined me as they couldn't afford to lose the £30 a week wage. I've never called in the favour.

After this, apart from the strange revue *In at The Death*, in which Dusty Hughes brought together Julie Walters and Victoria Wood for the first time, Bradwell has been the only director to lure me down the Goldhawk Road. *The Fosdyke Saga* had them queuing round the block. We tore up most of Alan Plater's script at the start of rehearsals and rewrote it ourselves, but Plater's canny agent refused us a slice of the royalties. The show prompted a learned piece in *New Society* which claimed that we had redefined the course of modern theatre. Really we were just pratting about, but pratting about sort of skilfully and in a life-enhancing fashion, so the audience's lives got enhanced too. I played seventeen different roles in *Fosdyke*, often nipping off one side and reappearing immediately on the other as somebody else. I soon figured that the less skilful the distinction made between these characters (e.g. a downtrodden miner closely followed by King George V), the bigger the laughs. A luvvy would have missed the point.

In *Wilfred*, an actor talked gibberish on the first night, but, as the play was written by Peter Tinniswood, the audience (and critics) thought it was part of the action. Afterwards, in the Yin Ho, my denture fell apart on an over-crispy slice of duck and I had it repaired next day by a Chinese dentist called Mr Phang, whom I found on King Street. I'll never forget the taste of his fingers, the toilet was actually in the surgery. Another actor talked gibberish on the first night of *Oven Glove Murders*, but this time the audience knew exactly what magnitude of cock-up they were witnessing and most critics mentioned the event in their reviews the next day.

When a show is going well at the Bush, the place becomes the centre of the universe. The laughs are astounding, the silence electric. Acting there made me never want to work in a big theatre again. You just can't see any detail watching a play in the Olivier. On the other hand, the paranoia before a first preview is terrifying, because you just know that the focus is so intense that you can get away with nothing. You have to be honest and open and warm and brave or the audience will switch off and long for a pint of Fringe. They'll start fidgeting about, suddenly aware of the discomfort of the place, and knock their beer glasses over in the meaningful pauses. Despite the decline in the quality of violence in the pub, I just love the place. I'm waiting for number six. Look out for me.

Philip Jackson

* * *

Howard Gibbins asked me to join him to help run the Bush in 1975. Luke Randolph joined us to do the accounts, on which Howard had lavished tremendous attention and a blizzard of Tipp-ex. Brian McDermott, who'd set the place up with his adaptation of John Fowles's *The Collector* a year or two before, was occasionally about, but mostly away dealing with his acting career.

My first show was *Hitting Town*, a one-act play by Stephen Poliakoff which was sharing an evening with Blanche Marvin's production of Tennessee Williams's *This Property is Condemned*. We built the set ourselves, I made the sound tape (leaning out of the window at three a.m. to get the sound of the traffic going round Shepherds Bush Green), and the dustbin we took from outside the quick printer's shop in Shepherds Bush Road. We lifted the condiments from the local burger joint.

It was a big hit (in spite of tensions between the leading lady and the director, to whom she said during the technical rehearsal, 'I don't see why you should be being paid so I can teach you how to direct.' He's now a prominent TV director, (which may have proved her point) and elegant literary London stamped upstairs to the airless theatre and watched us change sets at the interval. When *Hitting Town* went on tour Antonia Bird was the stage and company manager.

Michael White, who took Stephen's subsequent play *City Sugar* from the Bush into the West End, replacing John Shrapnel with Adam Faith, promised new air-conditioning as our payment for the transfer.

No one ever fidgeted as much as Stephen, who had particularly irritating habits of snapping paper spills and eating biros. We bought him a dozen biros to eat during rehearsals of *City Sugar*, and eight months afterwards found all twelve, chewed to destruction and stuffed down the back of a second-hand sofa we'd been proud to acquire for nothing.

Tommy, who ran the pub downstairs, had the racing on television in the afternoons, echoing through the smells of beer and pub food. When he left, the pub's takings went up by £6,000 a week.

The first time I went to the Bush I saw Tim Albery, Ken Morley, Howard Lew Lewis, Mary Sheen and Nick Edmett in Andy Smith's *Aladdin*. Every time Tim, who was (and I suppose still is) a very tall man, came on stage, a pensioner in the front row muttered 'Oooh, look out, here comes Lofty'. Ken was the comic genius of the group: unpredictable, mesmeric, unapologetic, filthy and warm. I loved him then and still do, but now from afar.

We had no idea, Luke, Howard and I, about performance indicators, or target marketing, or anything other than trying to find and help new talent. So we needed help with administration. Luke invited Robert Breckman, who was making himself a great name helping subsidised companies, to be the auditor. Laurence Harbottle, who had been Binkie Beaumont's lawyer, was already chairman. These two, with glamourous offices near one another in South Molton Street, represented the real world that had to be satisfied. What they thought of the shitheap through which they tiptoed for every board meeting they were too gentle to detail.

The conditions in the office, apart from the occasional splurge on a new sofa, were not good, though about the same as many other fringe theatres. There was one big room which trebled as dressing-room, meeting-room and offices, with the loo in the pub downstairs (There was no loo on the far side of the stage. If you were marooned during a show there was usually a milk bottle for comfort, and if the milk bottle had been forgotten there were always the stairs.) When Hull Truck came to do a show (*Oh What!* and *Bridget's House*) they used the office as their front room during the day, so we had them about while we were reading scripts, checking actors' availabilities, laughing or applying to the Arts Council.

The Truckers discovered that the public toilet on the Green opposite was a famous London cottage, so each day they opened a book on how long each visitor would be staying. Benches and seating were put into our first-floor bow window, and the Truckers loudly celebrated each startled caller to the cottage when he left. That didn't help the Arts Council applications either.

Our Drama Officer was Peter Farago (later, bizarrely, to be the director of the live stage version of *'Allo 'Allo*), and I've a constant memory of discussing our crises with him at the Council's elegant offices in 105 Piccadilly, when Arts Council officers had world enough and time.

Luke once sent an ACGB request for information back with a note saying that we were too busy filling out their previous form to have time for this one.

Always scripts, and more often than not the ones we were sent had the rejection notes still inside them from the Royal Court (where David Leveaux was literary manager) or the National or the RSC or Hampstead or or the Riverside. We set up an informal monthly meeting of literary managers, to compare notes, but it kind of fell apart because of our lack of influence. Only Tynan (not one of the group), who had been close to power at the NT, had ever had the authority to deliver what he promised. The rest of us could only make nice noises.

I did what I could to encourage Anthony Minghella, who at one stage seemed to send a script every fortnight: great, heavy, wordy, worthy, unstageable messes, with a real writer behind them. Did I do any good? I always thought that genius would make its own mark, and that if I didn't spot it, someone else would, or it would force its way through my neglect like a mushroom through tarmac. And there Anthony is now: craggily, uncompromisingly successful and certainly without any help from me.

Mike Bradwell and I, and Alan Plater and Bill Tidy plotted *The Fosdyke Saga* in the basement of Tidy's Southport house. Or rather, we drank too much and played a game I can't remember at his billiard table, while his silent but Italian brother-in-law padded through on his way to plaster the kitchen. And later Phil Jackson created Roger Ditchley to the life while Penny Nice hurled raw tripe at baying audiences in the hottest theatre in the hottest summer in London.

David Mouchtar Samurai directed Donald Sumpter, Caroline Blakiston, Jeff Chiswick, Stuart Fox, Tony O'Donnell, Oliver Smith, Jonathan Coy and me in Andy Smith's version of Brecht's *Edward II* in a tent on Shepherds Bush Green during a blistering summer of IRA bombs. At the dress rehearsal Caro's generously supplied pâté turned to maggots in the pan between lunch and tea, on the first night the drought broke and we played to the background sirens of the fire brigade from Shepherds Bush Road station racing round the Green to deal with floods all over London, and on tour (Young Vic, Oxford Playhouse, Christ's Hospital, Berwyn Arts Centre where I fell off the scaffolding, broke my ankle and was married two months later). Caro became so bored with what she was doing that she deliberately left her underpants off during the show, and gave us another kind. New, new.

Mel Smith (same feelings as for Ken Morley) directed Gaye Brown, Yvonne Gillan and Marian Fiddick in Terence Greer's

Nobody Knew They Were There. Nobody ever did know, or if they did they didn't care, for nobody came. New, new.

Roddy Maude Roxby and Ben Benison improvised new comedy every night with a troupe from the Royal Court Theatre Upstairs. John Bull's Puncture Repair Kit came; the pre-Bennett moodiness of *For Sylvia* from the Edinburgh Festival; the solo play *Billy the Kid* from Cardiff Arts Centre (the first night of which was attended by Howard, Luke, me and six critics, and the artist lost his nerve and wouldn't stop firing his rifle at us, until the critics, who you might have thought could take it, were huddled together like refugees), David Gale and Hilary Westlake from Lumiere and Son with *White Men Dancing*, the set of which was filched from building sites round Hammersmith and consisted of yards of chicken-wire and thirty rats. The rats didn't like being asked to scuttle through their chicken-wire runs above the audience's heads, and all stayed in one place like a furry Chinese paper lantern, defecating enthusiastically.

Simon Stokes arrived, and when he suggested that the Bush should start advertising in the *Daily Mirror* I knew it was time to leave. A year too long, twelve months too short.

If anyone's memories conflict with anything I've said here, it's because I'm lying.

Peter Wilson

* * *

The Bush Theatre is a small black box containing a number of steeply raked seating modules on which it is not always clear – indeed it is not intended to be clear – whether a particular step is intended for one's own bottom or the feet of the people sitting behind. I am mildly claustrophobic, intermittently sciatic and six foot four inches tall.

It is thus a surprise to realise that my most enduring relationship with the Bush is as a member of the paying public. On the other hand, and although two of them were not Bush premieres, the three plays of mine the theatre did in the 1970s add up to a distinct body of work.

I began writing stage plays in the early seventies, a period now rightly seen as the Prague spring of subsidy, a time when the streets of the capital (and those of other cities) blossomed theatre spaces in almost chokingly verdant profusion, presenting bewilderingly various works of dramatic art at almost all hours of day and night. In those days, it was said, it was just about possible to write a three-to-five-hander, at under an hour in length, so dreadful that nobody at all would want to put it on. But it wasn't easy.

So my first London work – the two-hander *Two Kinds of Angel* – was performed in a basement theatre (imaginatively called The Basement Theatre) actually beneath a Greek Street strip club; my second was presented in a little theatre (capriciously titled The Little Theatre), somewhere near St Martin's Lane. But my first consistent relationship was with the Pool Theatre in Edinburgh (the point of whose title was never clear to me) who had first done the Little Theatre play and which also premiered a full-length pantomime satire I'd written about Britain's entry to the common market, *Tedderella*, in December 1971. An intelligent teenager could probably reconstitute the entire play from the DNA of its title: suffice it to reveal that Ted Heath was the eponymous waif, Enoch Powell, Buttons, Harold Wilson and Roy Jenkins (then anti and pro respectively), the bickering uglies, and Geoffrey Rippon (the minister principally responsible for negotiating Britain's entry to the common market) was the Fairy Godmother. The Prince was called Charmant and Dandini became Brandini (Willy Brandt – geddit?) and there you have the whole thing.

The Bush was at this stage run by the engagingly entrepreneurial Nick Newton and Brian McDermott, who decided to revive the play to coincide with Britain's entry to what was then called the Common Market on 1 January 1993. This event was officially accompanied by a festival dubbed the Fanfare for Europe; I was involved in a kind of mini-counterfest to this jamboree, both with *Tedderella*, whose view of our entry was jaundiced, as well as a short play co-written with Howard Brenton for the Royal Court Theatre Upstairs, tastefully titled *A Fart for Europe*, which also managed to keep its enthusiasm for the community under strict control. Nick and Brian's production concept for the play was initially alarming to me: in collaboration with director Michael Wearing (whose future career as a BBC producer was to include *Boys from the Blackstuff*, *Our Friends in the North* and *Middlemarch*) they planned to engage two drag artists to play Harold Wilson and Roy Jenkins. My fear was that the keenness of the political satire embodied in these two characters might well be obscured by other qualities of the performers, which proved to be the case. As, however, Jean Fredericks and Tony Chantell were a great deal funnier – and keener – than my sharpest satirical barb I decided I was ahead of the game.

As a result of the success of *Tedderella*, Nick and Brian asked me to write a *Tedderella II*, which I declined, feeling that the risks involved in getting away with *Tedderella I* had been considerable enough and I shouldn't push my luck. As 1973 went on, however, another subject with rich satiritical potential was emerging across the Atlantic, as Richard Nixon's second administration was becoming increasingly throttled by the Watergate election-rigging scandal. Again, once you have the idea of basing a satirical review of the Watergate story on Richard III (retitled, naturally, *Dick Deterred*) then the thing virtually writes itself. Merrily, I set about transposing Hastings into Nixon's campaign manager John Mitchell, Buckingham into his Chief of Staff Bob Haldeman and the little princes into Democratic Presidential hopefuls George McGovern and Ed Muskie, all in referentially muscular blank verse, when Nick Newton rang up to announce proudly that he engaged composer Graham Field to write the music. 'What for?' I asked. 'The songs', Nick replied. I then had to go back through a two-thirds completed play, removing a speech and adding a song every five pages. This is not the way to construct a musical, but in Graham's capable hands you couldn't see the joins. The show was again directed by Michael Wearing, transferred to the ICA for a season, and would have had an American production but for the untimely resignation of its central character in August 1974, thus acceding to the work's principal political demand before – in the US at least – it had yet been made.

My third Bush play was, like *Tedderella*, a retread of an existing piece. I had originally written *Summer Sports*, a trio of aggressively hostile pieces about sport and sportsmen, for the Birmingham Arts Lab (and the actor Alan Hulse) in 1975. *Summer Sports* was revived in a season of short plays performed in tents in and around the then undeveloped Globe Theatre site, again directed by Mike Wearing. Shortly afterwards, its last and longest scene – set in a Wimbledon locker room and titled *Ball Boys* – had started its long and happy solo career. In 1976, the then Bush director Dusty Hughes asked me to extend *Summer Sports* into a fuller evening, called *Blood Sports*, and involving (in its first performance) Simon Callow in full jodhpured drag and Simon Stokes doubling a dead tennis star and a large black dog. This play continues to be performed as a whole from time to time: and on its own, the occasionally updated *Ball Boys* remains far and away my most produced work.

My experience of the Bush in the years then and since was largely of plays of acute social observation of contemporary mores, presented in lovingly naturalistic detail. It's striking to me in retrospect that the three works of mine presented there were all broad-brush cartoon parodies. Like most writers I remain open to a little gently parodic humour (and put the *Dick Deterred* experience to good use in writing a happily-ended *Romeo and Juliet* as the first-part closer for the RSC's adaptation of *Nicholas Nickleby*). But I haven't written a full-scale parody since *Dick Deterred* and I probably don't feel too much the worse for it.

Comedy is a different matter. I suppose when you cross the continental divide of a playwriterly career, it's understandable to want every work to have the gravitas of serious intent, just in case you fall under a bus on the way to the first preview. There is also an argument that almost all contemporary dramas are essentially comedies, or at least comic, whatever the pretensions of their authors. I have written one play that aspired to the genre, and several that were intended (and succeeded) in making people laugh from time to time. But I haven't written anything quite as full-throatedly, up-frontedly and on-the-nosedly rib-tickling in intent as the three plays I wrote for the Bush between 1972 and 1976. Perhaps, who knows, one day.

David Edgar

* * *

There are the remains of a small theatre in the complex of the ancient ruins of Knossos in Crete, near a bronze bust of Sir Arthur Evans, the nineteenth-century archeologist who did so much to uncover the complex. Time, mediterranean piracy, and earthquakes have shivered everything above ground but the seating arrangement of the Oldest Theatre in the World is preserved. It is domestic in scale and startlingly like the Bush theatre itself: an L-shaped bank of seats.

I'm sure that the Cretan Oldest Theatre in the World will soon lose its title. As global warming reveals more of our inheritance, twenty-first-century archeologists, squelching over suddenly melted permafrost will no doubt stumble across evidence of a previously unsuspected but powerful ancient culture, whose purpose at first they can only begin to guess at. In the midst of the remains will be a small building containing tiered seats on two sides, hewn from mammoth tusks. I predict the Siberian Shaman Theatre (circa 23,000 BC) will have few concessions to comfort, and the shorter arm will be pointing to the north pole, for it will be the ur-theatre, the mother of all theatres (except of course those tiresome concrete slabs excreted by Denys Lasdun), the template for its subsequent sister temples of the muse in Χρετα, and Londinium.

The strange thing about having associations with a theatre for almost all of its twenty-five years is how solid and complete that feels, compared to the constant toing and froing of managements and makeovers in the bar downstairs. The Bush Theatre remakes itself once a month in the interest of illusion, and down below, the pub follows behind, an awkward dancing bear, in the footsteps of illusion, most recently serving up ales which marketing men have piously adorned with memorable (they hope) theatrical attributes. I'm only surprised that the short, sad lives of Luvvie's Mild or Thespian Ale are not appointed to conclude in conveniences titled Stagedoor Johnny's Wee House, and Tinkerbell's Tinkle Room. Honestly, where is your sense of humour?

However, co-existence with the elbow-nudging vernacular has always been part of the theatre: I am sure that Mammoth

Tusk Theatre in Siberia resounded to the same complaints about itinerant traders in their yurts outside selling watered stoups of reindeer piss as Druid's Bliss, and bringing down the tone of the *amanita muscaria* collective mushroom trances.

I have so many memories of my own plays done at the Bush but the memory that comes to mind most immediately is of Dusty Hughes's own wonderful play *Commitments*. Alan Rickman, flipping his forelock in weary and forebearing tolerance as George Irving bitterly denounces the shallowness of his own existence playing simple Geordie fishermen in successive fish-finger advertisements. Aching pathos and comic disillusion, the unbearable need to dissemble: the human condition.

I also remember Lynda Marchal. She played the drunken Mabel in my play *The Soul of the White Ant* with such energy, witnessing it was akin to standing in a gale. Lynda later went behind another Bush, as it were, to re-emerge as Lynda La Plante, an extraordinarily successful writer, for TV. In *The Hole In Your White Pants*, as we called the play, Simon Callow played the low-browed journalist Pieter de Groot, in generously proportioned khaki shorts. Filled with the character's innocent, self-important curiosity Simon would use his forefinger to sample the melting contents of the deep-freeze. During the show Simon also pasted up photographs of his own father all about the foyer. In the photos, Simon's father was dressed in similar shorts to the ones his son wore on stage. Where the white pants stopped, the father's right leg prominently displayed a missing knee-cap. Since all the world's a stage, I wouldn't be a bit surprised, if one day early next century the knee-cap is found, mysteriously wedged between rough-hewn Siberian mammoth tusks in a small prehistoric theatre in northern Siberia.

Snoo Wilson

* * *

My debut at the Bush was in a transfer from the old Soho Poly of Snoo Wilson's *The Soul of the White Ant*, expanded to full-length with the addition of a lurid scene by the roadside, during which I was required to quaff a cocktail in which a variety of salads and a small umbrella floated in a liquid looking, and indeed tasting, very much like calamine lotion; it was called a Pink Flamingo (or Punk Flamungo as my character, the knobble-kneed Jo'burg journalist Pieter de Groot, would have said). The play was full of the rough magic for which the author is so justly famous, and it was my introduction both to the Fringe – of which I was flatteringly held eventually to become, for a while, the King – and to the Bush, which became my spiritual home, theatrically speaking, for some years. At that time, the theatre was at the beginning of the long journey from high-spirited chaos to ruthless efficiency and matchless production values at which it has now arrived. Though the journey was right and inevitable, there was a certain charm to the chaos, to the informality, of those early days, and it was still then possible for me to wander into the office with a play in my hand and ask to be allowed to do it and a month later we would be on.

The first time I did that was with Richard Quick's one-man show called *Juvenalia*, in which the right-wing Roman satirist was supposed to have slipped through the time warp to harangue the audience for some seventy-five minutes in a DJ, in verse, under a revolving glitter-ball on a stage made up to resemble a seaside cinema. Strange to relate, the show worked, both artistically and commercially. As part of the deal, I had agreed – my arm hardly needed to be twisted – to play Princess Anne in David Edgar's parody of *Equus* (*Hippos*, it was called) as part of *Blood Sports*, a collection of four short plays on politico-sportive themes. This also worked. One that didn't work was my Charles Bukowski show *Ejaculations*. It would have done, I have always believed – the original politically incorrect man, Bukowski wrote like an angel, a sort of hobo Jeffrey Barnard – but on the first day of rehearsals we received a telegram which read simply: 'Absolutely not. Bukowski.' We never found out why. This was perplexing, and also vexing, but only mildly. We just moved quickly along to the next thing.

Although matters were beginning to get rather more serious by 1982 – Simon Stokes, Jenny Topper and Nicky Pallot now formed the triumvirate, and were slowly transforming the place into what it has since become – it was still possible for me to be having supper with them and Snoo and for them to tell me that the director of Snoo's new play *Loving Reno* had just dropped out and for me to say, well, Snoo and I could co-direct it and for them to say, sure, why not? I had never directed anything in my life, and had never intended to, but, hey, anything to help a chum out of a spot. I was in the middle of shooting *Amadeus*, and this necessitated occasional departures to Prague, but it all went terribly well, and it became clear about halfway through that I liked being a director very much indeed, rather more than Snoo did, in fact, and so that's another thing I owe the Bush: I don't believe that I'd ever have directed anything had things not fallen out as they did. Astonishingly, Snoo and I were nominated by the ever-eccentric James Fenton as Most Promising Newcomers of the year for our production. Snoo immediately retired from directing; I stuck with it, with all the usual subsequent joys and miseries.

Everything at the Bush was still done on a shoestring, but it was a shoestring of seemingly limitless dimensions. Grant Hicks had designed an ambitious set which was simultaneously an airport lounge, an amphitheatre and the inside of a cranium. It was hugely complicated and strange, but, fashioned out of materials begged and borrowed and very rarely bought, it was installed to an impressively high level of finish – as it had to be; sets at the Bush were inevitably submitted to very close scrutiny. There was no question, in those days, of any limitation on the hours that the actors or the theatre staff would work; as a production came close to opening, all outside life, any attempt at regular meals or sleep, was abandoned, and an increasingly hag-ridden team, sustained largely by roll-ups and pints from the pub below, would doggedly ensure that the latest vision was realised in that tiny little black room above the pub.

The pub itself really was, in those days, a pub, run by stout Irish Tommy and his incomputably large family. He and indeed all of them were robustly indifferent to what was actually going on in the room above, though perfectly friendly and delightful to all of us who worked there. The local clientele of the pub, equally oblivious of the dubious goings-on upstairs, were less tolerant of the influx of poncy theatre buffs coming between them and the next pint at around eight o'clock. The lavatories were kept properly pungent and awash with misdirected urine; no concessions to West End standards there. Of course it was tedious for the theatre lot to be yoked to this counter-culture, but it was also healthy, in its way. A certain roughness in the experience prevented it from drifting away from life altogether. Backstage, conditions were on the primitive side of rough. The dressing-rooms were on the other side of the auditorium from the stage; a small cupboard, modestly divided into male and female with a curtain held up by gaffer tape. During *The Soul of the White Ant*, Clive Merrison had first to cover himself with soil, then to wash himself spotless, in this cupboard, with all the rest of us dancing around him. No matter how large or small your part, you had to sit there from beginning to end of the show – although it was possible to get round to the other entrance, the one by the door, by going down the back stairs and running, in costume and make-up, down the Goldhawk Road and back through the pub, forcing one's way through the seriously alarmed regulars, by now on their fourth or fifth round of the evening. Nightly I made my entrance as Princess Anne by this route, with ponytail and jodhpurs, to much rubbing of eyes.

The stage manager for a large portion of my time at the Bush was the charismatic Dutchman, Bart Cossee, the shy focus of many fantasies, no whit discouraged by his habit of wearing black string vests through which his rippling musculature was sharply visible. He was of that breed of stage manager who, having had a maximum of two hours sleep and half a sandwich, risk life and limb twenty times a day, wiring up live fittings, swinging from the rafters, heaving vast skips around, and then quietly and nonchalantly sip a pint at two o'clock in the morning. Heroes, they are, and the Bush was entirely staffed by such.

After *Loving Reno*, I had two last stints at the Bush, both as a performer. The first was in another obscure one-man show, *Melancholy Jacques*, this time about the philosopher Rousseau, a sublimely cryptic meditation in which the audience were made to feel as if they were overhearing – barely – an almost incomprehensible private monologue on the subjects of art and love. Again, astonishingly, this seemed to work, and cast a considerable spell. One night the tent in which I was supposed to be spending the night, brewing my Nescaff, burst into flames; neither I nor the audience were at all animated by this, as I placidly doused the flames with Evian water, not interrupting my meditation for a minute. The second show was even more incendiary, though not quite so literally. It was *Kiss of the Spider Woman*, which, again, I had brought to the Bush, and which it had taken Jenny and Simon and Nicky exactly half an hour to decide to do. A genuine masterpiece – oddly neglected – by the novelist Manuel Puig, it was given an exquisite production by Simon Stokes, with Robin Don's masterly set which converted the auditorium into the interior of an Argentine jail, the textures scrupulously and perfectly realistically painted by the great, late, team of Gordon Stewart and Andrew Wood. Mark Rylance and I enacted the story of the improbable and tender romance that blossoms between Molina, the camp little queen, and Valentin, the determinedly heterosexual revolutionary hero, incarcerated in the same cell, and despite indifferent or non-existent notices (it was widely ignored by the broadsheets) it played to bursting houses, in an atmosphere of emotional intensity that I had never before, and alas, have never since, encountered in any performance of which I was a part. The Bush is able to generate, given the right play, and the right production, a mood which is like none another, not even in comparable theatres; despite the least comfortable seats in London, perhaps the world, and an odd L-shaped configuration, and primitive air-conditioning, and the roar of the Goldhawk Road's traffic, and the occasional throb of a distant rock band, there is a complicity between performers and audience which is both intimate and epic, and which somehow fans the actors into blazing life, and which has informed an astonishing range and scale of work. There was talk at the time of transferring *The Kiss of the Spider Woman* to another theatre, but much as I loved the piece, I was glad it never happened. The experience that Mark and I and the few hundred people who saw the show that sultry summer was unique, and uniquely right. Pure Bush. There's nothing quite like it.

Simon Callow

* * *

At one time artistic directors used to commission and receive scripts, and put them on if they thought they were good enough. They learnt about the plays along with the writers. The Bush was a prime example of where this could happen. To some extent, in some theatres but by no means all, this has changed. Writers have begun to deliver unfinished scripts, since they know they will be interfered with. It's not healthy for good writing or for the theatres putting on new plays. Good plays at their best are a singular vision. They are not improved by a committee.

Robert Holman

* * *

Our most recent visit to the Bush was to see Joe Penhall's *Love and Understanding*. It was playing to deservedly packed houses and we got there in good time to bag decent seats on the front row. Our legs dangle a bit but you have to make sacrifices otherwise how do you know it's Art?

Many of the people in the audience seemed to be first-time visitors. They stared up the steeply-banked terrace of seats looking for empty spaces.

'Do we have to climb up there?' said one of them, with the incredulity of a woman more accustomed to the gentler inclines of the Barbican.

'Yes,' I said, 'that's how you know it's Alternative.'

Ronnie Scott used to say he got his back problems from bending over backwards to please Stan Getz, the famous American tenor player. The Bush is right up there with Getz. The theatre should take commission from the osteopaths of north London.

Back in the sixties and seventies I used to have arguments with my agent, the late Peggy Ramsay, about the Bush and similar intimate venues like Peter Cheeseman's Victoria Theatre in Stoke.

'The audience is simply too close, darling. The actor only has to *breathe* and it's absolutely hypnotic,' she'd say.

'Isn't that a strength?' I'd ask, warily. 'Wouldn't Sam Beckett say all drama is about humanity trying to breathe?'

'Read Ibsen, darling,' she'd say then hang up because Sam Spiegel was on the other line.

The debate continues to this day. The core of it is that you don't prove you're a proper, grown-up playwright until you've written a big play with a big cast for a big theatre, with a proscenium arch. The problem is that persuading big theatres to put on big new plays was never easy and over the last couple of decades has become almost impossible.

Like all the best arguments I find it easy to agree with both points of view, according to the phases of the moon and what's been in the *Guardian* that day. It remains one of humanity's enduring metaphysical debates along with the comparative merits of Chaplin and Keaton, Jack Hobbs and Len Hutton, Ella Fitzgerald and Billie Holiday.

It's become conventional to say that what the Bush does best is to present intimate and naturalistic views of humanity under stress: Closely Observed Strains, as Michael Billington might say. It's a half-truth, on a par with the idea that what the Northern writers of the sixties and seventies were depicting was Gritty Realism: anyone who thinks that needs to have a closer look at grit, reality and the North.

But all that being so, it's paradoxical that the two pieces I wrote for the Bush were, according to all this designated wisdom, totally wrong for the size and shape of the venue. *The Fosdyke Saga* (1976) and its sequel, *Fosdyke Two* (1977), both dramatised from the great Bill Tidy's celebrated strip cartoon in the *Mirror*, were so far over-the-top that Donald Wolfit, in his prime, would have been fired from the company for reticence. None of the actors breathed: they were too busy gasping.

At the time Mike Bradwell was running the original and brilliant Hull Truck Theatre Company and I was living along the road in Larkin country. One day we travelled to Southport to meet Bill Tidy. We had a drink in Bill's studio. Then we went to a pub for a drink. Then we went to an Italian restaurant for a drink and some pasta. Then we went back to Bill's house where we had a few more drinks and played snooker. The only thing I remember is Bill's brief: 'Your job's to glue my balloons together, so why don't I leave it with you?'

Of the production itself, there are scattered but poignant recollections, each of them unique in the theatre's history.

Philip Jackson discovered he was playing twenty-two named characters and planned to write to the *Guinness Book of Records*. Penelope Nice performed an exotic striptease dance culminating in her producing a sledge hammer, which was then hurled backwards across the stage and caught one-handed by ace drummer and lethal pool player, Charlie Grima. During rehearsals, Jane Wood realised she was the only one in the company without a song to sing, so I wrote her a compensatory sonnet, modelled on Wordsworth's 'Westminster Bride' ditty, except this one was about Manchester. It began:

Leeds hath not anything to show more fair
Thick as short planks be he who would pass by
A sight so noxious in intensity
Manchester now doth like a string vest wear
The dankness of the morning . . .

And so it goes, for fourteen lines. It's my only sonnet in print and I'm very proud of it.

It should also be noted that the *Fosdyke* shows were the only time in the theatre's history that the audience and cast were encouraged to throw *real* tripe at each other, and also the only shows that ended with an audience singalong, as we all joined in the anthem:

Tripe it is grand
Tripe it is noble
In every land
Tripe it is global
Better by far
Than fowl, fish or weevil
Let there be tripe
And banish all evil.
Fosdykes Arise
Fosdykes Arise

Lift up thine eyes
See the Fosdykes Arise.

Bernard Wrigley, aka the Bolton Bullfrog, who wrote the
music, later recorded the song for one of his albums which
meant I shared a tiny composer credit on an LP, just like
Lorenz Hart or Johnny Mercer. This had long been one of my
seven ambitions. I met Bobby Charlton around the same time
so that was two ambitions achieved within a year.

The *Fosdyke* shows later went on a national tour and during
our week in Hull, a local tripe factory brought out a special
souvenir edition of tinned tripe. My sister recently came across
one of these, still in mint condition after twenty years. The
question is: should we call in the authorities to organise a
controlled explosion or keep it in a safe place until the Bush
opens its Heritage Trail?

Alan Plater

*   *   *

Bush CV: Acted in *The Fosdyke Saga* (1976/77), *The Paranormal
Review* (1978), *Lone Star & Private Wars* (1980/81), *Progress*
(1984). Wrote *Coming Clean* (1982).

In my first appearance at the Bush, I had to throw tripe at the
audience. In my last appearance, I had a bottle of wine poured
over my head and Struan Rodger's tongue stuck down my
throat. The intervening eight years provided many other fond
memories.

I've much to be grateful for to the Bush. It not only gave me
some great opportunities as an actor, but also launched my
career as a writer. It's a space in which I've always enjoyed
performing and, indeed, watching others perform. My work
there over the years provided me with invaluable experience.

I'm spoilt for choice for high points. I once played an
armchair that rolled around the stage talking to God in a show
called *The Paranormal Review*. At the time I didn't see anything
particularly unusual in this. There was – how shall I put it? – a
certain heady atmosphere amongst most of the cast during the
run that made playing a piece of talking furniture seem quite

normal. It was only later I realised the show was a challenge to one's sanity. On the first night, the author, Erik Brogger, discreetly handed me a note. It said he thought I was the best thing in it, but not to tell anyone else. The smug smile soon froze on my lips as I realised he'd delivered the same message to the whole cast.

The press night of my first play, *Coming Clean*, was pretty memorable. The house lights went down, the first sound cue didn't happen and the stage lights didn't come up. I was sitting in the darkness clutching Jenny Topper in a state of high anxiety, wondering if my writing debut was ever going to be allowed to begin. It eventually did and the stage manager was eventually sacked. Fortunately the rest of the performance went well. The space served the play a treat. The close-range eroticism of certain scenes had a charged intimacy which the Bush is so effective at generating.

But the happiest memories happen to be the first memories. Turning a famous comic strip into a stage show is a tall order, fraught with difficulties, but somehow *The Fosdyke Saga* worked. In fact, it was one of the theatre's biggest successes and was like a party every night. It is still the most enjoyable show I've done.

There was, of course, the occasional low point, like the show that never happened: *She Was Only A Grocer's Daughter, But She Taught Sir Geoffrey Howe*. It had first-rate writers and cast, but as we rehearsed, the project somehow disintegrated before our eyes, eventually disappearing without trace.

The good moments, however, far outweighed the bad, and it's a great pleasure to say thanks and best wishes for the next twenty-five.

Kevin Elyot

* * *

I was first approached to work at the Bush in the spring of 1978 by Dusty Hughes, who invited me to contribute to a revue he was directing called *In At The Death*. I went to a meeting, I think it was at Snoo Wilson's house; all the men involved were in the garden building a shed, and it was the first time I had ever heard the word 'macho'.

I didn't really want to be in the revue, because I had been an out-of-work comedian for four years, and three weeks at the Bush seemed like committing to do a decade in *The Mousetrap*. But I thought the cast seemed quite jolly, and you could leave your car in a lorry park on Wood Lane for thirty pence a day, so I was in.

The revue was supposedly based on the news from a certain week in June that year, 1978, and every item was supposed to be concerned with death, but I did notice that a lot of the stuff people sent in was on very old paper, and had references to Anthony Eden tipp-exed out.

I wrote three songs, one about a recently widowed old man, one about a teenage joyrider, and one about Guy the Gorilla, who had just died in London Zoo. For my fourth item, I asked Dusty if it would be OK if I wrote a sketch. I hadn't written one before, and I think I was expecting him to say, 'Get out of here! The impudence! I never did . . .' and generally carry on like Mrs Bridges in *Upstairs Downstairs*.

He kindly let me write a sketch, and because I'd pretty much had it with death by this point, I did one about sex set in a library. I wrote it in one lunch-time in the theatre, and as there happened to be a typewriter on the set, typed it. I didn't type anything again for twenty years, but what has made that sketch a landmark for me was that it was the first time I found my voice, my way of writing comedy. It was a wonderful feeling, after quite a few years of being told I would never make it, and being unable to move forward in my career at all, to know inside I had connected with something that was going to make it all work.

Julie Walters and Alison Fiske were in the sketch with me, and I have to say it did go a bomb every night. One line I remember from Alison as the concerned middle-class woman to Julie the panicky library assistant who thinks she might be pregnant was 'Where are you in the menstrual cycle?' to which Julie replies 'Taurus.'

Backstage was weeny and grubby and if you wanted a wee you had to go down into Goldhawk Road and mingle with the audience in your costume, which, if you were as I was dressed in grey flannel shorts and ankle socks, was a bit dodgy. So the ladies of the cast tended to rely for short-term relief on handy beer glasses which from indolence we would leave on the window-sill of Dusty's office. This led to the often heard cry 'Don't drink that lager!'

It was during that three-week run that I was asked by David Leland to write something for his new-play season at the Crucible Theatre in Sheffield, and because I didn't know it was supposed to be difficult I just wrote one, and that was bought by Peter Eckersley, the head of drama at Granada, and he commissioned another one . . . I haven't been out of work since then really. So thanks Dusty and the Bush.

My favourite memories are of parking up in the lorry park, and then having an egg and tomato sandwich in the pub before the show, and of Julie calling out over a urine encrusted window-sill to Harold Pinter, who was standing in the street outside 'Hey, Harold, you write plays, don't you?' He gave her a quick pause (I think it was from *The Homecoming*) and moved away smartish.

Victoria Wood

*   *   *

Dec 6th 1978

To: Mr Dusty Hughes
From: Erik Brogger

Dear Dusty,

    This is a letter of agreement between Erik Brogger and Mr Dusty Hughes, granting permission to perform <u>The Paranormal Revue</u> at the Bush Theatre. Of course, implied in this letter of agreement is Mr Brogger's understanding that he will receive free cigarettes and lager at the

pub and the chance to shake his head and
say: 'Three thousand miles for this!'

Sincerely,
Erik Brogger
121 Bank Street Apt. K
New York, N.Y. 10014
United States of America
(the best)

* * *

It was a Sunday. The usual decibel levels of seven people in a
room 20' × 12' (the Bush Theatre) simultaneously using power
tools to drill, saw and hack had been constant for the past four
hours. A new show was in preparation. The five-weekly fit up
was in full swing against a tight deadline and on a budget of
less than £1000 for set, costumes and props. As ever, we'd
been to the BBC tip and were recycling their old bits of
scenery, removing wiggle pins et al in order to get at the good
bits of timber.

The team, three artistic directors (technical skills variable),
three stage managers (all trained at least in the use of power
tools) and a designer were showing signs of wear and tear from
the get out on Saturday immediately after the farewell drinks
with the outgoing company, four hours sleep and a body clock
craving Sunday lunch.

Jenny Topper was mistress of the lunch routine, the
collective when and where. Time had not been called but I
began to be aware of a less frenetic atmosphere and, looking
around, realised that the boys had disappeared. Perhaps they
were on the street unloading the van again, no. On the roof, in
the timber store, in the office? No, no and no.

They were eventually tracked down to the back bar of the
Bush Hotel finishing off a surreptitious drink following
allegedly one of the ruder routines to be witnessed in a strip
show. The regular strippers were not usually in the first flush of
youth and were accompanied by a wizened fellow with a few

strands of hair and about as many teeth who stood impassively by collecting discarded items of clothes.

On this occasion someone much fresher and more fragrant put in an appearance. She'd dropped off some Finborough Theatre leaflets at the theatre before going back downstairs to do her strip routine. Clearly a woman of not so hidden talents, she helped the finances of the unfunded theatre by occasional forays into the lighter end of entertainment. And, by all accounts, it was extremely rude and her polio-damaged leg deterred neither her nor the punters among whom were the one male artistic director of the Bush and his stage management companions. They had a whale of a time – and tucked into lunch with renewed vigour.

Nicky Pallot

*   *   *

It was an extraordinary night. First previews at the Bush were always fairly wired events, fairly gladiatorial, with more adrenalin than beer sluicing round the building.

Sometimes they would go off half-cock; a taut mixture of missed cues, technical fumbling and tight acting. Everyone would stand around in the dressing-room afterwards swilling Australian chardonnay and mouthing the right platitudes; 'that's-what-previews-are-for' and 'you've-got-to-miss-them-to-score-them'.

Sometimes they'd be disasters. A new play would meet a living, breathing audience for the first time, and the living, breathing audience would utter a silent, but resounding NO. The pub would be empty when you came downstairs, and all the staff would be wearing insane grins, like old skulls. They knew there was six weeks more of self-denial to come. 'No, the show's great, the critics just didn't understand it, houses are good-ish . . . really, where did you hear that from? . . .'

And sometimes they would fly. And none has ever flown farther or higher than the first preview of *Beautiful Thing*.

It would be wrong to say you could feel the ground moving, it wasn't like that. It was more as if some large hand took hold of the little black box the hundred people sat in, wrenched it out of the old Victorian building that surrounded it, took it out above London, above its theatrical and social context, and chucked it hard and high up into the stars, where it floated around for a couple of hours, exhilarated by the view.

It was largely the laughter, which pounded out of everyone, until your eyes wept and your head ached from the sheer noise. But it was more than that, there was a quality of joy, pure joy, which surprised as much as it pleased. Nobody could believe they were allowed to be that happy. Or that a modern story, a modern play could so deftly, truthfully and skilfully take them up rather than down.

Of course press night wasn't the same. All the fashionable madmen came, and they all raised their pedantic cry 'Life's not like that', 'Where's the pain?' 'It's wish fulfilment' – a bunch of middle-aged, middle-class neurotics telling Jonathan Harvey that his version of working-class, gay life was not truthful. But once they'd cleared out of the way, the amyl nitrate in the heart of the play gushed back into the auditorium, and every night would be the same glee-filled trip to the stars.

It was never regarded as such, but for me, the first preview of *Beautiful Thing* was one of the more significant nights in post-war theatre. In one night, the empty space became the full room. New writing, and particularly political new writing, would never be the same again.

You have to understand the context from which it escaped. *Beautiful Thing* was the crash of a wave that had been rising for several years. It was a wave of reaction to the Miserabilist Tendency that had predominated for almost a decade before. Cowed by the monster Thatcher, much of English theatre went into various forms of hiding during her reign.

There was the Classic hideaway, where contemporary concerns were buried underneath a vague 'relevance' and an ineffectual interaction between, say, seventeenth-century Spain and modern England. The upside of this was a return to big stories: the downside was an over-reliance on spectacular sets, post-modern costuming and Eastern European choral singing. The collapse of the iron curtain led to a universal ransacking of such effects. Fresh-faced graduates would come over all Polish, and the appropriation of others' suffering would supposedly add dignity and emotional authenticity to the event.

There was the Physical Theatre hideaway. Much of this was and is exquisite, formally inventive and brave; much of it is meaningless gesture, pure affectation without content. Some of it has expanded the boundaries of what we think is possible in the theatre; some of it has allowed Oxbridge graduates to show off how good they are at pretending to be chickens. Because of its substance-less nature, it proved highly popular for sponsors and the ruling ideology. Money and Conservatives never minded theatricality, or expressionism, or shock: what terrified them was life.

And then in the world of New Writing, there was the retreat of the Miserabilist Tendency. This dry, dusty hideaway housed a ton of dead drama; state-of-the-nation plays rehearsing arguments already settled long before the audience arrived; journalistic plays on single issues; work plays exploring the tensions in a DHSS/minicab/newspaper office; ghastly plays of opinions; autobiographical therapy theatre dressed up as confession, and the long endless nights where the left would argue all night with the radical left, and dawn would break, and someone would burst out crying. Small subjects, small plays.

Two principal sins bedevilled this school of writing. First was the odd twentieth-century idea that *argument* is at the centre of theatre. This is a peculiarly British phenomenon which seems to result from too much exposure to George Bernard Shaw at an early age. While the rest of the world absorbed the influences of Chekhov, Ibsen and Strindberg, and learnt that theatre is about texture, relationships, idiom, imagination and the poetics of action – in short – *story* and *life*: while the rest of the world got that, we got George Bernard Shaw. Big plots, long arguments, large points – a tremendous amount of wind, whirling around a complicit self-satisfaction that everyone's intelligent enough to know what's going on.

The marriage between philosophy and theatre always struck me as deeply uneasy, but for a while, for a couple of decades, any play that didn't sport a loud and long thesis was seen as deeply illegitimate. You needed a point to survive. No wonder audiences dwindled, tired of being lectured at, or having things explained to them.

The other great sin in many of the new plays of this period, and other forms of theatre, was *fake pain*. We live in a world of rampant cruelty, waste and injustice; we see it in every place, at every level. It's a given. We also, especially in this country, live in great comfort, surrounded by tolerance, generosity and compassion. We often seem to find this harder to deal with than the downside. We certainly hate to admit it.

It's not perfect, it's far from perfect, it's often hideously imperfect, but show it to a Romanian, or a Georgian, or a Peruvian, or a Moroccan, and tell them about how much suffering there is here, and you'll notice a funny look creep into their eye. Yet, in theatre, this didn't stop wealthy, healthy, middle-class folk looking at some inane subject like pensions or architecture or spying or newspapers and finding more rottenness than in any Denmark, more pain than in any holocaust, more apocalypse than any Hiroshima.

Our suffering is of course legitimate, but it is not the only thing that legitimises us: our joy does too.

Those who did have something genuine to complain about, the gay community, the ethnic minorities and, not to baulk at an enormous generalisation, women, managed to produce some of the best work of this period. They also managed to move in from the edges to become the mainstream. One of the reasons was they wrote stories. Another was they knew enough about real pain not to need to 'fictify' it.

With *Beautiful Thing*, Jonathan Harvey bravely went into classic old miserabilist territory. With young gay love as his theme he went on to a housing estate in a working-class enclave, and there he found joy and love and wit and tolerance and compassion and justice. He didn't ignore the difficulties that surrounded these people, but was happy to show that they could triumph over them. He also wrote a simple story simply – there was no argument, no analysis, just sympathy and truth.

Of course the old miserabilists found it very hard to take this seriously. If they did they were out of a job. So all the people who spent their lives attending conferences chaired by David Edgar on The Death of Theatre or The Death of Language or

New Writing or Queen Victoria or whatever had died that week, all those people rallied round to diminish Jonathan's achievement. They called it over rosy or unintellectual. Their reaction was rather in keeping with the Old Left's sneery reaction to Tony Blair. What they couldn't stomach was that this was genuine populist theatre – not dire Marxist cabaret, nor sentimental junk or guck – but an evening that everyone could love.

Of course *Beautiful Thing* wasn't the only play that put life before argument, nor is it necessarily the greatest. There was a whole host of writers who preceded Jonathan in breaking the shackles of Marxist critique or reductionist pointmaking. There was Billy Roche with his widening spread of compassion; Sebastian Barry with his remarkable modern myth-making; Roy MacGregor with his wise humanist politics; Catherine Johnson with her savage humour; Philip Ridley's extraordinary, decadent fantasy worlds; Chris Hannan's violent conjunctions of art and life; Richard Cameron's limpid stillness; James Stock's intellectual fireworks – the list is long, much longer, and full of wonder.

And of course, since *Beautiful Thing*, there has been the most profound explosion of new dramatic talent that we have seen for many a long decade. The profusion of mid-twentysomethings who have burst on to our stages has revitalised our theatre. We do not know which plays will survive – we can never know that. What we think is great today may be laughed at in a hundred years. *Beautiful Thing*, as I said, is not necessarily the greatest of all these, but it arrived happily at the crucial moment, when the old conventions were crumbling, and something had to give to allow the new state of feeling its necessary space.

A lot of people wonder how and why this explosion started. The culturally obtuse say it started at the Royal Court, which is rather like saying jungle, ragga, trip-hop and grunge all started on *Top of the Pops*. It didn't start at the Bush either: it started with the writers, working things out alone with their VDUs.

Of course, this is not a prescription for everyone to go out and write Happy Plays. Jonathan Harvey himself went on to write a savagely dark tragi-comedy *Rupert Street Lonely Hearts*

Club. Nor is there a necessity to do away with analysis altogether. All the best Bush plays would be hard as well as easy, they would have insights that are not immediately apparent, nuggets of difficulty that would keep the plays out of the audience's greedy grasp. The dangers of going too far towards life and story are apparent at the moment, where people who write nothing more than conflated potboilers get talked up as major artists.

We cannot have tracts, nor can we have potboilers. Having escaped the clutch of doctrine, we cannot splash around too lazily in life. *Beautiful Thing* was the tip of the battering ram which knocked down the wall of dogma and defeatism which had surrounded theatre. It was the brightest colour of a whole host of colours and shades and hues that had been trying to infuse some variety into what had become a very grey room. Happily they succeeded.

The Bush, and the people who worked there, were lucky and privileged enough to be in the right place at the right time. We were able to open the door to an outstanding generation of writers, and we were happy to watch the flowering of so much insight and imagination and wit and truth.

To have been there at the Bush at the moment things changed was a source of huge delight.

Dominic Dromgoole

* * *

Three Poems

Someone Wants to Kill Me Again

Someone wants to kill me again.

When we embrace
I feel bullets
where vertebrae
should be,
nails
sharp as razors,
and teeth grazing

my skin
with chainsaw
delicacy.

Their breath
smells of napalm,
their sweat,
petrol,
and their dandruff
is distinctly
gunpowder.

These thoughts
used to scare me
but now
I'm merely thrilled
for I'm never more alive
than when I'm waiting
to be killed.

The Seams

Your love
was a needle
and thread
that stitched me
into myself,
sewed up my eyes,
mouth, ears, nose,
anus:
every orifice safe
and leakless.

Darling,
this embroidery
is camouflage,
not armour.
It helps me disappear
but does not protect.

One day,
I know,
your loving will stop
and I'll fall apart
at the seams.

Getting Through The Day

Sometimes I wonder
how I'll get through the day
without putting my fist through glass.

Believe me.
I watch the sunrise
knowing there'll be
gashed knuckles,
severed fingers
and the sound of someone
begging for mercy
before it sets.

My thoughts are full
of razors and hammers
and all the ways
to do permanent damage
to fragile things.

It's true.
At night I dream
of puncturing skin
and wake up
instinctively reaching
for the screwdriver.

Listen.
When I look
in the mirror
I see the savage
in all its glory.
It's terrible to be alive, it says.

Sometimes I wonder
how I'll get through the day
without putting my fist through that glass.

Philip Ridley

* * *

If you have ever caught a black cab from London to Bristol, you will have had plenty of time to think about why you love the Bush. I've been a Bush-Baby (© Michael Billington) for nine years which makes me a Bush-Boiler now, I suppose. I've had two plays produced – *Boys Mean Business* and *Dead Sheep*, and I'm writing a third, *Shang-A-Lang*. I'm going to have THE BUSH 4 EVER tattooed on my thigh, because it's the best, and it's the best because of the people who work there.

When you have a play on at the Bush, you feel part of the place, and that doesn't stop with the end of the run. I've got my Thames Best Play Award for *Dead Sheep* up on the wall, and I've just checked the date – 1991. Which is a bit of a shock – I haven't written for the Bush in six years, but I still feel like a Bush writer. (Or two – hey, let's make a night of it) I can't do justice to the Bush experience in words, it's more a sort of primeval roar, but here's some random Good Times, in no particular order:

Boys Mean Business on the beach in Weston-Super-Mare.

Winning Thames TV Best Play Award for *Dead Sheep*.

Going to Butlins with Mike 'Two Breakfasts' Bradwell.

The Baby by Chris Hannan.

The *Dead Sheep* works-outing to Somerset.

Dominic breaking into Jenny's dad's flat at dawn, to show me the first review of *Dead Sheep* – it's a cracker!

Brian, Nicky, David, Dominic, Nick, Deborah, Joanne, Mike . . .

TAXI!!!

Catherine Johnson

* * *

Bogman Danny lit up a wild cheroot and watched it glow in
the dark like a snake's arse. 'I remember,' he said, 'when that
place was just – a place! Doing no harm to man nor beast.
Empty as the eyes of God. And, see it now!'

We were sitting on the Green, watching the electric sign for
the Bush Theatre glow also in the dark. Below it, a door
opened and people spilled out into the street. You could tell
they'd just been to a play, they had that forlorn bewildered air
to them. One man delicately flexed a black shiny shoe and
looked down at it.

'He's had a backside sittin' on that toe didn't agree with
him,' observed the Bogman. 'The bum of culture numbs your
tootsies!!' he bawled over at the startled man who moved
quickly away towards a parked Saab.

Saturday night ritual. I, a sometime writer for the theatre
and Danny, Derelictus Rex of Shepherds Bush, chewed the fat
while the lime green light of a Chinese takeaway lit us up like
two gargoyles. 'Tell me about the succession?' I asked,
knowing it well but loving the repetition. Danny pondered.
'First there was Queen Jenny, then there was Prince Dominic
and now – Michael the Protector.'

A brooding silence fell on the Green, it was the moment for
us to make our weekly pilgrimage, Danny would howl and
protest but he'd do it just the same, up the windy narrow stairs
festooned with ticket stubs, on hands and knees crawl past the
sentinel at the desk and then into the silent, newly vacated
theatre. Time to go . . .

We looked around the place. 'I love it when a theatre's
empty – feels . . . natural somehow,' remarked the pensive
Bogman. Me, I was remembering the first time I came to the
Bush, a Ron Hutchinson play about an Irish showband, it was
like a boxing ring, an arena, no place to hide, no place to be
pretty stage left, and then a lot later on, my own two plays and
me, wetting myself and Deborah Aydon dealing out the tickets
like a riverboat gambler, and me, wetting myself, sitting on
someone's feet, praying they were waterproof, oh yes the moist
bum of culture right enough and the Dromgoole guffaw which
signalled the first night, round one, and there's no place to hide
– 'Pssst . . . this auld piece that's on now, what's it called?' '*The*

Rock,' I replied. We looked at the set. It looked like a big rock.
So far so good.

Danny walked away and assumed a formal attitude opposite
me. 'Who are you going to be tonight?' I asked. Prompt
response, 'Buffalo Bill.' Shit. That meant I was Martha of the
Vineyards. Again.

Danny smoothed back his hair with a trembling hand, every
Saturday we did this but he still got nervous. His untitled play.
We'd been running it for two months now, late every Saturday
night, of course the sentinel saw us sneak past, the Bush all
knew, but they figured an old boy off the Green had as much
right to have his moment as some tosser from Stanlake Road
like myself.

A clearing of the throat indicated a first line imminent. I
assumed the posture of Martha. Danny spoke . . .

> *Men of violence have ripped the drawers*
> *off Mother Nature these many years but,*
> *by the pearl handles of my old six shooters,*
> *I, Buffalo Bill, promise you, Martha of the Vineyards*
> *that I will make of your earth a verdant place . . .*

and more of the same and the mind wandered. I was
remembering *White Woman Street* which chilled me to the bone,
the Billy Roche plays – a trilogy to break your heart, critics
huddled together like slugs in the rain, a little boy who came
near death for crunching his way through three packets of
crisps during the second act of my play, *The Chinese Wolf*, but
always the feeling of an arena where the writer is going to be
backed up like Wyatt Earp at the OK Corral – a diffident
cough brought me back on course. Danny was banging in the
last nails . . .

> *Love like mine, it goes so deep.*
> *It is a well, I invite you now*
> *To drown yourself within . . .*

And indeed a great feeling of love rose in my breast and I
thought that of all the great mad plays the Bush had put on,
the new writers it had cradled and fiercely defended like a
wildcat mother, nothing, nothing so much became it as this

Saturday night performance of Bogman Danny's *magnum opus*. I looked up and it seemed to me that three celestial beings hovered above in the patchwork air, Queen, Prince and Protector, each waving an empty wine glass – in approval or just looking for a refill? Perhaps a bit of both.

Time to go . . .

David Ashton

* * *

I write about Yorkshire because it's where I'm from. I started writing full-time for the theatre after doing eighteen years as a drama teacher in Scunthorpe. It was a none too auspicious start – I got a commission from another London Fringe Theatre after I'd won the *Independent* Theatre Award for a play I wrote for my students which we took to Edinburgh. That award included a three-week slot in said London Fringe Theatre. We sold out. They offered me a commission. I thought, this is it, let's go. But then, of course I made the fatal mistake of desperately wanting to get it right for them, writing what I thought they would like, what would look good on that stage. I got so wound up with it, rewrites and so on that it finally disappeared up its own arsehole. I'd blown it. My first professional commission. Thankfully, someone somewhere had seen some of my work before and gave the Bush the nod. And for that, Mike, I will be forever grateful.

Pond Life was set in about eight different locations, including a carp lake in the middle of the night, where a monster carp is caught. And it was Yorkshire. And everybody in it was daft as a brush. And four of them had to go on a carp fishing expedition with full tackle – rods, line, hooks, et cetera, connect with, fight and land a twenty-pound carp.

If I'd have touted that idea round the fringe theatres in the hope of a take, nobody would have touched it with a bargepole. Impossible to stage. Not for the Bush. If we need a lake, we'll build one.

And so I was introduced to Simon Usher, director, and Anthony Lamble, designer. Together we've now done four productions at the Bush. Each one has been a brilliant experience for me. I always marvel at the way it all comes together, the way that tiny cramped space fills with life. Of course, I know how it's done, but I still marvel. It has not a little to do with the fact that everyone involved in this tiny theatre is absolutely dedicated to putting on the best possible productions of the work of new writers they discover and nurture. I have no doubt at all that the team at the Bush taught me an enormous amount about the craft of writing – about, for example, the importance of what to leave out. 'Bury it', Mr Dromgoole would say. So I'll bury the gushing praise . . .

Over thirty years ago, at Doncaster Poetry Society, watching Hugh MacDairmid down a bottle of malt, sitting next to this beatnik with a Sloppy Joe jumper and fedora, who kept standing on his head to scratch his beard, I never dreamed I'd work in the theatre. All I had in common with the beatnik was a love of words. I was delighted when he got the job as artistic director of the Bush. It's a terrific feeling to be working with him thirty years on. Here's to more first-night wallowing in sentimental stupor.

Richard Cameron

* * *

When the Bush agreed to do *Beautiful Thing* in 1993, I seriously doubted their taste. The Royal Court had rejected it, Hampstead weren't keen, and the National felt there wasn't enough angst. One thing they were united in was that the ending was dreadful. It was only when I met Dominic Dromgoole and Nick Drake that I felt comfortable enough to ask just what was wrong with my ending. Dominic said 'Well it ends on a question.' When I looked at their copy of the script I realised that someone in my agent's office had been sending out the script with the last forty pages missing.

With the final pages reinstated (and a lot of people, critics mostly, thinking the proper ending was even worse) the play went into production. I told my mum and dad that I had a play on at a very prestigious theatre in London. They came down from Liverpool and we went for a 'pre-theatre supper' (I believe it's called) at the Pizza Hut on the Goldhawk Road. At the end of our meal the waitress asked 'Did you enjoy your meal?' My dad, who loves complaining, and using name badges as a tool for social interaction, replied 'No, Tina-Marie. The pizza was mediocre, the music was obtrusive, we *won't* be coming here again.' When he'd upped and left, my mum whispered to the waitress, 'It's all right, we're from Liverpool.'

They were never that keen on pubs, so went straight upstairs to the theatre and didn't even come down at the interval. They'd probably expected my name in lights, plush carpets, a royal box and a special souvenir programme. What they got instead was my name written in chalk on a board above the cigarette machine, someone's knees in their backs, crap air-conditioning and a few words photocopied on a piece of paper. Still, they liked the bit where the lighting changed and a load of people came on and talked. They didn't like the swearing, 'You didn't get that from us.'

My memories of that time were of drinking too much, and hearing Patricia Kerrigan warming up onstage via the Tannoy in the dressing-room, doing an almost Buddhist chant of 'Remember the money, remember the money . . .' . . . which, knowing the Bush's wage-packets, can only have been a reminder to herself to pick up the fiver she used as a prop in act two.

I also remember the lock-ins at the pub, thanks to a very friendly licensee who loved the play. On the last night he organised a disco, and whilst I was giving it plenty of welly on the lambada floor, some actors were crying, some were jubilant, and the general manager was giving a very drunken rendition of 'I've Been To Paradise (But I've Never Been To Me)' on the ukelele.

I like to think they were quite impressed with my lambada skills that night because they then asked me back to be their writer in residence.

Being a writer in residence means that they chuck a load of money at you and you write them a serious, groundbreaking piece of meaty drama, hopefully with a couple of murders in, preferably with a stunning vehicle for a TV star in it, and if you're lucky, something with West End Transfer stamped all over it. I wrote a play called *Boom Bang-A-Bang*, about a load of queens getting together to watch the *Eurovision Song Contest.*

When choosing a director for *Boom Bang-A-Bang*, Dominic listed a load of blokes who I'd never heard of, and then said 'There's always Kathy Burke, she's not done much directing before, but you'd probably get on.' On the bus home I read my stars in the *Standard* and it said 'Take the outside chance, a bird in the hand is worth two in the Bush.' Kathy was duly sent a script, and I soon realised that horoscopes can sometimes be true.

I'm very grateful to the Bush for introducing me to two fantastic directors: Hettie Macdonald, who went on to direct the film version of *Beautiful Thing* as well, and of course Kathy Burke. It's such a joy to work with directors who are so good with scripts, and work with you to making them even better. As a writer, you can't really ask for anything more.

If there's one thing the Bush had under Dominic's rule, it was good taste. Good taste in scripts. Good taste in marrying writers with directors. Good taste in knowing which actors would suit the intimacy of the space. I'll always love that little corner of Shepherd's Bush Green, but I wish to God they had the good taste to sort the air-conditioning out.

Jonathan Harvey

*   *   *

My first visit to the Bush was to see a two-hander called *Through the Leaves*. It featured simulated sex on a kitchen table, a blowjob to orgasm and some of the best acting and writing I'd ever seen. Really great work. But there was something else.

The venue. I'm a cheap date for small, dark places but in that tiny, cramped, unforgiving microscope of an auditorium, there's a magic created that's unobtainable elsewhere.

Whether it's the steep raking, the intimacy, the concentrated focus of a huddled mass, I don't know – you can't analyse this stuff – it just is THE best theatre in London, bar none. And if you really want a reason then try this.

Emotional truth.

If real, it's electrifying. If faked, it's met with a sense of disbelief and disengagement that the actor feels equally instantly. There's no two ways about it. You've been a cunt. And you know it.

You can't fake it in the Bush. Whether you're just starting out or you've got a string of awards and a heavyweight reputation that lets you coast along on autopilot – it doesn't matter. The Bush will always find you out.

And thank fuck for that.

Richard Zajdlic

* * *

Posting your first play is nutty. I remember walking towards a pillar-box in Camberwell and thinking, maybe some little ritual wouldn't go amiss. I could drop the package on the ground and step over it, or post it upside down with my eyes closed, or kiss it three times and do a little shimmy as it disappears. Perhaps something like that would bring me luck? Perhaps it would bring me bad luck? I kept it ritual-free. I felt as if I'd thrown a pebble into the Atlantic. I was sure I'd never hear a word.

As it happened, I got a very nice letter from the Bush a few weeks later, saying something like, 'Thank you, be patient, be very very patient, your life's work is at the bottom of our enormous slush pile', and a few months after that – by which time I'd moved, got a new job and given up all hope – I got what can only be described as The Magic Phone Call from Joanne Reardon, the literary manager, who asked me to come in and talk to her and the then artistic director, Dominic Dromgoole, about rewriting what would eventually become *Clocks and Whistles*. So began my life as a playwright, and it's very satisfying to be able to sum up that difficult and heady time in a few words, as if it was all a piece of cake.

The Bush is an important theatre. The list of playwrights who have worked there is mind-boggling. Yet its importance is underrated. Maybe that's because they don't care about new waves or movements or writing booms or image or angry young voices or large pay cheques or critics or glamorous first nights or comfortable seats or rituals there – they just care about talent, hard work and good writing.

Still, I kissed my programme and did a shimmy in Shepherds Bush Green on press night, just for luck.

Samuel Adamson

* * *

I can remember on my twenty-second birthday rather cheesily remarking to a girl I was seeing at the time, that I'd probably remember that birthday for the fab afternoon we'd spent in the pub. Of course, what I didn't know as I kissed her goodbye and headed off home was that that afternoon Dominic Dromgoole had rung my newly acquired agent to say that the Bush Theatre would like to do my play. It won't be much of a surprise to learn that I don't remember too much of that evening's return to pub where I spent the afternoon!

What do I think about when the Bush Theatre pops into my head apart from remembering that birthday?

Spending most Friday or Saturday evenings while *Serving it Up* was on crashing on the floor at the house where Sandra and Jill (from the Bush) lived in Streatham.

The church hall rehearsal room in White City when the stage manager, the assistant director and myself got the giggles in rehearsal and were shamefully sent out by Jonathan, the director, to the kitchen!

The bit in the play at the end when Nick tells Sonny by mistake he's been shagging Val. The audience always saw what was going to happen thirty seconds before it happened, and I always loved watching people recoil with hands covering mouths as they realised one mate was going to tell the other mate he'd been shagging his mum!

Being delighted when Dom told me he liked my play, and feeling a real tit when he said the title was crap. But . . . *1995 (Let Them Eat Cake)*? He was right.

Noticing that Dominic Dromgoole could scratch his balls with one hand, his hair with the other, and rub his feet together – all at the same time.

Meeting Mike Bradwell for the first time and drinking three pints of lager very quickly as I was scared!

In the office before a casting session gossiping about getting off with a thirtysomething girl at the weekend – and how funny that was – and then noticing that the previously smiling Deborah, Jill and Joanne were now not looking at me as kindly as they had previously.

All of the staff at the Bush being fab to me when I lost two stone post-*Serving it Up* and none of them taking the piss out of me having put it back on since.

The special matinee of *Serving it Up* for a coachload of teenagers from Hackney. Their sense of humour and compassion was quite humbling.

Being excited as I nearly ran across the Green to get to the newly refurbished Bush Theatre's opening.

Jack Tinker's wonderful review of my play. I'll be lucky to ever get a review like that again.

Meeting Trevor Griffiths (a playwriting hero) on the press night of his play, and only managing to drunkenly say 'All right, mate?' Then playing I Have Never in the production office, finally spilling out onto the Green with Dom, Vicky, Sandra, and Kath in the early hours as the sun rose on a beautiful June morning.

Crying and trying to hide it during *All of You Mine* as 'Abide with Me' played, only to notice most of the people sitting around me wiping their eyes too.

The brilliant *Knives in Hens*.

Hugging Mike Bradwell. I suspect it's a nicer experience than being 'Trevved'.

All of my mates being gutted when I told them I'd met Kate Beckinsale.

I could go on.

But what does all this mean?

I'm not sure but I think it means good writing, laughter, compassion and people.

That sounds vague but I know those are the main reasons why I love the Bush and I think that's why the Bush found me and I found the Bush.

I hope to be around for the fiftieth.

David Eldridge

*   *   *

St Nicholas was my second play at the Bush. It was a one-man play performed by Brian Cox. I directed it.

Given Brian's busy schedule we broke the rehearsal period up. One week on, two weeks off, another week, another break, and two weeks before we opened. Consequently we rehearsed in a number of different places.

The first was the Riverside Studios in Hammersmith. I didn't know Brian. I was nervous. He was very enthusiastic and put me at my ease in rehearsal. We drank a lot of tea. This first week was quite lonely. I was in a town I didn't know very well and there wasn't a full cast to associate with. We knew we had to rely on each other.

The weather was freezing, it was the first week in January and night fell at five o'clock. I'd sort of make my way half-heartedly back to my digs knowing full well I wouldn't be able to sit there for long. It felt like every night was Sunday night and I hadn't done my homework.

I'd mooch down to Shepherds Bush and annoy the Bush staff into coming out for a drink. I had a right couple of hangovers that week. And I reckon that helped me stop worrying about the fact that my play was about a theatre critic who falls in love with an actress and ends up working for vampires. I was too tired to worry.

The next place we rehearsed was a church hall in White City. We were very cold. There was a large fan heater but it made so much noise we couldn't work with it on. It heated the air rather than the room. You could leave it on for two hours and as soon as you turned it off, you might as well have been outside. (No, it was warmer outside.)

By this time there were more of us in the room, our assistant director Helen and our stage manager Zoë. Things were a bit more chatty. Brian told us stories about working in famous classical productions and Hollywood movies. And we just sort of drank our tea.

Brian was working with an accent coach from Dublin. For a week or two he sounded like he'd lived in a caravan in every county in Ireland. Especially when he got tired. But he worked his bollocks off and began to sound quite good as the production neared. He reminded me of an uncle I had in Dublin.

We spoke about the play. We liked the character. He was honest. We felt sorry for him. We were afraid the critics would attack us for portraying one of their number in such a degrading fashion. I was also afraid they'd knock me for not writing an ensemble play which many of them suggested I do after my first Bush production, *This Lime Tree Bower*. And that had three characters. We veered from strutting arrogance to stumbling cowardice and back again.

We started doing interviews.

Brian came to Dublin. We walked around the places where I imagined the play happened. We did some shopping. Brian tried his accent out.

The next place we rehearsed was Latvia House. This was a cultural centre for Latvian expatriates near Hyde Park. I felt at home there. It might have been something to do with my Catholic upbringing. Latvia House was full of images. Depictions of battles, portraits of dignitaries, emblems with birds on them. We were in a large first-storey room with a wooden floor and high windows. We could open the windows and step out on to a balcony where we could smoke.

There was a place nearby where we could get sandwiches and so on. Brian and I sat there one lunch-time and became intrigued with the waitress's accent. She was very beautiful, very dark, she sounded Eastern European. I told Brian she reminded me of what the vampires might be like in the play. Brian said, 'She's Russian.' He had done a lot of work in Russia and was a bit of a Russophile. He called her over. I was going, 'No, Brian, don't . . .'

Brian goes, 'Hi. Are you Russian?'

She goes, 'No. Not Russian,' and walks off without elaboration. Perhaps even a little insulted. I said, 'Brian, that's quite a gift you've got there. You want to cultivate that.' Brian just laughed and began eyeing the cakes.

We finally moved to the Bush itself for a few rehearsals before previewing. We went into town and bought a costume. Brian wore it all the time. (He even got food on it one night before going on. An elderly man beside me in the audience asked me if the stains were deliberate. I said yes.)

Brian threw a party at his house. We were made to take our shoes off on arrival. At first I was annoyed, thinking this was some bullshit religious observance until Brian told me to relax, it was just so we'd feel the benefit of his underfloor heating. There was a lot of champagne. The deal was that every time a bottle was empty it was placed on one of the stairs. We wanted two empty bottles on every step, one on the way up, one on the way down. It never reached the bottom. Someone nicked the champagne.

A group of us ended up in the back garden, still in our bare feet in what must have been four or five degrees. Those of us not used to champagne invented a character who wants to impress everyone with his rubbish take on the finer things in life. This is what he was like:

'Champagne is a beautiful drink. I often feel it is like liquid beer. I was in a restaurant recently. I called the waiter over and said, "I'm about to propose to my girlfriend – but I need a stiffener. Bring me a bloody Mary, and don't be too stingy with the whiskey. Or the apple juice. Because I'll know, and I'll kick your fucking head in."'

We left at about seven in the morning.

We opened. Press night had about twenty-five critics. I sat waiting for the moment when Brian says, 'Mmm. I was a bollocks to all the other critics. And I'll tell you why, because it was this: They were all cunts.' I could remember writing that line one afternoon when I was living with my girlfriend in Leicester. I could remember my mischievious self-satisfaction, thinking what a great fellow I was altogether. And now here it was ringing out over a room full of critics. There was a silence like someone had pressed the detonator and nothing happened. And then bang, the place erupted. We were all playing.

Brian was fantastic.

I was terrified about how we were going to be received in the papers. Were we having a cheap jibe at an easy target, or were we exploring the nature of reason and responsibility? To tell you the truth I couldn't be sure any more. If the reviews were bad, I probably wanted the play to be me getting my digs in first. If they were good I wanted the play to induct me and Brian into a community that included artists, audiences *and* critics for however long it lasted. I was a picture of fickle self-preservation.

The morning the reviews came out I was on my way to a reading of my new play, *The Weir*, at the Royal Court. I bought the papers on the way. And I immediately knew we were all right. They knew they'd seen a brilliant piece of acting from Brian, and thankfully that spilled over to include the things he had been able to bring out in my writing. They were bigger men and women than most of us usually give them credit for. But we all suspect that from time to time, in our more self-confident moments perhaps.

I walked into the Royal Court every inch the young-playwright-about-town. More than a bit smug.

Towards the end of the run I went back to the Bush after a sobering few weeks in Dublin. Dominic Dromgoole, who had commissioned *St Nicholas* before going to work at the Old Vic, came to see the show with his partner Sasha and their new baby, Grainne. Grainne was about four weeks old and too young to be left with a sitter. My girlfriend, Rionach, offered to mind her in the dressing-room during the show so Sasha could see it and still feed the baby at the interval.

I sat there for a while in the dark dressing-room while Rionach walked around with Grainne in her arms. She said, 'She keeps moving so she can hear my heart.' She slept there, spreadeagled across Rionach's chest. Over the intercom we could hear Brian's performance and I wondered which was putting Grainne to sleep, Rionach's heartbeat or the dead weight of my writing. But I didn't really care. The child in Rionach's arms. And me dripping in lousy perspective.

Conor McPherson

The Bush Plays – A Chronology

1972

THE COLLECTOR adapted by David Parker (aka Brian McDermott) from the novel by John Fowles

PLUGGED IN by John McGrath, presented by 7:84 Theatre Company

PLAYS FOR RUBBER GOGO GIRLS by Chris Wilkinson, presented by the Portable Theatre Workshop

WHEN WE DEAD AWAKEN by Henrik Ibsen, presented by the Portable Theatre Workshop

THE BALLYGOMBEEN BEQUEST by John Arden and Margaretta D'Arcy, presented by 7:84 Theatre Company

MONSIEUR ARTAUD by Michael Almaz

THE RELIEF OF MARTHA KING by David Parker

FORGOTTEN DREAMS and END OF THE ROAD by Patrick Broughton

TERRIBLE JIM FITCH and LAUGHS ETC by James Leo Herlihy

STRUT AND FRET by Paddy Fletcher, presented by Incubus

MALCOLM by Lewis Nkosi, presented by Vukani Theatre Company

THE PROSECUTION by Arthur Mamaine

PICKWICK'S CHRISTMAS PARTY by Brian D. Barnes

CHRISTMAS CAROL by Frank Marcus

FOR THE LOVE OF PIAF with Magdalena Buznea

FOR SYLVIA written and directed by John Harding and John Burrows

COWBOYS NO. 2 by Sam Shepard, presented by Wakefield Tricycle Theatre Company

THE WHITE WHORE AND THE BIT PLAYER by Tom Eyen

KINGDOM COME, THE ART AND CRAFT OF POR-NOGRAPHY by Neil Hornick, presented by the Phantom Captain

THE REPRISAL by Eamonn Smullen, presented by 7:84 Theatre Company

MUSIC HALL, presented by the Post Prandialists

1973

TEDDERELLA by David Edgar
DRACULA by Stanley Eveling, David Mowat, Robert Nye,
Bill Watson, Alan Jackson, Claris Ericson, Jack Shepherd
SKIPPER and MY SISTER AND I by Howard Barker
LIFE IN A CHOCOLATE FACTORY by Richard Drain,
presented by York Shoestring Company
MAN FRIDAY by Adrian Mitchell, presented by 7:84 Theatre
Company
IN TWO MINDS by David Mercer
THERE'S ALWAYS ROOM IN THE NICK by Jonathan
Marshall
HOW TO SURVIVE IN THE NICK by Jonathan Marshall
STIFF AND SILENT by John St Clair
THE POPE'S WEDDING by Edward Bond, from the
Northcott Theatre Exeter
HUDSON'S AMAZING MONEY MAKING STEAM
DRIVEN RAILWAY PANTOMIME by Richard Drain,
presented by York Shoestring Theatre
LIMBO by Richard Drain
HALLOWE'EN by Leonard Melfi
RAMSAY MACDONALD – THE LAST TEN DAYS,
presented by Belt and Braces
TROUBLE ON THE NIGHT SHIFT, presented by Sal's
Meat Market
ESKER MIKE AND HIS WIFE AGILUK by Herschel
Hardin, presented by Factory Theatre Lab., Toronto
BAGHDAD SALOON by George F. Walker
THE MAGIC OF PANTALONE by Maria Sentivany
THE BALD PRIMA DONNA by Eugène Ionesco
UNDER THE BAMBOO TREE by Tina Brown
THE TURQUOISE PANTOMIME presented by Lindsay
Kemp
DEATH AND THE DEVIL by Frank Wedekind
PHASE THREE AND A BIT (Revue)

A WET WINTER NIGHT'S DREAM by Jonathan Marshall
GOOD TIMES by Roy Minton

1974

FLOWERS devised and directed by Lindsay Kemp
OPERATION ISKRA by David Edgar
DICK DETERRED by David Edgar
SCENE by James Dawson
JACK ... THE FLAMES by David Gale, presented by
Lumiere and Son
REPORT TO THE ACADEMY adapted from Kafka by
Tutte Lemkow
ONCE UPON A FIDDLE by Tutte Lemkow
A NAVAL OCCASION by Henry Woolf
RETROGRIM'S PROGRESS by Chris Langham
SUPERMALE by Alfred Jarry, from the Derby Playhouse
THE INSOMNIAC by Andy Smith and David Samourai
SECRETS by Richard Crane
SOMEONE ELSE IS STILL SOMEONE by Bernard
Pomerance
STALLERHOF by Franz Xaver Kroetz
GREASY SPOON by Chris Langham and Richard Fagen
* ASIDES by Alan Drury
* THE CARNATION GANG by Stephen Poliakoff
* THE SILENT MAJORITY devised by Mike Leigh
* MARBLES devised by John Chapman, Tim Fywell and
Nigel Williams
(* = Temporary Theatre Company Season)
THE KNOWLEDGE devised by Mike Bradwell, presented by
Hull Truck Theatre Company
TRAVESTIE AUS LIEBE by George Rosagut, presented by
Action Theatre Munich
FRIENDS ROADSHOW
SAWDUST CAESAR by Andy Smith
THE MOSHE DAYAN EXTRAVAGANZA by Michael
Almaz, presented by Pool Lunch Hour Theatre from Edin-
burgh

FRIENDS AND STRANGERS ALIKE by Michelene Wandor, presented by Paradise Foundry

PHIL TEDDY'S FUN PALACE, presented by Sal's Meat Market

STORY TELLERS by Terence James

THE KNOCKABOUT PUNCH AND JUDY SHOW by Andy Smith

1975

WILD ANIMALS FROM MEMORY – presented by Sal's Meat Market

END OF THE WORLD NOW – a Wakefield Tricycle production

LADY CHE – an Action Theatre production

THE COMBINATION – a revue

MY MOTHER SAYS I NEVER SHOULD – a Women's Theatre Group production

THIS PROPERTY IS CONDEMNED by Tennessee Williams

HITTING TOWN by Stephen Poliakoff

LOUD REPORTS by John Burrows, John Harding and Peter Skellern

WHITE MEN DANCING by David Gale, a Lumiere and Son Production

KITTY HAWK by Leonard Jenkin, a Wakefield Tricycle production

NOBODY KNEW THEY WERE THERE by Terence Greer

SHEPHERD'S PIE 'A Festival Hot Pot on Shepherds Bush Green', including a Bush Theatre production of Brecht's EDWARD II and Hull Truck's GRANNY CALLS THE TUNE

DECENT THINGS by Richard Crane

BLOOD RED MY SUNSET by Andy Smith

FIST OF FROZEN LIGHTNING by Andy Smith

CITY SUGAR by Stephen Poliakoff

OH WHAT! devised by Mike Bradwell for Hull Truck Theatre Company

THE KID by Keith Woods
MOBY DICK by Keith Johnstone
I'M NOT WALKING presented by Sal's Meat Market
THE SLEEPING QUARTERS OF SOFIA by David Gale, a
Lumiere and Son production

1976

EVEREST HOTEL by Snoo Wilson
WORK TO ROLE – a Women's Theatre Group production
OPERATION WORDSWORTH – Mr Pugh's Velvet Glove
Show
THE HARD STOOL by Tony Haygarth
MAGIC AFTERNOON by Wolfgang Bauer
FELONS by Nicholas Edmett and Joe Griffiths
WINTER VISITORS by Andy Smith
THE SOUL OF THE WHITE ANT by Snoo Wilson
LADYBIRD, LADYBIRD by David Pownall, a Paines Plough
production
GEISTERBAHN by Franz Xaver Kroetz
GIN TRAP devised by Sarah Pia Anderson and Sheila Kelly
WOULD YOU LIKE TO BE AN ANGEL? by J. Alexander
Ryan
BLOOD SPORTS by David Edgar
JUVENALIA by Richard Quick
OPEN TO QUESTION – a Phantom Captain production
WAX by Howard Barker
THE NAKED OBSESSIONS OF . . . John Dowie and The
Big Girl's Blouse
SOON by Colin Bennett
BRIDGET'S HOUSE devised by Mike Bradwell for Hull
Truck Theatre Company
THE FOSDYKE SAGA by Bill Tidy and Alan Plater

1977

CHARLIE AND BUCK – a Sal's Meat Market production

OUT! ON THE COSTA DEL TRICO – a Women's Theatre Workshop production
GERMAN SKERRIES by Robert Holman
COME JUBILEE by T. Bone Wilson
VAMPIRE by Snoo Wilson
BLISTERS by Sarah Pia Anderson and Sheila Kelly
HAPPY YELLOW by Tina Brown
ARE YOU NOW, OR HAVE YOU EVER BEEN? by Eric Bentley
HAPPY BIRTHDAY WANDA JUNE by Kurt Vonnegut Jr
ROSIE by Harald Mueller translated by Steve Gooch
PSYCHOSIS UNCLASSIFIED by Ken Campbell adapted from the story by Theodore Sturgeon, presented by the Science Fiction Theatre of Liverpool
PILLION by Paul Copley
ENGLAND, ENGLAND – a musical by Kevin Coyne and Snoo Wilson
WRITER'S CRAMP by John Byrne
FOSDYKE TWO by Bill Tidy and Alan Plater

1978

A BED OF ROSES devised by Mike Bradwell for Hull Truck Theatre Company
ONLY MEN SHAVE by John Dowie
OUTSIDE THE WHALE by Robert Holman
ZIGOMANIA by Tony Bicat
ON THE OUT by Tunde Ikoli, a Foco Novo Production
EEJITS by Ron Hutchinson, transfer from Sheffield Crucible Theatre
RUNNERS by Ian Brown
IN AT THE DEATH by Dusty Hughes, Snoo Wilson, Ken Campbell, Nigel Baldwin, Ron Hutchinson and Victoria Wood
FIRST BLUSH devised by Sarah Pia Anderson, transfer from Sheffield Crucible Theatre
THE TRANSFIGURATION OF BENNO BLIMPIE by Albert Innaurato

LOVED by Olwen Wymark, a Wakefield Tricycle production
A GREENISH MAN by Snoo Wilson
THE DALKEY ARCHIVE by Flann O'Brien, adapted by
Alan McLelland for Hull Truck Theatre Company

1979

THE PARANORMAL REVUE by Erik Brogger
THE COCKROACH THAT ATE CINCINATTI by Alan
Williams for Hull Truck Theatre Company
INDEPENDENCE by Mustapha Matura, a Foco Novo
production
SUBJECTS FOR INTERROGATION by Frederick Harrison
THE TAX EXILE by Jonathan Gems
LAST RESORT devised by Sarah Pia Anderson
AMABEL by Terry Johnson
PEOPLE SHOW NO. 82 – JIM'S GYM
WEDNESDAY by Julia Kearsey
WILFRID by Peter Tinniswood

1980

OOH LA LA! devised by Mike Bradwell for Hull Truck
Theatre Company
DUET FOR ONE by Tom Kempinski
VIADUCT by Paul Copley
THIRD FLIGHT by Michael McGrath, a CV One produc-
tion
THE ESTUARY by Robert Holman
COMMITMENTS by Dusty Hughes
ABRACADABRA HONEYMOON – a Phantom Captain
production
LONE STAR and PRIVATE WARS by James McClure
MEAN STREAKS by Alan Williams for Hull Truck Theatre
Company
MORE OUT THAN IN by Bernard Kops, a CV One
production

1981

A PERFECT RETREAT by Bernard Krichefski
THE DAY WAR BROKE OUT by Peter Tinniswood for
Hull Truck Theatre Company
GOLDEN LEAF STRUT by Julian Garner
THESE MEN by Mayo Simon
TAPSTER by Paul Copley
THE LAST ELEPHANT by Stephen Davis
STILL CRAZY AFTER ALL THESE YEARS devised by
Mike Bradwell, a Bush Theatre and Hull Truck co-production

1982

THE NUMBER OF THE BEAST by Snoo Wilson
THE MISS FIRECRACKER CONTEST by Beth Henley
DEVOUR THE SNOW by Abe Polsky
THE DOUBLE MAN by Ed Thomason
BREACH OF THE PEACE by Marcella Evaristi, Gerard
Mannix Flynr, Jonathan Gems, Dusty Hughes, Tunde Ikoli,
Heathcote Williams – a Paines Plough production
COMING CLEAN by Kevin Elyot
A VIEW OF KABUL by Stephen Davis

1983

HARD FEELINGS by Doug Lucie, a co-production with
Oxford Playhouse
KATE by Daniel Mornin
THE NINE NIGHT by Edgar White
CRIMES OF THE HEART by Beth Henley
LOVING RENO by Snoo Wilson
THE TOOTH OF CRIME by Sam Shepard, a Black Theatre
Co-op production
TOPOKANA MARTYRS' DAY by Jonathan Falla
TURNING OVER by Brian Thompson

1984

UNSUITABLE FOR ADULTS by Terry Johnson
CANDY KISSES by John Byrne
PROGRESS by Doug Lucie
THE DIAMOND BODY – an Operating Theatre production
WHEN I WAS A GIRL I USED TO SCREAM AND
SHOUT by Sharman MacDonald
MELANCHOLY JACQUES by Jean Jourdheuil, an Almeida
Theatre production

1985

GERTRUDE STEIN AND COMPANION by Win Wells, a
Gertrude Stein Company Production
RUMBLINGS by Peter Gibbs
COPPERHEAD by Erik Brogger
THE BELOVED, a performance by Rose English
CALIFORNIA DOG FIGHT by Mark Lee
KISS OF THE SPIDER WOMAN by Manuel Puig
THROUGH THE LEAVES by Franz Xaver Kroetz
A PRAYER FOR WINGS by Sean Mathias

1986

THE OVEN GLOVE MURDERS by Nick Darke
CHINA by Mark Brennan
WATCHING by Jim Hitchmough, a Liverpool Playhouse
production
THE NEST by Franz Xaver Kroetz
MAKING NOISE QUIETLY by Robert Holman
THE GARDEN GIRLS by Jacqueline Holborough
REQUEST PROGRAMME by Franz Xaver Kroetz
ASHES by David Rudkin

1987

AN IMITATION OF LIFE by Claire MacDonald and Pete
Brooks
MORE LIGHT by Snoo Wilson
LOVE FIELD by Stephen Davis
PEOPLE SHOW NO: 92 – WHISTLE STOP, co-production
with the People Show
EFFIE'S BURNING by Valerie Windsor
TATTOO THEATRE by Mladen Materic, Open Stage
Obala Company, Sarajevo
MYSTERY OF THE ROSE BOUQUET by Manuel Puig
IT'S A GIRL by John Burrows, Dukes Playhouse, Lancaster,
production
DREAMS OF SAN FRANCISCO by Jacqueline Holborough

1988

FIVE SMOOTH STONES by Steve Shill
HANDFUL OF STARS by Billy Roche
RAPING THE GOLD by Lucy Gannon
THE BRAVE by Sharman MacDonald
A BRIGHT ROOM CALLED DAY by Tony Kushner
ROOSTERS by Milcha Sanchez Scott
HEART THROB by Caroline Hutchinson

1989

THE FATHERLAND by Murray Watts
UTOPIA by Claire MacDonald
THE ONE SIDED WALL by Jane Cresswell and Niki
Johnson
THE WAY SOUTH by Jacqueline Holborough, by arrange-
ment with the National Theatre Studio
THE MARSHALLING YARD by Ted Moore
SONGS OF SOWETO, an evening of South African music
LOOKING AT YOU (REVIVED) AGAIN . . . by Gregory
Motton, Leicester Haymarket production

BOYS MEAN BUSINESS by Catherine Johnson
POOR BEAST IN THE RAIN by Billy Roche

1990

STREETWALKER by the Babel Theatre
JACKETS II by Edward Bond, Leicester Haymarket production
MILL FIRE by Sally Nemeth
ALICE'S DINER by Alice's Diner Theatre Company
THE TOUCH by Peter Lloyd
THE EVIL DOERS by Chris Hannan
THE WAKE – Balloonatics
DANCING ATTENDANCE by Lucy Gannon

1991

THE PITCHFORK DISNEY by Philip Ridley, Trystero Productions
THE FALLEN ANGEL by Franz Fuhmann
CROMWELL by Brendan Kennelly, Theatre Unlimited
OUR OWN KIND by Roy MacGregor
THE KISS OF LIFE by Michael Crompton, Exchange Productions
DEAD SHEEP by Catherine Johnson
BLUE NIGHT IN THE HEART OF THE WEST by James Stock, Plain Clothes Productions
A BRIGHT LIGHT SHINING by David Ashton
BELFRY by Billy Roche

1992

THE MARVELLOUS BOY by Public Parts
THE CUTTING by Maureen O'Brien
DIGGING FOR FIRE by Declan Hughes, Rough Magic Theatre Company
WHITE WOMAN STREET by Sebastian Barry

POND LIFE by Richard Cameron
PHOENIX by Roy MacGregor
JACK'S OUT by Danny Miller, co-production with Barmont Productions
MISOGYNIST by Michael Harding, Skehana Productions
EXILE by David Ian Neville, Studio Earth Theatre Company
THE WEXFORD TRILOGY: repertory production of A HANDFUL OF STARS, POOR BEAST IN THE RAIN and BELFRY by Billy Roche

1993

WAITING AT THE WATER'S EDGE by Lucinda Coxon, Pangloss Productions
SMALL TALK ABOUT CHROMOSOMES by Theatre Pur
NOT FADE AWAY by Richard Cameron
NEW MORNING by Declan Hughes, co-production with Rough Magic Theatre Company
THE CHINESE WOLF by David Ashton
BACKSTROKE IN A CROWDED POOL by Jane Coles, in association with the Royal National Theatre Studio
BEAUTIFUL THING by Jonathan Harvey
THE BABY by Chris Hannan, co-production with Wild Iris Theatre Company
KEYBOARD SKILLS by Lesley Bruce
THE CLEARING by Helen Edmundson

1994

THE CUT by Mike Cullen, Wise Guise Theatre Co
BAD COMPANY by Simon Bent, London Stage Company
DEMOCRACY by John Murrell
DARWIN'S FLOOD by Snoo Wilson
RAGE by Richard Zajdlic
IN THE HEART OF AMERICA by Naomi Wallace
THE MORTAL ASH by Richard Cameron

TWO HORSEMEN by Biyi Bandele-Thomas, co-production with the London New Play Festival
RAISING FIRES by Jenny McLeod

1995

KILLER JOE by Tracy Letts, co-production with Hired Gun Theatre Company
THE PRESENT by Nick Ward
TRAINSPOTTING by Irvine Welsh, adapted by Harry Gibson
TRUE LINES by Bickerstaffe Theatre Co
CROSSING THE EQUATOR by Jane Coles
BOOM BANG-A-BANG by Jonathan Harvey
TWO LIPS INDIFFERENT RED by Tamsin Oglesby
ONE FLEA SPARE by Naomi Wallace
KNIVES IN HENS by David Harrower, co-production with Traverse Theatre

1996

GOLDHAWK ROAD by Simon Bent
SERVING IT UP by David Eldridge
CLOCKS AND WHISTLES by Samuel Adamson
RESURRECTION by Maureen Lawrence, a Paines Plough Production
WHO SHALL BE HAPPY . . .? by Trevor Griffiths, Mad Cow Productions
THIS LIME TREE BOWER by Conor McPherson
KISS THE SKY by Jim Cartwright
BURIED TREASURE by David Ashton

1997

ALL OF YOU MINE by Richard Cameron
ST NICHOLAS by Conor McPherson

LANGUAGE ROULETTE by Daragh Carville, Tinderbox
Theatre Company
LOVE AND UNDERSTANDING by Joe Penhall
WISHBONES by Lucinda Coxon
GOLIATH by Bryony Lavery from the book by Beatrix
Campbell, Sphinx Theatre Company
DISCO PIGS by Enda Walsh, produced by Corcadorca
Theatre Company
MACKEREL SKY by Hilary Fannin
CARAVAN by Helen Blakeman

This chronology was researched by Helen Raynor

MACKEREL SKY

Hilary Fannin

To Giles and Peter, with love

Mackerel Sky premiered at the Bush Theatre, London, on 1 October 1997. The cast was as follows:

Tom	Gillian Raine
Mamie	Ruth Hegarty
Stephanie	Viviana Verveen
Madeleine	Emma McIvor
Jack	Ben Palmer
Ted	Mal Whyte

Directed by Mike Bradwell
Designed by Poppy Mitchell
Lighting by Jenny Kagan
Sound by Simon Whitehorn *and* Angela McCluney

Characters

Tom Brazil, *grandmother*
Mamie Brazil, *mother*
Stephanie Brazil, *Mamie's daughter*
Madeleine Brazil, *Mamie's daughter*
Jack Brazil, *Mamie's son*
Ted, *a neighbour of the Brazils*

Voices: radio announcer, bailiff

Act One

Scene One

Dublin, early 1970s.

A living area. In the centre, a formica-topped table. Elsewhere, fibreglass curtains, leatherette seats, a washing machine, a goldfish bowl, lots of mirrors. An uneasy room, empty, seemingly abandoned. Clothes and brown paper bags are strewn about. On the walls, there are framed photographs of discernible family groups. One large photo is of a glamorous woman in her twenties embracing a man in naval uniform whose head has been cut out of the picture. There are two doors, one upstage right leading to the street, the other downstage left leading to the rest of the house. In general, the set should tend towards an expressionistic view of semi-detached urban life.

Enter **Tom**. *She is thin, nicotine-soaked, in her seventies. She wears large-sized men's slippers, emphasising her frailty. She carries a rifle. She goes to the washing-machine, a top-loader with a heavy hand-wringer, opens it and removes a birthday cake from inside.*

Enter **Mamie**, *a glamorous woman in her forties. She is dressed for outdoors in a fun-fur coat and carries a small lipstick case with a mirror.*

The two women look at each other.

Tom Happy birthday.

Silence. **Tom** *replaces the cake.* **Mamie** *applies lipstick.* **Tom** *moves downstage, sits and lights a cigarette.*

Mamie They'll kill you, you know.

Tom I know.

The doorbell rings. Neither woman moves to answer it. It rings again.

Mamie (*calling*) Stephanie.

Enter **Stephanie**, *adolescent, watchful, direct, theatrical. She wears a feather boa. She is carrying a life-size cardboard cut-out of her* *father in naval uniform, intact except for a gap in the shape of an arm across his torso. She places the figure on the floor.*

Steph   What?

The doorbell rings.

Mamie   Door.

Steph *opens upstage door to* **Ted**, *a car-coated benign man.*

Mamie   Ted.

Ted (*as a greeting*)   Happy bir . . .

Mamie (*moving to upstage exit*)   Thanks for the lift, Ted. Arriving by bus is so pedestrian. Stephanie, do your homework and don't let your grandmother shoot anyone. We'll eat . . .

Steph   When?

Mamie   What?

Steph   When will we eat?

Mamie   Later.

Steph   At tea-time?

Mamie   Sure.

Steph   You'll be home for a family tea?

Mamie   Yeah.

Steph   At six o'clock?

Mamie   I'll . . .

Steph   Come home for a family tea?

Mamie   Jesus!

Steph   Say it.

Mamie   Stephanie!

Steph   Just say it.

Mamie   At six o'clock, I'll be home for a family tea.

Steph   Thank you.

Mamie (*under her breath, as she pockets a china ornament*)   Christ.

Ted (*to* **Tom** *and* **Steph**)   I may, em, that is to say, I may drop . . .

Steph   Back?

Tom   Dead?

Ted   Back. Yes, I may drop back.

Mamie   Stephanie, put your father away. Ted?

Mamie *exits with* **Ted**, *taking with her a hatstand that has been standing next to the door.*

Tom   Go away and I'll give you ten bob.

Steph   I don't want your money. They'll kill you, you know.

Tom   I know.

Pause. **Tom** *cleans rifle.*

Steph   Madeleine got a night-and-day dress. It's so cool. It's reversible, you can wear it out, you know, to the shops or somewhere and then you can go to bed in it 'n you don't even have to take it off. But Anna Roache said that Madeleine looked like she was going out in her nightie, and anyway Mamie said 'oh take it off', and then Madeleine got sick all over the toilet and a bit in the hall 'n she said she was allergic to smoked mackerel, which she wasn't the last time Jack brought it home. And now Mamie's not even speaking to her.

Tom   I'm surprised the old bitch was out of the bath long enough to notice.

She loads the gun.

Steph   You're not supposed to talk like that. You better hope that God doesn't have a good memory.

Tom   Old barefoot holey hands doesn't bother me. I'm not going anywhere that he has any influence.

Pause.

Steph   I got you something.

Tom   Keep it.

Steph   It hasn't been anointed.

Tom   What is it?

Steph *takes* **Mamie**'*s lipstick box with mirror from her pocket.*

Steph   I just stole it from Mamie. She'll think she dropped it. See, you'll like it, the mirror is just long enough to see your mouth 'n you don't have to look at the rest of you.

Tom (*holding mirror*)   I had a beautiful mouth, you know. Wouldn't give you tuppence for it now. I'm rotting. Ah yes, the garden gate's closed for Maud. They won't steep my old head in formaldehyde, they won't wear scraps of me around their dirty necks.

Steph   Sister Colette said dying brings you closer to God, that his eternal love grows stronger the closer he gets.

Tom   She's speaking from experience, is she?

Tom *takes aim at a large photograph of* **Mamie**.

Steph   I'm setting the clock for two. (*Setting it and placing it next to the radio.*) What exactly is a revival?

Tom   Nothing your mother will ever experience.

Steph   Oh.

She gathers paper, scissors, schoolbag et cetera. During the rest of the scene, she alternates between making a paper-chain and doing her homework.

We had religion in the dinner room yesterday 'cos Sister Mary Wiseman cut off the top of her little finger with the guillotine. And anyway, Sister Mary Coleman had us

instead and we were doing Eden. And Sister Mary
Coleman said that after Eve gave in to her temptation,
everything in Eden withered and died, and there were
storms and plagues of locusts and stuff. And instead of just
hanging around, Adam and Eve had to 'toil' in the garden
– and Louise Tobin burst out laughing, and Sister Coleman
said 'Louise, I would like you to tell the class just exactly
what you find so amusing.' And Louise was mortified.

Tom   Poor little sisters of the halitosis. Should be rolled
down the hill in a barrel of spikes.

Steph   Look, Tom, right now this minute, God is in this
room listening to every word you say.

Tom   He is, is he?

Steph   Yes. And every mean and dreadful thing you say
causes him actual physical pain.

Tom   Druids and numbs – a pox on the lot of them.
Angels of death. They'll bleach you and scald you and
shroud you in linen. What'll you do then? Count your
beads and wait for Gabriel? They're not getting their milky
hands on me. I don't want their fat lips praying over me.
Spooning their gruel into me. Their wet bread and
dripping.

Steph   That was the olden days, Tom, it's not like that
any more. Gruel is banished, you get soup 'n a roll now, 'n
the butter is shaped like little golfballs. It's not the same as
when you were growing up, it's just not the same.

Enter **Madeleine**. *She is in her late teens, fashionable, provocative
and reluctant. She is wearing a diaphanous gown and is carrying
tights, underwear et cetera, which she drapes over the cut-out of her
father. She sits, one bare foot on the table.*

Tom   There was a convent in our town. A hundred girls
sent there by the Inspector of Cruelty. Given to the numbs
for safekeeping, and beaten and starved and paraded
through the streets on a Sunday morning in their antique
boots and their shabby black dresses. Their skinny little

wrists. You smelt them before you spotted them. Poor little children of Eve.

Maddie (*painting her toes, legs exposed*) Stephanie, what's our father doing out? He's giving me the creeps.

Steph What happened them?

Tom Who?

Steph The poor little children of Eve.

Tom How the hell do I know? (*To* **Maddie**.) Is that the night side or the day side?

Maddie Night.

Tom You're early.

Steph What happened the little girls?

Tom I don't know, Stephanie, what happens to anybody? You live and die.

Maddie What time is Mamie's revival at?

Steph Two.

Maddie I didn't know you could get revived on the radio.

Tom You can't.

Steph Imagine that signal, right, like a big beacon beaming across the shipping lanes, and then imagine if my dad was lying in a shiny wooden bunk, right . . .

Maddie Whittling down his willow stick, whistling 'The Lonely Boatman'.

Steph And then he'd hear Mamie . . . (*Singing.*) 'How are things in Glochamarra?'

Maddie Forget it, Steph. You've got more chance of meeting the Dalai Lama.

Steph Sister Colette said if you trust in Jesus, you can have anything you want.

Maddie   She obviously never met the old man.

Tom (*mimicking* **Steph**)   'Sister Colette said if you trust in Jesus, you can have anything you want.' Well, maybe if you ask him nicely, he'll return my six silver inlaid teaspoons in their mahogany box.

Steph   He didn't take them. Mamie sold them to pay the telephone bill. Anyway, that's too temporal.

Maddie   What?

Steph   Too temporal. (*To* **Tom**.) You'd have to ask Saint Anthony about that. Jesus mainly deals with spiritual needs.

Tom   She sold my teaspoons?

Maddie   Oh no, we haven't been cut off again? It's so embarrassing.

Tom   I don't even use the telephone. Everyone I know is dead.

Steph   Well, Mamie needs the phone. Her agent might call.

Maddie   Don't make me laugh. It'll distress my epidermis.

Tom   My china dog with horsehair whiskers?

Steph   She pocketed it on her way out. We all have our crosses to bear, Tom.

Maddie   No, please, not more God. I can't stand it, Stephanie, there's something wrong with you. Why aren't you out playing chasing or something? (*To window.*) This place stinks.

Steph   Actually, I'm trying to do my homework.

Maddie   Stephanie, are they my fishnets?

Steph *moves upstage to a large fish-tank containing one goldfish which survives despite sharing its habitat with* **Steph**'s *sea artefacts. One of these is a green glass buoy suspended in the fishnets draped over the side of the tank.* **Steph** *pulls the fishnets out of the water.*

Steph   Duncan looks worse.

Tom   Company depresses him.

Maddie   They're all saggy!

Tom   I know the feeling.

Maddie   It's not fair, Stephanie, why can't you leave my things alone? I hate this bloody house – nothing is anywhere. Where's the iron? And how come we never have any biscuits?

Maddie *has found the ironing-board and now assembles it.*

Steph   Mamie's birthday cake is in the washing-machine.

Pause.

Maddie   Why? Why is Mamie's birthday cake in the washing-machine?

Steph   It's a surprise, made it myself, sieve and mix forty-four candles, we're having a family dinner, Mamie said. It's for jelly.

Maddie   What's for jelly? The birthday cake?

Steph   Yeah.

Maddie   Good. I'm starving.

Steph   The iron is in the coal-bunker.

Maddie   Why?

Steph   Me 'n Jack were practising fusion.

Maddie   Get it.

Steph *exits downstage right.*

Tom   Eddie Coot draped in candlewick – a hell of an apparition for a barely continent old woman at one o'clock in the morning . . .

Maddie   It was raining. His clothes got wet.

Tom   Mackerel vomiting?

Maddie Who told you? It was off.

Tom *places her hands over her mouth – i.e. speak no evil.* **Steph** *returns with the iron.*

Steph What does 'happiness is a tight pussy' mean?

Maddie What?

Steph Last night, when Eddie Coot brought you home, he had a T-shirt 'n it said 'happiness is a tight . . .'

Maddie You should've been in bed.

Steph I was. I got up. I thought you were Mamie.

Maddie It doesn't mean anything, it's silly . . .

The alarm on the clock goes off very loudly. **Steph** *turns the alarm off and the radio on.*

Tom (*to* **Maddie**) The revival. Place your bets.

Lar (*radio announcer*) Trathnona maith a cairde agus welcome. Welcome to Radio Eireann Light and 'Songbook', bringing you easy-listening favourites live from the studio. Brought to you courtesy of Flahavans The Progressive Oat.

Steph (*mimicking*) 'Flahavans The Progressive Oat.'

Tom Shh, don't mock the afflicted. Let's hear her.

Lar Delighted to have with us today the gorgeous glam lamb of the cabaret circuit, Mamie Brazil. Mamie, you never look a day older.

Tom Glam lamb?

Maddie Shh.

Mamie It's my family, Lar, they're a great bunch. Honestly, we're like a shower of kids. They keep me young, Lar. No doubt.

Lar Absolutely.

Mamie I mean, when I'm hanging out with my girls,

people say to me: 'My God, you could be sisters.'

Lar   Fantastic. Now, Mamie, a little bird told me that you're planning on hitting the circuit with great gusto this year . . . (*Changing to 'in-depth interview' voice.*) We've missed you, Mamie. What kept you away so long?

Mamie   Well, Lar, as anyone who knows the real me will tell you, my family are my everything.

Lar   The offers stop coming . . .

Mamie   Well, no, Lar . . .

Lar   The phone plays dead . . .

Mamie (*controlled*)   No.

Lar   You watch your maracas lose their lustre.

Mamie   Lar!

Lar   Sorry, Mamie, you were saying?

Mamie   Family, Lar. Hell, Lar, there are times when kids need their mom – and when that time came, Lar, as it does for every mother, well, darn it, I just hadda be there for them.

Steph   Give me some mackerel. I want to vomit.

Lar   It hasn't all been a bed of roses, has it, Mamie?

Mamie   It has not, Lar, it certainly has not.

Lar   Mamie Brazil, still singin', still swingin'. What have you got in store for us today?

Mamie   An old favourite, Lar – 'Glochamarra'.

Guitar accompaniment starts. **Mamie** *sings 'How Are Things in Glochamarra?'* **Steph** *rolls around clutching her stomach as if she's been shot. The song continues under the dialogue.*

Maddie (*turning down radio*)   Why does she do this to me?

Steph   It's for her profile.

Maddie Why does she have to have a profile? Everyone else's mother manages without one.

Tom She is not everyone else's mother.

Steph Does Eddie Coot's mother have a profile?

Maddie Of course not, she's a Protestant. She has clean windows and a gravy boat and she makes her Christmas cake in August. She doesn't need a profile.

Tom Your grandfather was a Protestant.

Maddie So you've told us.

Steph What else?

Maddie What else what?

Steph Has Eddie Coot's mother?

Maddie Fitted sheets, cocker spaniel, hostess trolley.

Steph A cocker spaniel!

Maddie Protestants always have cocker spaniels.

Tom Shined shoes, soft hands – you could tell him a mile away.

Steph You do realise that he's probably still in limbo?

Tom I'll give you limbo.

Steph *holds up the paper-chain she has been making. It says 'HAPY BIRTHDAY MAMIE'.*

Maddie If either of you mention God, I'm leaving. There's two Ps in 'happy'.

Steph (*peeved*) It's all right for you, Maddie. You've time to mend your ways, but Tom is in mortal danger.

Maddie Of what, eternal damnation? It'll suit her, Stephanie. Will you iron my hair?

Steph No. Listen. (*Reading from copy book.*) 'My Pet, by

Stephanie Brazil.'

Tom   Mine. He's MY pet.

Steph   I know he's your pet, but I don't have a pet, do I? And the title we were given was 'My Pet', so, if you don't mind, I'll write about yours.

Tom   Be my guest.

Steph   My Pet, by Stephanie Brazil. 'Small yet sturdy/ Orange, not gold/My pet's name is Duncan/He's not very old.'

Maddie   That's going to bore Sister Colette to death.

Tom   A divine purpose.

Steph   Do you mind? – 'Alone in his fish-tank/By night and by day/With no lady fishes/To light up his way.'

Maddie   Christ.

Steph   'With no lady fishes/To light up his way/The glow of our friendship/In his little soul/Is the light through the darkness/In his lonely bowl.'

Pause.

Maddie   It's awful, Steph.

Tom   I'd rather you didn't write about my fish again, Stephanie.

Steph *turns up radio.*

Mamie   I've taken the knocks, Lar, the rough with the smooth, but I'm not afraid to look life in the eye. To say yes, yes, I'm flawed, I'm battered, I'm bruised, but I'm a fighter, Lar, and, God willing, I'll fight to see another day.

Lar   In a word, Mamie, what's it all about?

Mamie   Family, Lar, family and faith.

Fade out. Pause. Lights up.

Scene Two

Same room. Evening of the same day.

The paper-chain with the words 'HAPY BIRTHDAY MAMIE' has been strung up. An occasional balloon floats around. **Steph** *is sitting by the fish-tank.* **Tom** *is at the window, gun pointed indoors at an imaginary child downstage centre.*

Tom (*talking to imaginary child*)   What's wrong with you? You've the colour of decay and the smell of camphor. (*To* **Steph**.) What's wrong with that child? I told him not to come again. (*To imaginary child.*) Barley sweets from Dr Brazil, is it? That's some malady, that you can suck it away. And you can leave your dog at the door, there's nothing in Dr Brazil's black bag for dogs, sick dogs or sound. (*To* **Steph**.) Pretty child, always has an umbrella. Of course, his father's from Limavady, that's all that's wrong with him. Came up from Limavady in a big black car. Should have been dispatched long ago.

Enter **Jack** *through upstage door. He is in his early twenties, thin and hopeful, wearing an oilskin jacket and carrying a canvas bag. From the doorway, he watches* **Tom**, *then looks over to* **Steph**, *who shrugs.*

Tom (*to* **Steph**)   I told him, I told him, I don't want their dirty lives in my kitchen, bringing their germs and their infestations. Soft man, easy to love, is it? Easy to love when you grow up smelling leather. Oh, they loved him all right, their yellow-skinned Doctor Brazil, with his soft hands on their mange.

Pause.

I should never have married a gentle man. I didn't deserve him. (*Looking out of the window.*) There, look at them bringing their diseases, lapping at him. (*To imaginary child.*) Out. Out! Join the rancid queue for ointment, your grey skin on fresh bones. Don't look at me . . . (*To* **Steph**.) That child is as bold as brass. (*To imaginary child.*) Don't you wave your brolly at me, my man.

Jack (*going to* **Tom**)   Do you think he'll get the weather
he's expecting?

Tom   You're back, are you? You're late for your surgery.
There's running sores all over my parlour. They should
wait in the yard for you, air their afflictions. (*To imaginary
child.*) Will you stop your nonsense! He won't leave me
alone. I don't know what he wants. Go home, will you ...

Jack (*a little self-consciously, bringing imaginary child to door and
opening it*)   Off you go. Safe home, be a good boy and, eh,
don't forget to take your medicine. (*Calling.*) Watch the
puddle.

Steph *shakes her head.*

Jack (*opening his bag and taking out a wrapped gift*)   Where's
Mamie?

Steph (*shrugging*)   She was supposed to be home at six.

Jack   Oh.

Steph   I made her a birthday cake. (*Gesturing to the
machine.*) In the washing-machine.

Jack   You made her a birthday cake in the washing-
machine? Fair play.

Steph   No. I made her a birthday cake *that's* in the
washing-machine.

(*Referring to* **Jack***'s gift.*) What is it?

Jack   A lesser spotted dogfish.

He goes to the washing-machine and takes out the birthday cake.

Here, Tom, did you ever hear this one? 'She was only a
fish-gutter's daughter, but she'd barrel a pike in her
knickers.' No? Not to worry. Have a piece of cake.

Steph *unwraps the gift: it's a bottle of gin.*

Steph   Good week then?

Jack   Steamed, dropped, netted, pulled, sorted, boxed,

twenty-five seventy-five, half-share, great week.

Tom They never feed me, you know.

She accepts a bit of cake.

You're not my husband, are you?

Jack *shakes his head.*

Tom Remind me; no, don't. I know who you are. Jack. Decay, Jack; my mind is being eaten by the mice of decay.

Jack Bummer.

Tom Are you the fish-gutter?

Jack Half-share deckboy – 'The Granuaile'.

Tom You look like your grandfather; you have the yellow Brazil skin. Soft hands, sad-eyed. You won't last, none of them did.

Jack I thought I took after my mother.

Tom Do you sing and steal from the elderly?

Jack Not simultaneously.

Tom You're a Brazil.

Jack (*to* **Steph**) So, what's the story?

Tom Your father is a fine, healthy, beautiful man. My blood, of course. Marvellous teeth. Do you remember him?

Jack As little as possible.

Steph I think she's hungry.

Tom Who's 'she'? The cat's mother?

Jack Steph?

Steph (*sighs*) Maddie's upstairs shaving her legs. She's seen Eddie Coot every single night this week, even yesterday when she was throwing up your smoked mackerel. Mamie got revived on the radio. You missed 'How Are Things in Glochamarra?'

Jack Darn.

Steph And a stirring 'Guandalamera'.

Tom A son can be a spectacular disappointment. Your father, on the other hand, has balls, tenacity.

Jack I think we should feed her.

Tom He should never have married your mother. Vain, powdery little woman trying to hold back the tide . . .

Jack The tide, is he? Last week, he was a great butting oak and we were tangleweed in his roots.

Steph Mamie might bring home a chicken.

Pause.

But somehow I doubt it. I've eaten so many fish, I feel like a whale.

Jack They're a bit hard to get home on a bicycle.

Steph Do you think we could eat the Cuban missile crisis food? It's been under the stairs for years.

Jack I dunno. Do you want me to phone the White House?

Steph You can't. We've been cut off.

Steph *exits through downstage door to look for food in the cupboard under the stairs.*

Tom I walked three Irish miles to school every rain-soaked day of my childhood to be beaten. They never beat the tradesmen's children. They stood my brother up on the desk and that great bastun of a teacher knocked him senseless to the floor with his dirty red fist.

Steph (*offstage, shouting*) There's eight tins of Arctic salmon in here, a bottle of baby beetroot and some chocolate instant whip.

Jack Mamie expected a cessation of hostilities by tea-time.

Steph (*coming back in with tins of salmon and a bottle of baby beetroot*)   People don't survive nuclear wars anyway. We wouldn't have survived with a thousand tins of Arctic salmon. After a couple of days, people just melt.

Tom   They never beat the doctor's son. That's what I want, I said, a doctor's son.

Steph *turns on the radio. The original version of 'Guandalamera' is being played.*

Tom (*rifle aimed at radio*)   Thief, spoon-stealer . . . Cheap-shoed, shoddy-minded, witless tart.

Steph   It's not her, Tom.

Jack (*above the music, which is quite loud*)   Mamie been pawning the silver again?

Steph   Since Monday: six silver spoons, one china dog and my confirmation medal.

Tom   The standard lamp and the hatstand.

Jack   Right.

He turns the music down, then nods towards **Tom** *and the rifle.*

Are we expecting bailiffs?

Tom   Why my son ever married that woman is beyond me. She drove him out, you know, with her squalid small-mindedness.

Jack (*opening the salmon tins and beetroot bottle*)   I don't remember him needing much encouragement.

Tom   You can't expect a man of his calibre to shuffle in the muddy bed of domesticity.

Jack   I thought shuffling in muddy beds was his speciality.

Tom   All these woeful people with their back rashers and the body of Jesus. My son couldn't breathe here, he couldn't breathe. All part of his training, you see, to despise the masses.

Jack   Have you ever heard from him, Tom?

Tom   Beautiful young cadet. White teeth, white shirt.

Jack   Have you ever heard from him, Tom?

Pause. **Jack** *hands* **Tom** *an opened tin of salmon and a fork.*
Tom *puts the gun down and eats from the tin.*

Tom   You're right, you do take after your mother. Your
eyes are too close together. I suppose you'll want to join
the entertainment industry.

Jack   Still, you can't fault the bastard for style. No
sentimentality, no curiosity, no regrets. He might as well
have drowned, Tom, because he disappeared into those
waves as mercilessly as rock.

Tom   Speaks the fish-gutter.

Steph   What do you mean, disappeared into those waves?
He didn't drown.

Jack   No, Steph, he didn't drown. He just kept going.

The doorbell rings.

Tom   (*slamming down the tin of salmon violently*)   Listen, fish-
gutter, your father is a navigator.

Jack   (*going to door*)   Oh my God, Steph, our father is an
alligator.

Tom   You're a fool, Jack.

Jack *opens door to* **Ted***, who holds a bunch of lilies.*

Jack   The question is, Ted: if he's such a shit-hot
navigator, how come he never found his way home?

Ted   Ah, there you are, yes, home from the high seas.
Well . . .

Jack   Are they for me? How thoughtful.

Ted   Thank . . . I mean no, no, they're for your mother.
A small token, you know, of my . . .

Steph   Appreciation?

Tom   Infatuation?

Jack   Esteem?

Ted   Esteem. Thank you, yes.

Jack   Come in, Ted. Have a piece of cake.

Ted (*coming in*)   Well, I shouldn't really intrude on a family occasion.

Jack   And what family occasion would that be?

Tom   For Christ's sake, man, you're here so often the fish could forge your signature.

Jack   Make yourself at home, Ted.

Ted   Thanks.

He takes a seat. Silence.

Mamie's ... em ... ?

Steph   Out.

Ted   Right. I think there's two Ps in 'HAPPY'.

Steph   I know.

Pause.

Ted   Good gutting this week then?

Jack   Exceptional.

Steph   He's not a fish-gutter, he's a trawlerman.

Tom   Apparently.

Jack   Half-share deckboy on the H&H, Ted, filling the miscellaneous boxes.

Ted   Indeed.

Ted *looks mystified.*

Steph   The H&H, Ted, is a section of the navigational grid just north of Anglesey: treacherous waters, large sharks

. . . and cross-currents, mullets, conditions rarely good to variable.

Ted   I see.

Tom   Said the blind man.

Jack   Your cake, Ted. Unfortunately, my mother is not here to join us, but maybe you'd like to make a wish for her.

Tom   Or maybe you'd like to wish for something useful.

Ted   (*accepting cake*)   Thank you.

Steph   It's no joke, you know, being a half-share deckboy.

Ted   I never imagined . . .

Steph   Sometimes, in the dead of night, Jack has to haul bulging nets out of the water with his bare hands, while the 'men' sleep off their drunkenness . . .

Ted   (*mouth full*)   Really?

Steph   And once, right, with the waves crashing on to the open deck, he pulled out this enormous pike . . . with teeth . . . a blind pike with a head like a mallet.

Ted   Goodness.

Steph   It runs in our family, you know. Water.

Tom   Blind pikes! My son pitted himself against nature, dizzied her with grit.

Jack   And that's no mean feat.

Tom   You've doll's hair and a bicycle; what would you know about danger?

Ted   I once had occasion to take the ferry to Llandudno.

Silence.

Not a great adventure, I realise, but it certainly made me respect the seafaring man. Water, water, everywhere, as they say.

Jack   It's a phenomenon all right.

Ted   It's in your blood, of course. I must say, I always resented getting wet. Lacked a certain ruggedness, I suppose. Your father, on the other hand, from my memory of him, strode around these streets as if they were too small for him. Looking at the weather; land-locked, you assumed. Exuded ruggedness, if that's, em . . . Anyway, well, there he is, a seafaring man. Yes, no doubt.

Pause.

Steph   He sent me a postcard.

Steph *produces a battered card from her pocket and hands it to* **Ted**.

Jack   Steph, don't.

Steph   Read it.

Ted   I really don't want to intrude . . .

Steph   Read it.

Reluctantly, **Ted** *begins to read the card to himself.*

Steph   Out loud.

Ted   Tuesday, August sixth. Vessel, San Pedro. Forty-one degrees and twenty-five minutes north, eight degrees and fifty minutes west. Dear Stephanie, heavy weather in the Atlantic forced us to dock in Oporto on the south-west coast of Portugal. With winds gusting to fourteen knots and an inclement forecast, we have decided to hove-to and sample the delights of this historic town. Crew are in good spirits. Hope the same can be said of all on the home front. Your loving . . .

Pause.

. . . Dad.'

Steph   It's addressed to me, isn't it? He wrote it to me. It's my card.

Tom (*eating from the tin again*)   Rapacious old bastard. Well,

I hope it stays fine for him. I'm sure we'd all love to see the sea. Oh yessir, we'd be wrapped in wool on the wooden decks with the boys in their livery delivering gin.

Jack   Stephanie, the card is a fucking antique. You could barely read when he sent it; in fact, you could barely walk.

Steph   I don't care what you say, it's my card, he wrote to me, I am the one he wrote to. He did not write to Maddie, he did not write to Mamie, he did not write to you, he wrote to me. (*To* **Ted**.) Didn't he?

Ted   He wrote to you, Stephanie.

Maddie (*off*)   Jesus fucking wept.

She enters.

Stephanie, where is my luggage? Hi, Ted.

Steph   What?

Ted   Sorry, Madeleine, did I wake you?

Maddie (*puzzled*)   No. (*To* **Steph**.) My brand-new Green Shield Stamp luggage. (*To* **Jack**.) What are you doing here?

Jack   It's Saturday.

Maddie   Oh, right.

Steph   Why do you need luggage?

Maddie   Why do you think?

Jack   Mamie must have pawned it.

Maddie   I am going to remain really calm and not overstretch my facial muscles.

Jack   Are you leaving, Maddie?

Maddie   Yes. I've decided to live with Eddie Coot and be a Protestant. I'm going to be very serene and polish things.

Pause.

(*Loud.*) Oh my God, my luggage! I'll kill her! What does

she expect me to do? Turn up on his door like a bag lady? (*To* **Ted**, *who is still holding the postcard.*) Who's that from?

Ted   Your father.

Steph   Does this mean you're never coming back either?

Maddie   Christ, he's alive.

Jack   Not necessarily. The postmark's older than Steph.

Maddie   Oh. He wrote to me once: 'Something, something, squally showers.' She'll pay for this – eight hundred stamps plus post and packaging. I've been saving for it since I was ten.

Steph   What else?

Maddie   A facial steamer.

Steph   I mean, what else did the letter say?

Maddie   I don't remember. Anyway, he came home from that trip.

Steph   To have me?

Maddie   Well, I don't know if he planned to, but yes, they had you.

Steph   What was he wearing?

Maddie   What?

Steph   What was he wearing when he came home to have me?

Maddie   Jesus, Steph, I don't know . . . Hold on, I remember. He brought me a lamb, a little furry lamb . . .

Steph   Madeleine!

Maddie   He'd been to Norway. He said: 'A lamb for a lamb.' I bet that's why I'm a vegetarian. Jack, will you iron my hair?

Jack   No. You're *not* a vegetarian.

Maddie   I am now.

Jack   Since when?

Maddie   Yesterday. Ted, are you busy?

Jack   Is that why you threw up my smoked mackerel?

Ted   Not particularly.

Maddie   Is what why I threw up your smoked mackerel?
Ted?

Jack   Because you're a vegetarian?

Maddie   More or less. (*To* **Ted**.) Will you iron my hair?

Ted   I thought you were leaving.

Maddie   I am – but not looking like this.

Maddie *has put up the ironing-board during Scene One. She now
plugs in the iron, hands* **Ted** *a sheet of brown paper and, bending
over, lays her head on the board.*

Jack   Well, which? More or less?

Maddie   What?

Jack   Did you throw up my mackerel less because you
were a vegetarian and more because you were something
else?

Maddie   Yeah. Anyway, how do you know I threw up
the bloody mackerel? Ted, I'm not down here for the good
of my health.

Steph   Put the paper over her hair, Ted.

Ted   Oh . . . right.

Jack   So you're not a 'don't eat anything with a face'
fundamentalist?

Maddie   No.

Tom *and* **Steph** *mime ironing to a bewildered* **Ted**.

Jack   You're pregnant!

Steph   Oh my God.

Ted, *who had begun ironing, stops.*

Maddie   Ted – my hair! Of course I'm not pregnant; that's why I barfed all over the landing.

Jack   You barfed all over the landing because you're *not* pregnant?

Maddie   I couldn't be. I'm on the pill.

Jack   Where did you get it?

Maddie   Anna Roache. She got a year's supply in England when she was doing her nurse's exam. She gave me six months' worth for a fiver and my turquoise hot pants.

Jack   Cool.

Steph   Oh my God, Maddie, I beg you, don't take those capsules of evil.

Maddie   What?

Steph   Sister Colette warned us. Each capsule of evil, she said, contains a tiny serpent that eats the tiny unborn baby alive.

Maddie   Bollox.

Steph   Maddie, Maddie, it's true. Once there was this woman, right, 'n she left one of the pills out on the mantelpiece overnight, and the very next morning, when she came downstairs, the serpent was wriggling around a framed photograph of the woman's only child on her communion day.

Maddie   You're drowning in shite, Steph, you know. You really have to stop believing all their propaganda.

Steph   Do you believe in God, Maddie?

Maddie   Occasionally. Like if I'm really scared, you know, like walking past Victor Burke's house if it's dark. That guy is so fucking weird.

Jack   He's not weird, Maddie, he's just lonely.

Maddie   He smells . . . weird.

Steph (*to* **Jack**)   What about you? Do you believe in God?

Pause.

Jack   I don't think so.

Tom   All the fools touting gods, they're carpet salesmen. I told you already, Stephanie: you live, you die.

Steph (*to* **Ted**)   Well?

Ted   Well, I suppose it's a question for the individual.

Jack   What do you want, Steph?

Steph   Does Mamie believe in God?

Jack   Mamie? It depends who's asking her.

Pause.

What's wrong, Steph?

Steph   Someone is going to get blamed for this, someone is going to have to pay. We're being watched even now, even this millionth of a second we're being watched. He knows what's inside your head before you do; you can't hide from him. Someone is going to have to pay for all this. People can't just do what they want. What would happen if everybody just did what they wanted to do?

Maddie   I do.

Steph   Well, someone is going to have to take the blame. (*To* **Tom**.) I mean, what's going to happen to your soul if you shoot a bailiff?

Tom   It'll be seated at the right hand of the father.

Jack   Do you worry about us, Stephanie?

Steph   Yes, and I worry what will happen when you're dead.

Jack   What, that we won't get into heaven?

Steph *nods.*

Jack Maybe they'll let us in on your passport.

Steph (*very upset*) But what if I go wrong too?

Maddie I *do* remember him when he came home to have you. He wore red canvas trousers and he smelt of Sweet Afton.

Steph Did he ever see me?

Maddie No.

There is a knock on the street door.

Jack (*quietly*) Shit.

Tom *turns to the window with the gun. She is joined by* **Steph** *and* **Jack**.

Ted I'll get it.

Maddie Jesus Christ, my hair!

Jack Quiet.

Bailiff's Voice (*off*) I have a summons for Mrs Margaret Brazil. Acting under instructions from the county sheriff, we may use reasonable force to enter the premises.

Maddie Pretend she's not here.

Jack She's *not* here.

Maddie Right.

Steph (*calling out of the window*) I'm afraid our mother is ill. She's in hospital suffering from . . .

Tom Syphilis.

Steph From her appendix. You'll have to leave it for another day.

Van doors, chains, footsteps can be heard off.

Bailiff's Voice (*off*) In accordance with the bye-laws of this jurisdiction, and as we have tried and failed to present Mrs Brazil with this summons on three separate occasions, we will now enter the property to redeem goods to the value of her outstanding debts.

Jack   Well, dangle me chaps and call me Andy, the posse has arrived.

Fade.

Act Two

Scene One

Same room. Same day, late at night.

Low light. The room is empty of furniture, except for the table, which remains centre. The telephone, the lilies and the bottle of gin remain, and the cut-out stands downstage centre.

Jack *lies on the table making sea sounds.* **Mamie** *is standing next to the upstage door, having just come in.* **Jack** *sees her and begins to speak.*

Jack There's great solidity in a table, in the brush of a bus seat, in the flat of your bed on the flat of your back. In my wet bunk on the Grainne, I dream of ordinary things and they are fucking extraordinary. A bath mat, a black dog, a kiss.

Pause.

(*To cut-out.*) God bless you, rubber-booted scurvy man, you brown-skinned circumnavigator. You disappeared into your own arsehole and that's some trick for an alligator.

Mamie (*moving downstage, surveying the empty room*) I have a dream; it recurs. I'm running, light as a feather, up a staircase – beautiful, sweepingly beautiful, you know the kind, tap-dancing kind. Sharp and, at the top, when I reach the top, there are doors, high solid heavy doors reeking of promise. And I open them, and there is nothing, absolutely nothing.

Pause.

I had a cake in that washing-machine.

Jack We ate it. Happy birthday.

He hands her the bottle of gin.

Mamie Thanks. We should have a party: bring a bottle,

a glass and a chair. (*To cut-out.*) Did you send the flowers? I hate them. I hate lilies. The day I married, my mother insisted on lilies. They haunt me. I remember my father in his high bed: tiny, putrescent. There were lilies in his room to disguise the smell of death.

Mamie *looks around for glasses, revealing the emptiness of the cupboards as she does so. She finds a plastic beaker and a jug.*

Jack (*gesturing at the cut-out*)   Do I look like him?

Mamie   God, no, nobody was allowed to look like him. We couldn't blight his perfection.

Jack   I can't go back.

Mamie   Of course you can.

Jack   They're big, oily, brutal, half-witted, stinking bastards, as thick as the heels of a Mullingar heifer.

Mamie   Ignore them.

Jack   Ignore them! I scrape their shite off the sides, I . . . (*Receiving beaker of gin.*) . . . thanks. I breathe their white-arsed farts in my sleep.

Mamie   Pretend it's happening to someone else. You won't be a deckboy for ever.

Enter **Tom**.

Tom   Let's pretend it's *all* happening to someone else, will we?

Mamie (*turning*)   Where did you spring from?

Tom   That's *my* jug.

Mamie   It is not your jug.

Tom   It is so mine: 'Honeymoon Bundoran, God keep you.'

Mamie (*looking at words on jug*)   You can have it.

Tom *takes the jug and drinks from it.*

Tom   Ginger ale? No? Not to worry. Cheers.

Jack (*handing his beaker to* **Mamie**)   Cheers.

Tom   Please don't let me interrupt. I'll just pull up a chair and polish my six silver spoons.

Mamie   Tom . . .

Tom   Or maybe I'll put my china dog on a diamanté leash and have a stroll around Gorky Park.

Mamie   Why aren't you in bed?

Tom   Because, you blind trollop, I don't have one to go to.

Jack (*making room on table*)   Here, Tom, you can share my bier.

Tom   You must be mixing me up with someone else. *I* steer clear of offers of that nature.

Mamie   And what's that supposed to mean?

Pause. **Tom** *and* **Mamie** *look at one another.*

Tom   You didn't come back. We waited for you. At tea-time.

Mamie   Tea-time.

Tom   Where were you?

Mamie   Out.

Tom   Out where?

Mamie   That's none of your business.

Tom   I see. And are you sufficiently revived now that we might anticipate the imminent return of our belongings, do you think? Should we ready ourselves to embrace the prodigal silverware?

Mamie   Don't.

Tom   Only, in my day, we found that furniture enhanced the home.

Mamie   It's been a long day, Tom.

Tom   Two days and a night in Bundoran. Treacherous month, August. His shoulders browned, mine burnt – but Protestants tan well, it's elegant. So, dulcet Lar failed to revive you.

Mamie   Failed to revive, failed to excite and failed to delight. But the pungent Lar's most spectacular failure was on the humid leatherette of his family saloon.

Tom   Look, you doe-eyed strumpet, I want my six inlaid silver spoons in their mahogany box.

Mamie   You wouldn't have recognised an inlaid teaspoon that jumped up and bit you in the arse, if you hadn't pulled yourself out of the bog by your brassière straps.

Jack   Whoops.

Tom   You vile little hussy.

Mamie   Takes one to know one, Tom. Takes one to know one.

Jack   Oh, the manly joys of net-casting, pulley-pulling, barnacle-tightening, oilskin-sweating, hull-filling fishing pale to a salty indifference when you're scraping the scum-jellied rotting offal off the dull cod. It sucks, Tom. Gutting sucks.

Mamie   There will be no revival this time. I'm a beat behind, you know, just a beat behind. No – this time, there will be no resuscitation. You're on your own, all of you. I'm shut.

Enter **Maddie** *through downstage door.*

Maddie   Why didn't you tell me you sold my luggage?

Mamie   Madeleine.

Maddie   When are we getting the furniture back?

Exit **Tom** *downstage.*

Jack   Where's Eddie Coot?

Maddie   What? He went home ages ago. I vomited in his car. What's wrong with Tom? Will we be able to get it back tomorrow?

Mamie   Madeleine.

Maddie   I also vomited in his house. All over the scatter cushions. (*Picking up the jug.*) That's not milk.

Mamie   Madeleine.

Maddie   I think his mother was quite pleased – all that cleaning up to do, all that suspicion, all those recriminations to look forward to. I'm starving.

Mamie   Suspicion?

Maddie   Where's that cake?

Mamie   What suspicion?

Pause.

You've thrown it all away on that pusticular halfwit.

Maddie   Not necessarily.

Mamie   How can you do this to me? What am I going to tell people? Everyone thinks we're sisters.

Maddie   No, they don't. Nobody thinks we're sisters. (*To* **Jack**.) Did you eat it?

Mamie   They bloody do. Lots of people can't believe I'm old enough to have a daughter who menstruates, never mind one who parturates.

Jack   What's parturates?

Maddie   Lots of people like who?

Mamie   Like Lar, for instance. 'My God, Mamie Brazil,' he said, 'I can't believe you're the mother of teenage children. You look so damn ripe.'

Jack (*alarmed*)   Maddie, what's parturates?

Maddie (*to* **Mamie**)   Slow down, will you? I never

said . . .

Stephanie *has entered. Unnoticed, she stands very quietly at the back of the room. She wears a nightdress.*

Steph What's parturates?

Mamie Parturation, Stephanie, is when a woman rips herself open to produce offspring: screaming, breathing things that outlive you.

Steph Oh.

Jack You *are* pregnant.

Maddie Well . . .

Steph Thank God.

Maddie Look it up in your catechism, Steph, you've nothing to celebrate. If the serpent doesn't get me, the archangel will.

Mamie What serpent?

Maddie It doesn't matter.

Steph Anna Roache gave Maddie the pill. Sister Colette said . . .

Mamie Anna Roache has a squint. What does she need the pill for?

Jack She had that fixed years ago.

Mamie (*witheringly*) How can you tell?

Maddie Have we any chairs?

Mamie Don't bleat at me, Madeleine. You're born alone, you'll die alone. If you want sympathy, go and drown in the meticulous bosom of the Coots.

Maddie I don't want to drown in the bosom of the Coots.

Mamie Well, maybe you should have thought about that before you offered yourself as a chalice for their genes.

Jack   What are you going to call it?

Maddie   Led.

Mamie   As in astray?

Maddie   As in Zeppelin.

Jack   Right.

Mamie   Go to bed, Stephanie.

Steph   You're not alone, Maddie. Mary travelled this road when she received Jesus.

Mamie   *Con*ceived, Stephanie, *con*ceived. You open your *mouth* to receive Jesus. There's nothing immaculate about your sister's conception.

Maddie   Anna Roache needn't think she's keeping my hot pants. (*To* **Mamie**.) Did you bring home any biscuits?

A tentative knock at the upstage door can be heard, followed by a loud gunshot from the upstairs window. **Steph** *opens the door to reveal* **Ted**, *ashen-faced.*

Mamie (*shouting at ceiling*)   For Christ's sake, it's Ted. (*To* **Ted**.) She knows it's you. She's doing this deliberately. She's trying to kill me.

Ted   She's trying to kill *you*?

Mamie   You might as well come in. We appear to be having a vigil.

Ted   Thanks.

He enters the room.

Jack   Drink?

Mamie   Thanks.

Ted   Just a Mi-wadi, please, if you have it.

Mamie *receives a jug of gin from* **Jack**. **Ted**'s *request is ignored.*

Maddie   Did Tom try to shoot you again, Ted?

Ted   Yes.

Maddie   She doesn't usually miss. She must like you.

Mamie   Madeleine, get dressed.

Maddie   I *am* dressed. How's the family, Ted?

Ted   Well . . .

Maddie   Is Monica feeling herself again?

Mamie   Madeleine.

Ted   She's . . . well . . .

Maddie   Good.

Ted   No . . . she's . . .

Maddie   What?

Ted   She's . . .

Maddie   Back on her feet?

Ted   No, actually . . .

Maddie   Oh. Prolapse, was it?

Ted   No, relapse. She's dead.

Steph   We have no Mi-wadi.

Jack   Maddie . . .

Maddie   Oh my God, I'm so sorry.

Jack   Maddie.

Maddie   God, that's awful. Is there anything I can do?

Ted   That won't be necessary, Madeleine. She passed on last August.

Mamie   You were responsible for the lilies?

Ted   A birthday token. I . . . I thought they might be appropriate.

Mamie Most appropriate.

Ted Well . . . I'm not disturbing anything, am I?

Mamie There's nothing to disturb.

Jack The dispersal of our belonging has only just begun, Ted. You haven't missed a thing.

Maddie You never had kids, did you?

Ted No, we . . . we never did.

Maddie I think I'm pregnant. It's a bit of a bummer.

Ted Oh, I see . . .

Mamie (*suddenly losing her temper*) Jesus, Madeleine, this is not like getting your tonsils out. This is not losing your bus pass, for Christ's sake.

Maddie Well, it's not my fault. I didn't put it there.

Mamie You were there, Madeleine. What did you think you were doing, kick-starting time travel?

Maddie I was just being agreeable.

Mamie No. Saying good morning to the postman is being agreeable; helping quadriplegics across the road is agreeable; fornicating with Eddie Coot is stupid and irresponsible.

Steph *exits downstage, slamming the door.*

Mamie (*after* **Steph**) I'm sorry, Stephanie, I'm sorry. It's my birthday. It's been a very fucking stressful day, Stephanie. I don't need a moral adjudicator. I'm sorry they took your fish.

Steph (*off*) He wasn't my fish, he was Tom's fish . . .

She puts her head back round the door.

. . . and he had a name.

Fade.

Scene Two

Same room. Later the same night.

Mamie *and* **Jack** *have been drinking gin, but they are not drunk, just sharply strung and lucid.* **Jack** *is standing at the window,* **Mamie** *and* **Ted** *are downstage.*

Jack (*looking out of the window*) All along the shrubless road, the children of Prague are creeping off their dusty plinths; dozens of baby Jesuses are slipping off their mothers' sky-blue knees; Padre Pios, blessed virgins, John Kennedys, Padraig Pearses and St Anthonys are joining in the march, their paths illuminated by burning God hearts ripped off every kitchen wall from here to the post office. They're grazing their plaster feet across the dewy back gardens and gathering around the rustic to wish us all farewell. (*Turning to* **Ted** *and* **Mamie**.) Bought ten fags in McGrory's this afternoon, met Mrs Meany clutching her family pan. Conversational banter? Stop the lights.

'How's the mammy?'

'Fine.'

'She must be after getting a terrible shock.'

'No, really, she's fine.'

'Ah, God love her all the same.'

'No, Mrs Meany, God loves no one all the same. If God loved everyone all the same, he'd destroy competition.' (*Turning back to window.*) How I'll hate to say goodbye to the mottle-thighed neighbourhood. (*Opening the window and shouting.*) Offer it up, offer it up – you'll get it back rewrapped for Christmas.

Mamie *is searching through her bag.*

Mamie   I put it in here somewhere. Couldn't stand the tone. 'I've washed my hands of you' – that's all they're saying. So dispassionate. Poor Mr Wilson.

Ted   Mr Wilson?

Mamie My bank manager, patting my leather glove on the counter.

Ted *looks at her questioningly.*

Mamie He thought my hand was in it. Wasn't his decision. He's mad about me. Has a dreadful wife, looks like wallpaper. I've found it.

Mamie *takes a letter from her bag and hands it to* **Ted**, *who reads it.*

Ted Foreclosure. The bank are repossessing your house, Margaret.

Mamie Mamie.

Ted Mamie ... You have responsibilities – Madeleine, Tom. I don't think you should have to bear this burden alone.

Mamie They are no longer my responsibility.

Ted I know things haven't been easy for you in the past . . .

Mamie Damn right they haven't been easy.

Ted But now is not the time to throw in the towel.

Mamie I have no debt to my family.

Ted I'm not suggesting that you haven't struggled to keep your family together.

Mamie I am not accountable for that urine-soaked old woman upstairs. I didn't impregnate my daughter. I didn't leave.

Ted I know that . . .

Mamie I stayed and sang in every pox-ridden, grey-sheeted hotel from here to Letterfrak and back.

Ted Mamie, I . . .

Mamie If my children can bed themselves, they can feed themselves. This is no burden, Ted, this is liberation.

Ted   I want to marry you, Mamie.

Mamie   Don't make me laugh.

Ted   I mean it. I'm offering you my support and my commitment.

Mamie   No.

Jack   I'll marry you, Ted. I could do with the security.

Mamie   Anyway, I'm already married.

Ted   What about Stephanie?

Mamie   What about her?

Ted   She's young . . .

Mamie   She can come with me.

Ted   Where?

Mamie   You never had children, did you, Ted?

Ted   You know I didn't.

Mamie   Why?

Ted   I loved Monica, I respected her . . . privacy. She suspected children might destroy our equilibrium.

Mamie   Are you desperate for adventure, Ted?

Ted   Not for adventure . . .

Mamie   My husband was desperate for adventure, sniffing after every rancid tart he met.

Ted   I am not your husband.

Mamie   You see, children depressed him. He was never a child himself.

Ted   I've been alone all my life, Mamie.

Mamie   We'll eat you, you know. You're ripe. Your bones are full of marrow and ours are dry.

Jack   My bones swim in salt water.

Mamie (*to* **Jack**)   My bones swim in you.

Enter **Tom** *from downstage door. She is dressed for the outdoors and wears a hat. Looking very dignified, she is carrying a suitcase, her rifle and a boxed gramophone. The downstage door remains open.*

Tom (*to* **Ted**)   You're alive.

Ted   Yes, thank you.

Tom (*to* **Ted**)   You understand we are unblotting the suburban landscape?

Ted   Well, I . . .

Tom   You are a tepid man. You're lucky. The tepid shall inherit the earth. Now, tepid man, you may drive me to Kingsbridge Station. I'm going to catch a train.

Jack   Where to?

Tom   Fish-gutter's curiosity enough to kill the cat. (*To* **Ted**.) I'm ready to leave.

Jack   Where, Tom?

Tom   Home.

Jack   This *is* home. You've lived here for twenty years.

Tom   This purgatory is not my home.

Jack   No? Where's home for the dead doctor's wife? Limavady? They ran you out of their leafy town as soon as the first clod fell, Tom.

Tom   Home, home, my real home.

Jack   Where, Tom?

Tom   I come from somewhere, don't I? There will be a town. I'll recognise it.

Jack   You'll recognise diddly-squat. The country's full of haciendas and cheese sandwiches.

Mamie   Go to bed, Tom.

Ted   Actually, I do not consider myself a tepid man.

Mamie What?

They all look at **Ted**.

Ted I realise you all find me dull. You seem to place an enormous value on self-expression. Well, that's all very well, but you're not resolving anything. I may be dull, but I'm charitable.

Mamie Christ, Ted, not charitable. Charity is so opinionated.

Jack The dull should stay dull, Ted. Against the cloud of your monotony, my mother shines very brightly.

Mamie He's right, of course. I should have married a dull man in the first place.

Ted My offer stands.

Mamie What height are you?

Ted Sorry?

Mamie Short men are belligerent, generally. Tall men are distant, secretive. If I remarried, I'd marry a tall man with a stoop. (*To* **Tom**.) What's in the box?

Tom What did you do to my son? I had a beautiful son. You poisoned him with your perky idiocy, you smothered him with plastic pants and boiled milk.

Mamie I'm not playing, Tom.

Tom I can no longer live in your home. You've a mind like a shopping centre: cheap, compact, unnecessary.

Jack There is nowhere else to go, Tom.

Tom I'll remind you, fish man, that I have a past. I just have to find it.

Jack I dunno, Tom. Left unattended, the past can go very cold.

Tom How the hell would you know? You've your head in a haddock.

Jack   Memory and anticipation – I make sandwiches with them.

Tom   It's my misfortune to live in a family of fools. My son was deceived, extinguished by ignorance.

Mamie   Your celestial son fathered three children, one of whom the bastard's never seen, retched on suburbia and disappeared in a tugboat.

Tom   He was suffocated.

Steph *appears at downstage doorway.*

Mamie   *I* was suffocated, *I* was suffocated. I pushed the creaking pram up and down that road, watching their tight little lips whispering about me. I did summer seasons with fat girls who smelt of chips, and came home to whingeing children and your endless accusation.

Tom   Where will my son find me now? You've stolen his home, you've beheaded him. He should be beatified for marrying you.

Mamie   Your son is mortal and undistinguished. He's also gone.

Tom   He'll return. He is just . . . recuperating.

Ted   Tom, put down your case. Give me the rifle.

Mamie   He has no intention of returning.

Tom   How do you know that?

Mamie   He told me.

Pause.

Ship to shore. 'Mamie. Sand shifts. Stop. Salvage what you can. Stop. Trust your spirit floats. Stop. Sam. Stop.'

Silence.

Concise?

Tom   You found him?

Tom *puts down box.*

Mamie   I found him years ago. Hove-to in Lisbon, he said he was. Hove-to *with* Lisbon would be more like it.

Tom   You found him.

Mamie   One morning, in one undistinguished year, he sent Stephanie a card. Maybe he thought it was her birthday. It wasn't. But there it was, a picture postcard. Two little girls holding hands. One had a parakeet on her shoulder, and there was an address, of sorts, so I wrote to him, put 'urgent' on the envelope in great big bruising letters, and I told him . . . I told him I was tired. I thought . . .

Tom   Where is he?

Mamie   I never had hope, Tom. Hope is tricky, sleeps with disillusion.

Jack   You black-hearted bastard. Swap your babies for barnacles, feed your mother to the gulls.

Tom   You hurt me.

Mamie   And you me, Tom. And you me.

Ted (*to* **Tom**)   It's late. There'll be a train tomorrow, plenty of trains tomorrow.

Steph *enters the room.*

Mamie   Stephanie, what are you doing?

Steph   Maddie's thrown up again. She wants someone to read her a story. Is anyone using daddy? I'll take him upstairs if you don't mind. There's been a lot of changes today and he's probably a bit confused.

She picks up the cut-out and goes to the downstage door, then stops.

He never told *me* that he wasn't coming back. He's just looking for something . . .

Mamie   Stephanie.

Steph   No. Jesus said, he said knock and it will open, seek and you will find, ask and you will receive. It's only a matter of time. My daddy will be coming back.

Fade.

Scene Three

Same room. Next morning.

Jack *is dismantling the phone (removing the bell and gluing the receiver to the cradle). He wears his father's naval cadet's uniform.* **Steph** *is helping him with the phone.*

Jack *(imitating Lar, the radio announcer)*   Now, gentle people, for some heart-rending realism. Well, caller, you have a story of tragedy and tears – is that right?

Steph *(as caller)*   Yes, Lar, but as you well know, Lar, every cloud has a silver lining.

Jack *(as Lar)*   Indeed. You lost your mother, caller – is that right?

Steph *(as caller)*   No, Lar. I lost my dog. My mother was killed by a runaway train.

Jack *(as Lar)*   Tut, tut. You must have been devastated, paralytic with grief.

Steph *(as caller)*   Ah, I was, Lar, but it turned out Fido was under the bed the whole time.

Jack *(as Lar)*   Oh well, thank God for small mercies.

Steph *(as caller)*   That's what I always say.

Jack *(as Lar)*   No, that's what *I* always say.

Steph *(as caller)*   Oh right. That's what *you* always say. *(As herself.)* Why are we doing this?

Jack   It's an experiment.

Steph   I don't have to do it.

Jack   You do if you want to be cool.

Steph   Oh.

Jack   OK, we're ready.

Steph   How do you know you'll be accepted?

Jack   They'll accept anything. Ready?

Steph   Will you have to go through an initiation?

Jack   What?

Steph   You probably will. Actually, I believe it's pretty gruesome.

Jack   Yeah?

Steph   Yeah, apparently they pee in your orange juice when you're not looking, and then you drink it and you realise someone's mickey has been in it. And as well as that, right, they put snot in the sandwich spread. It's really disgusting. Also, you have to kill people if you're told to. Like, say your commanding officer said, 'Jack, I don't like the look of that little kid with the brown eyes and the limp,' you'd just have to shoot it.

Jack   I'm considering joining the Irish Navy, Steph, not the French fucking Foreign Legion.

Steph   Oh well, don't say I didn't warn you.

Jack *makes the phone bell ring three times.*

Jack   Go on. Loud. Sound shocked.

Steph (*very loudly*)   Oh, hi, Eddie. Maddie? I'm afraid she's vomiting at the moment. Can I take a message?

Maddie (*off*)   Hang on, I'm coming.

Steph   Really? That bad? Right, well, I can't say I blame you.

Jack   Shocked, Steph.

Steph   Oh my God, Eddie, you're not serious. That's

awful . . .

Maddie (*off*)   I'm coming!

Jack   She's coming.

Steph   What? That's terrible . . . oh my God . . . yeah, yeah, OK, Eddie, I'll tell her. Bye.

Maddie (*entering*)   Don't hang up . . . It's working. That's so brilliant. I'll phone him back.

Steph   Forget it, Maddie.

Maddie   Forget what?

Jack   It's Eddie's old lady.

Maddie   What about her?

Steph   She had a fit.

Jack   Lost it completely.

Steph   Said you were a tart.

Jack   Said you sullied him, made him do it.

Steph   Said they'd seen the last of you.

Jack   Said she's sick of you.

Steph   Said even the dog is sick of you.

Jack   Said you can take your Catholic vomit elsewhere, her bowl is full.

Maddie   Give me that phone. I'll fucking kill her.

She grabs the phone and realises the receiver is glued down.

You bastards. You're supposed to be nice to me. I might be in a delicate condition.

She sits.

Steph   We were just experimenting with your state of mind.

Maddie   Why?

Jack To see if pregnant people can be driven to hysterical, irrational acts of violence.

Steph Like shooting Mrs Coot.

Maddie And what if I had?

Jack You could plead diminished responsibility.

Maddie That uniform is too big for you.

Jack I'll grow into it.

Maddie In your dreams. Is there anything to eat?

Jack It was his first one, you know: 'white teeth, white tunic'. I'm joining the Navy.

Maddie How do you know they'll accept you?

Steph They'll accept anything.

Maddie They'd want to.

Pause.

I suppose we'll never see *you* again either.

Jack I'll be as faithful as a pigeon.

Maddie How will you know where to come home to?

Jack You can write to me, tell me where you are.

Maddie Sounds familiar.

Jack What else can I do?

Maddie Just gut fishes. Just stay where you are and gut.

Jack There is no 'where we are'.

Maddie Don't say that to me.

Jack I'm numb gutting, Maddie. I'm ready to float.

Maddie What will I do?

Steph Bloat.

Maddie (*looking at* **Steph**) I could bloat in the Coots'.

They've got a colour television.

Steph See?

Maddie I hope I *do* have something inside me. I hope it gets bigger than me. I hope it gets so big I'm obliterated. I hope it gets so fucking big I'll have to be hand-fed and washed.

Pause. **Steph** *makes the sound of a ringing phone.*

Jack (*as Lar*) Yes, caller.

Steph It's my sister, Lar. She's exploded.

Jack (*as Lar*) Dear oh dear.

Steph Actually, Lar, my whole family has exploded. There's bits of them all over the ceiling.

Jack (*as Lar*) Tut tut. And tell me, caller, is there anyone who could give you a hand cleaning them up?

Steph Not really, Lar. You see, my dad was eaten by a whale.

Jack Yeah? That's serious shit, caller.

Steph You're telling me.

Enter **Mamie** *with two cooked chickens.*

Mamie Form a tableau. It's the last supper.

Maddie But we haven't had our breakfast yet.

Mamie You know, Madeleine, you really are deeply conventional.

Jack Where'd you get the chickens?

Mamie Mrs Meany. With her sympathy, she said. I'm surprised she didn't make them into soup. Stephanie, you'd better pack.

Steph Why? Where are we going?

Mamie Summer season. Butlin's. You can have your own cabin.

Steph I don't want to.

Mamie Of course you don't want to. Only people with outdoor lavatories want to go to Butlin's. Do you think I want to sing 'Jake the Peg' with a prosthesis extruding from my fanny? Madeleine, stop looking gormless.

Steph I'm not going.

Mamie No?

Steph I'm staying here with Tom.

Mamie This is not our house any more. It belongs to the bank.

Steph I want to stay here with Tom.

Mamie We don't live here, Stephanie. We've been evicted. Madeleine, snap out of it.

Maddie Do I take it that I'm moving?

Mamie Yes.

Maddie And where do you suggest I go?

Mamie (*to* **Jack**) That uniform is too big for you.

Jack No it isn't.

Mamie It was his first one, you know. He'd fold it so delicately.

She laughs quietly.

Jack What?

Mamie Nothing.

Jack *remains looking at* **Mamie**.

Maddie I said where do you suggest I go?

Mamie I suggest you reside with your foetal relations.

Maddie What if I don't have any foetal relations?

Mamie Well, Madeleine, there's always the next time.

Jack Why did you laugh?

Mamie He was absurdly fastidious, you know. He'd contemplate anything with a pulse, but he always had a clean hanky. Stephanie, you'd better get a move on.

Steph What about Tom?

Ted *can be heard offstage as he approaches the upstage door.*

Ted (*off*) Mamie. Mamie.

He enters with a net shopping bag containing breakfast groceries.

Provisions for the troops. I thought you'd . . . (*Noticing* **Jack**.) Oh Jesus . . .

Mamie You were saying?

Jack Hi, Ted.

Maddie (*taking the bag from* **Ted**) You didn't get any Frosties.

Ted What?

Maddie Frosties.

Jack Ted?

Ted (*to* **Jack**) I'm sorry. For a minute, I thought . . .

Jack Have you ever seen a short policeman, Ted?

Ted (*confused*) No.

Jack No.

Mamie Ted?

Ted Sorry? Oh yes. Mamie, I came to tell you . . .

Steph What about Tom?

Enter **Tom**.

Tom What about me?

Mamie (*to* **Ted**) Yes?

Tom (*to* **Jack**) I've packed your lunch. God knows what time they'll feed you at. Your father will come down after his surgery. Lot of bleeders this afternoon – if you ask me, it's in-breeding.

Mamie   Ted?

Tom (*to* **Jack**)   Show me your teeth.

Ted, *unnerved, thinks he's being spoken to.* **Jack** *grins at* **Tom**.

Tom   You're very good-looking. I'm sure you'll have your own cabin.

Jack⎱
Ted⎰   Thank you.

Steph   I'm not going anywhere without Tom.

Ted   Mamie?

Mamie   Yes, Ted?

Tom (*to* **Jack**)   Be wary of the hoi polloi – they can be unpredictable.

Ted   Mamie, I . . .

Maddie (*eating a banana*)   Anyway, why can't *I* go to Butlin's?

Mamie   I can't afford you, Madeleine.

Ted   Mamie?

Maddie   God, that's so unfair.

Ted   Mamie?

Mamie (*shouting*)   What? (*Calmly.*) What is it, Ted? What old bone have you dug up for my approval?

Ted   Mamie, last night I didn't sleep. I . . .

Maddie   Neither did I. I was starving.

Ted   I went home to my long-fingered ghost . . .

Maddie   Your long-fingered toast?

Ted   Ghost. Ghost. My long-fingered ghost . . . (*To*

Mamie.) Isn't that what you used to call my wife?

Jack I thought her name was Monica.

Mamie It was.

Ted Even when she was alive, Mamie. My long-fingered ghost, you used to call her.

Mamie So I did.

Tom I was hoping for some chicken.

Ted She was there, clinging to the door-frames, watching over me, prescribing to me.

Mamie What are you talking about?

Steph Chicken. She wants some chicken.

Mamie Not her. Ted.

Maddie I want chicken as well.

Mamie Eat the ruddy things!

Maddie With what?

Jack Your long-toasted fingers.

Mamie Ted?

All except **Ted** *and* **Mamie** *begin to eat the chickens enthusiastically.*

Steph Eviction stinks.

Jack I dunno; certainly enlivens the neighbours.

Maddie Who would have believed it? A cooked chicken from Mrs Meany.

Mamie *Two* cooked chickens from Mrs Meany.

Jack Wonder what you'd have to do for a leg of lamb.

Tom Die.

Ted (*loudly*) Mamie ... please, I ...

Silence. The Brazils all focus on **Ted**.

I . . .

He coughs nervously.

It's funny; in McGrory's this morning, you know, I didn't know if I'd bought enough . . . provisions . . .

He coughs again. Everyone continues looking at him.

I . . . I felt . . . I was making provisions.

Pause. More coughing. **Ted** *tries to get himself under control.*

Well, one banana or five, so to speak. Six including myself . . . if I'm included, that is . . . If you'd . . .

Steph   Tom doesn't eat bananas.

Maddie   She *is* bananas.

Jack *and* **Mamie** *remain sharply focused on* **Ted**, *who has now got his coughing under control.*

Ted   You see, I remember you, Mamie. I remember you singing to your babies in the sunburnt back garden.

Mamie   I was singing to the damn pots and pans. I never knew *you* were listening.

Ted   Live with me. All of you.

Silence.

Maddie   Why?

Jack   There's a desperate inevitability about ending up in your father's pants, Ted. Dust to dust, wouldn't you say?

Mamie   Leave us alone, Ted.

Ted   God, Mamie, I remember you. I remember you pushing your pram up the bleached road . . .

Mamie   You remember that, do you?

Ted   I remember your defiance, the cut of you, your hip, your mouth.

Mamie   Jesus.

Ted You killed me with your beauty spot. You had a beauty spot, Mamie – is it any wonder they whispered about you?

Tom The dogs in the street whispered about her.

Ted The Aphrodite of our avenue. They thought exotic was a dab of Atrixo, then you slipped by and you made them weep. *I* wept, Mamie. I wept for you while my damp long-fingered ghost made the parsley sauce.

Mamie And do you know what I remember, Ted? The sliced venetian blinds at midnight, the eyes of the parish, a fat-kneed girl from Offaly smelling my hair. What were you looking for, Ted? A blunt fuck was beyond you.

Tom Hah!

Ted Don't say no to me, Mamie.

Mamie So what's your offer? A tangerine carpet and a biscuit tin? For what?

Ted You're past your prime, Mamie – that's my good fortune. I just had to bide my time, scratch in the ashes. You need me, Mamie, you all need me. You are my reward, Mamie, for thirty years with an alabaster virgin.

Mamie There are no rewards, Ted, for cowering mediocrity.

Ted But I have waited so long.

Mamie We've all waited, Ted, every surly morning, every dislocated night. For what? To be healed? Time doesn't heal, time embroiders.

Jack (*to* **Ted**) Every day on your way to work, you closed your wrought-iron garden gate and put your plastic sole on the accelerator of your neat little car. And every night, you lay on your sheet with your matching valance while your pyjama cord strangled your dick. My mother is right. There is nothing you can offer us, Ted. But accept our condolences on a majestically dull life.

Ted *sits down next to the cut-out.*

Mamie   It's his face in our palm lines, Ted. He's etched in grime on our necks.

Pause.

Tom   He told me once about a wind, a strong wind, blows from the north, blows abeam of Finisterre, picks up the Portuguese trades, swings west, follows the Gulf Stream, meets a piping wind from the Azores and blows to South America, could blow to Africa . . .

Pause.

Imagine that. Just imagine that.

Mamie   Go home, Ted. We've things to do, things to do.

Fade.

Scene Four

After a dead blackout, the lights come up centre to reveal **Tom** *and* **Steph** *in a pedalo on a lake.*

Pause.

Steph   Bowsprit, phosphorescence, crow's nest, launch – familiar to you, these words. Distance.

Jack said he's seen a wall of water crumble under the grey steel hull of his ship and heard dolphins laugh at his frailty. You never said – maybe you never heard them.

Mamie is going to cut a record: 'Songs for the Dispossessed'. I don't suppose you'll hear that either.

Jack agrees with memory. Memory and anticipation.

You can't remember me. You never knew me. And I always imagined you missed me, that our thoughts joined up like cobblestones. I imagined I could walk across a mackerel sky to you.

Even God gives up.

Maddie is leaving the past go cold, she is dispossessed of memory. There never was a baby to obliterate her, not this time. Lost in God's dispassionate pocket, Tom said.

She said on the telephone: 'I'm hectic'. Hectic, she said she was.

Jack said if you leave the past unattended, it can go very cold – but maybe Maddie's right, maybe that's the way it's supposed to get.

Oh! I nearly sank in the swimming pool! But I didn't. Funny if I'd died in four foot of chlorine, with the world full of oceans to drown in.

I have missed you and missed you, and not missing you will take a long time too.

Tom is still waiting. Every surly morning, every dislocated night. It's her vigil. I wait with her, but for something extraordinary, not for you.

Fade.

CARAVAN

Helen Blakeman

To my family and Jon
and those who've helped me along the way

Caravan premiered at the Bush Theatre, London, on 12 November 1997. The cast was as follows:

Kim	(*unconfirmed at time of printing*)
Kelly	Emma Cunniffe
Josie	Elizabeth Estensen
Mick	Nick Bagnall
Bruce	Pip Donaghy

Directed by Gemma Bodinetz
Designed by Bruce Macadie
Lighting by Dick Fisher

Characters

Kim, *aged 15. Fairly tall and rather busty. Sparky in temperament yet sensitive in nature. She dreams of better things.*

Kelly, *aged 19. Dark-haired, sturdy and short. Appears gentle and naive but is not as soft as she makes out. She looks for better things.*

Josie, *aged 45. Thin-faced and sharp-featured, she appears slimmer than she is. Ambition only centres around material items. She thinks she has found better things.*

Mick, *aged 20. Swarthy and casual. He has small hands and short legs. Can overpower but is very insecure. He takes whatever is given.*

Bruce, *aged 50. Well-built and sexy. He believes he knows most things better than anyone else but is mellowing with age. He finds and fights for what he can.*

Caravan, *aged 10. A young static made of corrugated metal, painted cream and subdued orange with a pale blue stripe. Her concrete stilts and rusty chains tie her down. She thinks her 'For Sale' sign could change her life – or at least her interior.*

The women of the play are from the south Liverpool suburbs, the men are from north Liverpool.

The play is set on a caravan park in Towyn, North Wales.

The set should consist of the cross-section of a caravan and the small piece of land in front of it. The action inside the caravan takes place in the main living area. The interior consists of two settees, at the back and stage right, with windows above them. A convertible bed, facing forward, centre stage is next to a small L-shaped kitchen area. A table and benches are at the front of the stage facing forward. Three doors lead off the room, stage left, to the bathroom, Josie's room and Kelly's room. The window of Kelly's room faces out to the audience. The front door of the caravan can be indicated through lighting.

Act One

Scene One: Caravan of Love

Music: 'Caravan of Love' by the Housemartins.

The caravan. A rainy afternoon in October 1994.

A 'For Sale' sign stands in the garden area outside the caravan. Two gas canisters stand near the steps up to the front door. The caravan is empty, although the table is scattered with newspapers, crockery and food – mostly packets of biscuits and bags of fruit. The convertible couch-bed displays a child's duvet cover. A cuddly Garfield toy sits on the pillow.

Kim *enters quickly, crosses to the door and enters the caravan. She is dressed for summer – a swimsuit, skirt and pumps – with a jacket over her head. Once inside the caravan, she throws the jacket onto the side settee. She straightens the bedclothes and hides the Garfield toy under the sheets. She embarks on tidying the table.*

Mick *enters. He is casually dressed and slightly wet. He carries two ice creams – one is half-eaten.*

Mick (*calls*) Kim!

Kim *goes to the door.*

Kim Are ya dead wet?

Mick *enters the caravan.*

Mick Nah, I run fast.

Kim D' ya want some money for that?

Mick No.

Kim Ya sure?

Mick Don't be soft.

Kim Ta.

Mick *goes to the back settee and looks about.*

Kim *sits on the edge of the bed, as if trying to hide the duvet.*

Mick   Is this ya mam an' dad's?

Kim   We got it out the *Echo*. I 'aven't got a dad.

Mick   It's not bad.

Kim   Me mum loves it. She thinks it's dead nice. Every time she comes in she goes, 'Ooh, me little palace.' She wants to buy it an' everythin'.

Mick   That'd be all right.

Kim   Ya jokin' aren't ya? I'd go off me 'ead comin' 'ere all the time with me mum an' me sister. (*She licks the ice cream.*) This is lovely.

Mick   I like mint choc chip.

Kim   Cold though. (*Pause.*) I'd rather be at 'ome an' go out than come 'ere. I'd rather go to town, wouldn't you?

Mick   I dunno. Depends.

Kim   Depends on the company.

Mick   Depends what's 'appenin'.

Kim   What am I like? Depends. She 'asn't even bought it yet.

Mick   So ya think she'll buy it then.

Kim   Dunno, depends. Depends on the money. (*Pause.*) Fancy 'avin' ice cream in the rain.

Mick   Cold an' wet.

Kim   Yeh, cold an' wet an' nothin' goin' on just loadsa sheep an' one-arm bandits.

Mick   That club's good. Ya should go. Three pound an' a bottle a Pils. An' birds get in for nothin'. Ya still get ya Pils like but ya can 'ave that in a ladies' glass. Or ya can drink it out the bottle if ya drink it out the bottle. Ya should go.

Kim   I'll 'ave to see what are Kelly's doin'. We always go out together on a Satdee.

Mick Whatever yeh.

Pause.

Kim Where are ya sittin'? 'Ere or there?

Mick I'm sittin' 'ere.

Kim I'll sit 'ere as well then.

Kim *sits alongside* **Mick** *on the back settee.*

Kim I'm freezin'.

Mick Ya wanna put some clothes on.

Kim I'm orright.

Mick It's blowin' a gale.

Kim It was nice this mornin'.

Mick Not that I'm complainin'. Ya suit that – (*He gestures.*)

Kim Cozzie.

Mick Yeh.

Kim Look at me. Goosies everywhere.

Mick You've got all ice cream on ya chin.

Kim There?

Mick No. By ya mouth. Come 'ere.

Mick *moves closer and wipes her chin.*

Kim Gone?

Mick No, there's more.

Kim *moves away, embarrassed, and wipes her chin. She looks at her hand.*

Kim Where?

Mick It's on ya mouth.

Mick *puts his fingers on her mouth. Pause. He kisses* **Kim** *as she holds the remains of her ice cream at a distance.*

Kim   Should I shut the curtains?

Mick   Nah, leave them.

Kim   Ya can see in. Ya can see in to everyone's.

Mick   Never noticed.

Kim *stands and draws the curtains of the back and side windows.*

Kim   Goin' dark now anyway.

Pause. They stand face to face.

D'ya wanna finish it?

Mick   Yeh.

He takes the ice cream from her. They kiss. He puts ice cream on her lips then kisses it off.

That nice?

Kim   Yeh.

Mick   D' ya feel horny?

Kim   Mm.

Mick   I'm glad I went up the beach today.

He kisses her, still holding the ice cream.

An' just when ya thought it was safe –

He swiftly dabs ice cream onto **Kim**'s *chest. She tries to back away.*

Kim   Nah – you – Mick, oh my God – it feels dead cold get a cloth –

Mick   Leave it. Let me see it. Lie down.

Kim *lies rigidly on the bed.*

Mick   It looks better on ya chest than on ya chin.

Kim   It's runnin' –

Mick   It's not.

He kneels astride **Kim** *and leans down over her. He balances himself with one hand and holds the ice cream with the other.*

Mind ya arm.

Kim   Mind that cornet.

Mick   I am. I'm savin' it for somethin' special.

Kim   Like what?

Mick   Like you.

Mick *kisses her neck and upper chest.*

Kim   'As it gone? (*Pause.*) That tickles, slow.

Mick   'Old that.

Kim *takes the ice cream from him and holds it straight up above her.* **Mick** *resumes removing the ice cream.*

Kim   Ya like doin' that, don't ya?

Mick   Mm.

Kim   Can ya move up a bit? All ya weight's on me leg.

Mick *moves slightly.*

Kim   You sure ya comfy?

Mick   Yeh. It's gorgeous.

Kim   'Ave ya finished?

Mick   D' ya want some more?

Kim   If ya want but 'urry up.

Mick *kneels up and takes the ice cream from* **Kim**.

Mick   What time's ya mum in?

Kim   Not for ages. They'll stop off at Rhyl for the bingo.

Mick   We're all right then, aren't we?

Kim   Watch it doesn't run out. I don't want no gunk on me bed. (*Pause.*) Are ya gonna do any more?

Mick   I'm tryin' to fuckin' eat.

Kim   Keep ya kecks on. You 'aven't got ice cream meltin' all over ya tit.

Mick *puts the remains of the ice cream in the bin and then resumes his position on top of* **Kim**.

Mick   Ya feel good, don't ya?

Kim   Yeh.

Mick   Sexy cow.

Kim   Ta.

Mick   Turned on?

Kim   Think so.

Mick   Yeh?

They kiss passionately.

Kim   Mick?

Mick   What?

Kim   I can't undo ya buttons.

Mick *kneels and undoes his flies.*

Mick   You're a horny bitch, d' ya know that?

Kim   Mick?

They kiss.

Ow. Me back.

Mick   Move over.

Mick *reaches into the bed and pulls out the Garfield toy. He drops it onto the floor and kisses her.*

Kim   Mick.

Mick   I like this skirt. The way it goes right up.

Kim *tugs her skirt down as* **Mick** *kisses her. She tries to move him off.*

Kim   Mick, I've never –

Mick   It doesn't matter. You'll be orright.

He kneels again and loosens his jeans. He lies back down and fumbles with **Kim***'s clothing.*

Are these knickers?

Kim   No, it's me cozzie.

Mick   Move ya leg a bit. That's it. Can ya feel that?

Kim   No. Leave it. Don't do that. No leave it now –

Mick   Move ya leg or we won't get nowhere –

Mick*'s actions become more forceful.*

Kim   God, no leave it now. That hurts. I don't want –

Mick   Move ya hand.

Kim   Ow.

Mick   Let me pull it to the side –

Kim   Ah, no – don't do that – that hurts –

Mick   That's it. That's better –

Kim   Ow –

Mick   Just relax – relax a bit – open ya – ohh, that's it, that's better –

Kim   No, Mick, no – get off me now – get off get off me –

Mick *puts his hand over* **Kim***'s mouth to silence her. She struggles and groans then stiffens and becomes still.*

Mick   Ohh, you're so fuckin' gorgeous – quiet now – orrhh, you'll make me come – Oh Kim – ah that's it – that's it – that's it – that's ohh –

He pulls away from her quickly.

Shit. I think some's gone on ya skirt.

He turns away from her and sits on the edge of the bed. **Kim** *holds down her skirt.*

D' ya think it was gonna be like that ya first time?

Kim   Dunno.

Mick   Ya were gorgeous.

Kim   Thanks.

Mick   Good the first time, innit?

Pause.

Kim   Was it all right?

Mick   Yeh. I pulled out.

Kim   Ta.

Mick   Ya didn't 'alf get me goin' when ya groaned.

Kim   It'll be orright, won't it?

Mick   As long as I don't 'ave to bring flowers the 'ospital when it's born. I'd feel a cunt.

Kim *stands and goes to the mirror, out front.*

Kim   Not goin' the fair now. It's pissin' down.

Mick   'Ave to make it another time.

Kim   It might go off in a bit.

Mick   I'll 'ave to get off.

Kim *edges her way towards the kitchen.*

Kim   Stay. I'll do ya tea. We could 'ave noodles an' curry sauce with veg in.

Mick   Me mam does me tea.

Kim   With peas an' carrots. Like vegetable curry. We

could get more ice cream for afters.

Mick   Ya mam 'll be back. I'll 'ave to go.

Kim   It'd be orright.

Mick   I'm in a rush for goin' out. I might see ya later.

Kim   Where are ya?

Mick   Up the top.

Kim   In millionaires' row? I've seen them. They've all got Dralon couches. I'll come an' knock. Where ya goin' after?

Josie *enters onto the terrace in front of the caravan. She is loaded up with bags of bingo prizes and cuddly toys.*

Josie (*calls*)   Kimberley, get 'old a these for us, babe.

Kim   Shite.

Mick   I'd better go.

Josie   Give us a hand, love.

Mick *goes to exit.*

Kim   No – she'll go mad. You'll 'ave to get out the winda.

Mick   What?

Kim   You'll 'ave to.

She goes to the back, draws the curtains and opens the window.

Go on. (*Calls.*) I'm comin' now, Mum.

Mick *goes to the window and climbs out.*

Mick   If anyone sees me –

Josie (*calls*)   Kimmy?

Kim   I've 'ad a lovely day. I'll see ya after or whatever.

Mick   Ta-ra.

Mick *exits.* **Kim** *closes the window.*

Kim (*calls*) I'm comin'!

Josie Are you in, love? Open the door it's only ya mam.

Kim *goes to the door and onto the terrace.*

Kim I thought you'd 'ave ya keys. 'As it stopped rainin'?

Josie Just. We've 'ad a crackin' day, weather aside. Ya shoulda come. Ya would've enjoyed ya little self. Grab 'old a them.

Josie *enters the caravan.*

Kim So it was good then?

Kim *re-enters the caravan, drops the bags and tidies her bed.*

Josie Got all me bags?

Kim Think so.

Josie I'm glad to be back. Me bleedin' feet are achin' off me. Are Kelly's gone the Amouré for a pizza. Fuckin' pizza mad she is. You'd think she'd 'ave enough a them in work.

Kim Did ya stop off at Rhyl?

Josie Stop off? I cleaned the fuckin' town out. Lovely bus driver we 'ad. Like Omar Sharif but not as greasy. An' the bingo was fuckin' marvellous. I'll just get me slippers.

She exits to her bedroom.

(*Off.*) 'E took a shine to are Kelly. Kept callin' 'er 'sweet'eart'. The couple sat behind us own one a these. Two rows down. They're 'ere every weekend peak season.

She re-enters the living-room and sifts through her prizes. **Kim** *sits on the edge of the bed, quite still.*

Imagine that, eh, Kim? Rhyl just down the road. The bingo, the bars. You could be clubbin' it down there next year. Make-up on, all dressed up. Are Kelly could take ya once she's passed 'er test. You'd pass for eighteen. You'd love it.

Kim Can I go out tonight?

Josie We were singin' on the way back. Omar didn't seem to care. They even 'ad a twistin' competition up the back. Didn't know till it was too late. I don't know who won but they wouldn't be as good as me, eh, babes? What you been up to then?

Kim Went up the beach, it was nice. Went the fair, it rained. Came back.

Josie Did ya meet ya nice friends from Frodsham?

Kim Yeh.

Josie Anyone new?

Kim No. I think someone else is in next door. They've got bikes an' everythin'.

Josie Just wait till I buy this place. I'll give them festoon blinds never mind bloody bikes. Bleedin' show-offs. Are Kelly can 'ave the make-up set. D'ya wanna a teddy off the grabbers? Ee are, put that on ya bed. That'll cheer ya up.

Kim *takes the cuddly toy and puts it on the pillow.*

Josie Ya dad woulda loved today. What's that on ya skirt? The life an' soul of it, wasn't 'e, Kim?

Kim What? Where?

Josie That's one thing I'll say for 'im. All white stuff down the back.

Kim Dunno. Ice cream.

Kim *sits on the bed.* **Josie** *lights a cigarette.*

Josie I 'ope it comes out. When I get ya dad's 'oliday insurance, I'll bloody buy this place. An' them clouds 'll part an' the sun 'll come out an' ya dad 'll be 'appy up there. 'E'll go, 'Josie's got a caravan an' that's what she's always dreamed of'. An' for once 'e'll be 'appy with me. We'll all be 'appy.

Scene Two: Saturday Night

Music: 'Saturday Night' by Whigfield.

The caravan, the following morning.

Kim *is preparing breakfast for two at the still-cluttered table. She places a banana, an apple and an orange on each plate. She is dressed as in scene one.*

Kim Ee are! (*She peels a banana and begins to eat it.*) It's lovely this. Dead posh muesli with extra nuts an' loadsa bits in.

Silence. This is a daily routine for her.

Ya milk's gettin' soaked up. If it goes all mushy it'll look like spew. So don't say I never warned ya.

Silence. She clears most of the clutter from the table.

It's says on the packet, 'Good for ya spots, good for ya shits, (*She calls.*) good for ya shags an' stops ya gettin' cancer.' Not bad, eh? Bet ya didn't know muesli could change ya life? (*Pause.*) Or would ya rather 'ave a sausage? I'd rather 'ave a sausage. (*Pause.*) Come on. Are ya gettin' up or what? It's dead nice out.

Pause. The curtains of the front bedroom window open. **Kelly**, *already dressed, looks out of the window.*

Right, Kelly. That's it. It's goin' in the cat. Why should I waste me mornin' waitin' for you when there's very important fish to fry?

Kelly *enters from the bedroom carrying a make-up bag and hairbrush. She is dressed for attention but looks rather dishevelled.*

Kelly We 'aven't got a cat.

Kim It's just a phase, a figure a speech.

She passes **Kelly** *a plate of fruit.*

Ee are. I was lyin' about the muesli.

Kelly I couldn't look at food.

Kelly *sits down on the back settee.*

Kim That's nice. After I've gone to all that trouble arrangin' ya breakfast fruit in alphabetical order.

Kelly Is that why the orange is in the middle?

Kim Ya lookin' at it the wrong way round, clever arse.

Kim *puts the untouched fruit on the table.*

Kelly Oh, shut ya face.

Kim Yeh, when you shut ya neck.

Kelly Well shut ya legs.

Kim Shut ya aarse.

Kelly Ah, just shut up, Kim, me 'ead feels like it's on the waltzers.

Kim Put some make-up on. You'll feel human then. You'll still look like a dog but at least you'll feel human.

Kelly (*quietly*) Shut ya hole.

Kim I'm goin' the beach in a minute, ya comin'?

Kelly Don't think so.

Kim Well wait till ya spew then see 'ow ya feel. Or do ya hair. (*Pause.*) I'll do ya hair. I'll do it nice. An' ya make-up. Ya can use them eye shadows off me mum. (*She picks up the make-up set.*) 'Earthy Shades.' Earthy colours are in. (*She reads.*) 'Winter dawn, frosty peach, golden towny.'

Kelly Tawny.

Kim Whatever. (*Pause.*) Come 'ead, don't be an aald aarse. Come the beach.

Kelly It'll be bloody freezin'.

Kim So? Ya on 'oliday.

Kelly Are you goin' like that?

Kim Yeh. Why?

Kelly   Ya skirt's all dirty.

Kim   Shit. I forgot about that.

Kim *picks up a small pile of clothes from the side settee.*

Kelly *stands and begins to do her hair in the mirror, out front. Through the following dialogue,* **Kim** *tries on various skirts and shorts over her costume. She stands on the back settee to view each one in the mirror.*

Kelly   Did you know that ya only supposed to take five items a clothes on 'oliday with ya?

Kim   Like what?

Kelly   A cozzie, a sarong –

Kim   A what?

Kelly   A big fancy sheet. A pair a shorts, a long skirt an' – (*She thinks.*) somethin' else.

Kim   Five bitsa clothes? Go 'way, you'd stink. (*Pause.*) There was a dirty big turd on the beach yesterday.

Kelly   Eugh. The dirty Welsh bastard.

Kim   It wasn't Welsh shit, it was in the sea. (*Pause.*) Everyone was runnin' away from it.

Kelly   An' ya want me to come with ya?

Kim   Just today. I don't wanna go on me own.

Kelly   You've changed ya tune.

Kim   Girls look better in twos. (*Pause.*) An' one can mind the bags while the other one goes in for a paddle.

Kelly   Ya must be jokin'. Paddlin' in squalid conditions? (*She sits.*) Move over.

Kelly *starts to make herself up.*

Kim   D' ya think this one or the shorts?

Kelly   That one.

Kim Ya 'ave a laugh. (*Pause.*) An' ya get a tan off the sea.

Kelly More like fuckin' beri-beri.

Kim No, ya do. If the wind's blowin'. Come with me, come on.

Kelly I can't. I'm goin' the fair –

Kim We can go there after –

Kelly To Rhyl?

Kim Who ya goin' there with?

Kelly Someone.

Kim Is it that Omar?

Kelly 'Ave I got taste?

Kim It's 'ard to say.

Pause.

Kelly Someone from last night.

Kim From that stupid cabaret bar? Eeeh, only queers go in cabaret bars.

Kelly No. From Fortnum's on the coast road.

Kim Is that that club?

Kelly Yeh. Free to get in an' a bottle a Pils.

Kim I'll kill me mum. I can't go nowhere.

Kelly Ya wouldn't a got in, babe. Tell ya what, I'll take ya to town once ya sixteen.

Pause.

Kim What was it like? Is it really, really brilliant?

Kelly It's orright. Not exactly the hottest spot north of Havana.

Kim But what like?

Kelly   It was good. We 'ad a scream.

Kim   I 'ate this. I 'ate this stupid 'oliday. Did ya cop for anyone?

Kelly   Yeh. Sandra an' Lisa were up dancin' an' I was leanin' over watchin'. An' then this gorgeous lad comes up to me an' goes, 'I don't 'alf know your face.' An' that was it.

Kim   What was?

Kelly   I just started neckin' 'im.

Kim   Ee, ya slapper.

Kelly   Wait till you get a bit older.

Kim   I'm old enough.

Kelly   'E even walked me 'ome. 'E's just gorgeous. Me 'eart was poundin' all the way.

Kim   All the way?

Kelly   All the way 'ome.

Kim   I 'ate livin' with you an' me mum. Ya either dead narky or yers are makin' a show a yerself.

Kelly   What's up your aarse, moaner?

Kim   I get dragged up the bingo an' the family bar an' all the time you're shaggin' –

Kelly   Snoggin'.

Kim   Is that all ya did? – An' me mum's up doin' 'Saturday Night' an' flirtin' with some stupid aald pig. An' when I went to bed she sneaked 'im in through the winda. I could 'ear them smoochin' an' laughin' an' doin' things.

Kelly   That was me, soft shite.

Kim   Ya brought 'im back 'ere?

Kelly   We never done nothin' so don't be gettin' ideas.

Kim   I thought it was me mum. I was prayin' to me dad

an' Our Lady to make 'im go an' everythin'.

Kelly   Well now ya know.

Kim   Ya mean, ya brought 'im back 'ere an' never done nothin'?

Kelly   No.

Kim   Would ya a done if there was no one in?

Kelly   I've only just met 'im.

Kim   I was only askin'.

Kelly   Do I look all right? 'E'll be 'ere in a minute.

Kim   What's 'is name?

Kelly   Wait till ya meet 'im, Kim. 'E's like me dad, all gentle like – (*She thinks.*) a gentleman.

Kim   'As 'e got a moustache?

Kelly   No.

Kim   Then why's 'e like me dad?

Kelly   It was just the way 'e ett 'is chips.

Kim   Did 'e get ya chips?

Kelly   Yeh.

Kim   It's nice isn't it, when they buy ya somethin' special.

Kelly   'Ow would you know?

Kim   I just think it must be nice. (*Pause.*) When's 'e comin' round?

Kelly   Now, soon. In a minute!

Kim   Does 'e wear trainees or shoes?

Kelly   Twenny fuckin' questions! I don't know!

Kim   Oh, I'm goin' the beach.

Kelly   So ya said.

Josie *enters from her bedroom. She wears silky pyjamas, a dressing-gown and slippers. She looks better than she feels. She stops and lights a cigarette.*

Kim   Oh shut ya face.

Kelly   Shut ya fadge.

Kim   Yeh shut ya minge.

Kelly   Shut ya tits.

Kim   Shut ya mary.

Kelly   Shut ya pits.

Josie   Now don't go bringin' politics into it.

Kelly   What?

Pause. **Josie** *thinks.*

Josie   I'm sure that HRT gets ya pissed.

Kim   Don't give none to are Kelly then.

Josie *sits at the table and surveys the clutter.*

Josie   Should a brought more food with us.

Kelly   Get some at the market.

Kim   It's all second 'and cakes an' mouldy veg.

Kelly   Does this top look stupid?

Kim   Yeh.

Josie   No.

Kelly   Thanks a lot. I'm already late an' you're sayin' me top's mingin'.

Kelly *exits to her bedroom.*

Josie   Where's she goin'?

Kim   The fair with some ug.

Josie   So she copped?

Kim That's what she reckons. (*Pause.*) She reckons she brought 'im back 'ere.

Josie I thought I 'eard someone raspin' with passion outside me winda.

Kim I thought it was you an' that fella.

Josie Be'ave yerself. Ya dad's still warm.

Kim 'E kept slidin' 'is 'and down ya bum.

Josie We was 'avin' a laugh. Bruce is a nice fella.

Kim You went with someone called Bruce?

Josie Went with?

Kim Ya kissed 'im. I seen ya. I seen ya kissin' 'im.

Josie Just to say goodnight.

Kim Ya were snoggin'. Propply snoggin'. I could see ya reflection in the arcade winda. Ya were laughin'. Ya were laughin' an' ya were kissin'. Ya were kissin' 'im an' ya 'ad ya hand on 'is arse. Ya were laughin'. Ya was, ya were laughin'. Ya stopped an' ya were laughin'. Ya make me sick. Ya just make me feel ill.

Pause.

Josie So I should stay on me own the rest a me life –

Kim There's no one like me dad.

Josie An' not 'ave friends?

Kim Some friend!

There is a knock on the back of the caravan. **Josie** *starts.*

Josie Who the shittinell's that?

Kim Kelly!

Kelly *bursts from her bedroom wearing a different top.*

Kelly Shit. Is this top tight enough?

Josie Who is it?

Kelly (*calling*)   It's open!

Mick *crosses in front of the caravan and heads for the door.*

Kim   It's are Kelly's fella.

Josie   Didn't know I was runnin' an open bordello.

Kelly *stands near the door facing* **Mick**, *on the steps.*

Kelly   'Iya.

Mick   Thought I'd got the wrong one then.

Kelly   Come in. I'm nearly ready.

Mick *enters.*

Josie   Come in, son. Sit down.

Mick   I'm orright.

Kelly   I won't be a minute.

Josie   Take no notice a me in all me glory. The state a this place an' all. The shame of it. You'll think we're a gang a gyppos.

Kelly *exits to her bedroom.*

Mick   Ya orright.

Josie   Introductions, Kelly.

Kelly *appears round the bedroom door.*

Kelly   That's me mum an' that's are Kim.

She exits.

Josie   Sit down, love. I don't know ya name.

Mick   Mick.

Josie   Sit down, Mick. I'm Josie, by the way. Move up, Kimmy, let Mick sit down.

Kim *moves along swiftly.* **Mick** *sits.*

Mick   'Iya.

Kim *looks away.*

Josie   Nice day for the fair.

Mick   Not bad. A bit dull now.

Josie   Weather's not bad, considerin'.

Mick   No.

Josie   Rhyl, is it?

Mick   Yeh.

Josie   Ya goin' on the bus?

Mick   I've got me dad's car.

Josie   Very nice. You'll 'ave to teach are Kelly.

Mick   Yeh.

Kelly *enters from the bedroom wearing a bumbag and carrying a small jacket.*

Mick   Ya ready then?

Kelly   All cleaned up an' ready to rumble. (*Checking the contents of her bumbag.*) Got me lippy, got me keys, got me money.

Josie (*forcefully*)   An' don't go on them chair-o-planes.

Kelly   As if I would.

Josie   Ta-ra, Mick. See ya again, son. Say ta-ra to Mick.

Kim   Ta-ra.

Mick   Nice to meet ya.

Kelly *and* **Mick** *exit from the caravan.*

Josie   Fancy are Kelly gettin' a bit of orright. I'm glad she's courtin'.

Kim   Courtin'? 'E'll be with someone else tomorrow.

Josie   You're just in a tizz, you are.

Kim   I'm not.

Josie   Well do somethin' with yerself an' don't sit there like a sack a spuds.

Kim   I'm not.

Josie   D' ya wanna come the market?

Kim   I'm goin' the beach. I told ya last night I was goin' the beach.

Josie   Eh! I like their 'angin' baskets. We'll 'ave them. This'll be a little palace when I get ya dad's insurance. All lovely fuchsias an' petulias. (*Pause.*) Nice nets an' all.

Kim   Nice yeh.

Josie   Ah well, no use gawpin' better start buyin'.

Kim   Curtains?

Josie   Cushions. Cushions are a start. An' I'll get some a them out-of-date noodles if they sell them. At least that'll cheer ya up.

Josie *exits to her bedroom.* **Kim** *sits. She starts to sing.*

Kim   'Saturday night, di-di-di-da-da da da dum, Be ma baby – It's party time an' not one minute can we lose, Pretty baby . . .'

She goes to her bed, picks up the quilt and sniffs it. She folds the quilt and pillows and places them on top of the bed with the cuddly toys. She sits at the end of the bed and looks forward. Pause.

(*Calls.*) Mum, 'ow long will ya be?

Josie (*off*)   You go if ya want.

Kim *goes to the table and clears the rest of the clutter.*

Kim (*calls*)   I'll tidy up first.

Josie (*off*)   Ta, Kimmy babes.

Kim *goes to the back settee. She picks up her bag and takes out a beach towel. She places it on top of the pile of clothes and tidies them away under the bed. She returns to sit on the edge of the bed.*

Kim (*calls*)   Mum.

Josie (*off*)   What?

Kim (*calls*)   Can I come the market with you?

Josie (*off*)   I thought ya were goin' the beach.

Kim (*calls*)   There's no point the sun's gone in.

Scene Three: Babies

Music: 'Babies' by Pulp.

The caravan. An evening in early March 1995.

The caravan is empty.

Mick *enters. He is followed by* **Kelly**. *She is dressed in an Asda supermarket uniform and wears a jacket.* **Mick** *wears a sporty outdoor coat. They each carry a case –* **Kelly**'s *being much bigger than* **Mick's**. *She also carries a small bag.* **Mick** *reaches the door of the caravan, stops and waits.* **Kelly** *hauls her case along throughout her dialogue. She stops occasionally to change hands or rest, then continues.*

Kelly (*in disbelief*)   An' then I 'eard it over the Tannoy, – 'Congratulations to Kelly on are fresh pizza counter – who got married to her fiancé Mick yesterdee. – Congratulations, good luck, best wishes, all that – from everyone in the store.' – Mick, I-felt-ashamed. Anyway, I was on checkouts today so no one knew it was me. – None a the customers looked at me 'Kelly Happy to Help' badge and went –' Oooh, are you the one? – Ah, it rained yesterdee didn't it? – Was it in a church? Fancy 'avin' to work the day after.' (*She picks up the case and quickly hobbles the last few yards.*) Uurgh, bloody 'ell!

She stops.

Mick   Why don't ya just say?

Kelly (*still holding the case*)   Say what?

Mick   Ya shoulda carried mine. Why didn't ya say?

Kelly   It's dead wifey. I didn't like.

Mick *picks up the case.*

Mick   Jesus Christ, Kel. What's in 'ere?

Kelly   Me clothes, me 'airdryer an' me 'eated rollers. Just essentials really.

Mick   Bleedin' 'ell.

Kelly (*gesturing the small bag*)   There wasn't even room for the 'oneymoon food.

Mick   The what food?

Kelly   The randy food. Ya know, food that gets ya goin'.

Mick   Ya what?

Kelly   Chocolate spread, avocado pears and Chinese oyster sauce.

Mick   Give me that an' I would be goin'. 'Ave ya got the keys?

Kelly   Oyster sauce is nice. I 'ad it at the Ming Sing on me eighteenth.

Pause.

Mick   Kelly, where's the keys?

Kelly   Oh yeh. I was gettin' them out then I told ya about work an' I forgot.

She reaches into the bag and brings out the keys.

Mick   Go on then. Open up.

Kelly *offers the keys to* **Mick**.

Mick   It's your mam's caravan.

Kelly   Not yet it's not.

Mick   Ya know what I mean.

Kelly Sorry.

Kelly *opens the door of the caravan, puts on the light and enters.*

Mick (*calls*) Didn't they 'ave a collection for us in work?

Kelly Who did?

Mick (*calls*) In work.

Kelly They're not that bloody quick. They might do when I go back. It smells dead musty, Mick, an' it's bloody freezin'.

She opens the bedroom doors.

Mick I 'ope so cos the dole don't believe in weddin' presents.

Kelly *goes to the front door and takes the large case from* **Mick**. *She puts the case in* **Josie's** *room.*

Kelly Or they might do once I've 'ad the baby.

Mick *enters the caravan with the small case and places it outside* **Josie**'s *room. He then relaxes on the back settee.*

Mick That's for the kid though not for us.

Kelly *takes the small case into* **Josie**'s *room.*

Kelly It is for us. It's for us as well.

Mick 'Ave a rest now, Kel. Come on.

Kelly *enters the living-room and takes a newspaper from her bag.*

Kelly Not much chance with you around. I got ya the paper.

Mick I don't want the paper. I want you.

Kelly Well 'ave it anyway.

Mick Sit down. Come 'ead. We 'aven't got long.

Kelly I thought we could keep it cos it's got the date on.

Mick Sit down. They'll be 'ere soon.

Kelly   I am. I forgot to get one yesterday. But it doesn't matter. We'll keep this one so we know what 'appened the day after.

Mick   Yeh, are honeymoon anniversary.

Kelly   News that gets ya goin'.

Mick   Ya shoulda got the *Sport.*

Kelly   That's just tits.

Mick   I know.

They kiss. **Mick** *begins to undo* **Kelly**'s *overall.*

Kelly   I love ya, Mick.

Mick   I know.

He takes off his shoes.

I've been waitin' all day for a good shag off you, Mrs Maguire.

Kelly *kicks off her shoes and lies down.*

Kelly   I know what ya mean.

Mick   Me bollocks are burstin'.

Mick *undoes his belt and flies.*

Kelly   Were ya dead angry last night?

Mick   I was dead 'orny.

Kelly   I just don't like doin' it in me mum's.

Mick   It'll be orright when we get a place.

Mick *kneels on the settee in between* **Kelly**'s *legs.*

Kelly   It'll be brilliant.

Mick *lowers himself down on top of* **Kelly**. *Pause.*

Mick   I know.

They kiss.

Kelly   D'ya think it'll be different cos we're married?

Mick   It'll be fuckin' excellent.

Mick *fumbles with* **Kelly***'s overall as she tugs at his jeans.*

Kelly   Shall I shut the curtains?

Mick   Just leave them.

Kelly   Shall we get on the floor?

Mick   If ya want.

They tumble awkwardly to the floor, still trying to kiss.

You on top?

Kelly   Yeh.

Kelly *establishes herself on top of* **Mick***.*

Mick   'Urry up. I just wanna put it in.

Kelly   Ah, watch me knee.

Mick   Take ya tights off.

Kelly   I will now. Move a minute – ow.

Kelly *stands and undoes the rest of her overall.* **Mick** *lies back, watching her.*

Mick   Mind the winda.

Kelly (*turning off the light*)   Flash 'Arry 'll be 'avin' a waz like there's no tomorrow watchin' us.

Mick   Just take it off, Kel.

Kelly   I'm gonna be bleedin' freezin'. An' don't you groan too much. 'E'll get off on that an' all, the dirty screff.

Mick   I couldn't give a shit.

Kelly   I know. I'll put me goin' away outfit on. Then you can take it off again.

Mick   Ya shoulda done it before.

Kelly *takes a tiny, stretchy dress from her bag.*

Kelly   Never 'ad time before. Ya can't get off them tills on a Friday.

Mick   Just 'urry up, they'll be 'ere by seven.

Kelly *takes off her overall and drops it round her feet. Her tights are more hole than gusset. She attempts to put on her dress.*

Kelly   We've got ages yet. I didn't want ya to wait. Ya were good enough gettin' ya dad's car. I just wanted to get 'ere an' it be just you an' me.

Mick *watches, amused, as* **Kelly** *battles with the dress.*

Kelly   Not that it will be for long. I'm gonna be bleedin' freezin' in this. I forgot to pack me weddin' bra an' all.

She tries unsuccessfully to squeeze it over her chest.

I shoulda got a twelve.

There is a noise outside the caravan. **Kelly** *stops.* **Mick** *listens. The door opens. It is* **Josie** *and* **Kim**.

Kelly   Christ! Who is it?

Josie   Surprise, lovebirds!

Mike *jumps up and sits on the settee.* **Kelly** *tugs down her dress.*

Kelly   Oh my God.

Josie   We managed to get the early train.

Kelly   Mam! Ya said after seven.

Josie   That's all right, isn't it?

Josie *enters carrying a suitcase and puts on the light.* **Kim** *follows, wearing a tracksuit. She carries a holdall and holds a cake box.*

Josie   You carry on doin' what ya doin'. Just pretend we're not 'ere.

Mick *is still making himself decent.*

Kim *stands near the door, still.*

Josie   Can ya manage that, Kimberley, love?

Mick   D'ya need a hand?

Josie   No, love. Do you?

Josie *puts down her case.* **Kim** *puts the box on the table. She marches past* **Kelly** *into* **Josie**'s *bedroom with her holdall.*

Kelly   'Sorry we're early. Did we disturb ya?'

Josie   'Aven't ya put the gas on? Christ, you'd freeze ya bits off in 'ere.

Josie *takes the case into the front bedroom.*

Kelly   'Aven't 'ad a chance.

Josie   What time did ya get 'ere?

Kelly   Before. (*Putting the overall in her bag.*) Won't be seein' that again for a week.

Mick   Ya not the only one.

Mick *lights a cigarette.*

Josie   Done much?

Mick   No.

Kelly   There's nothin' open.

Josie   Bruce said that. 'E's glad 'e's doin' double shifts. 'E said 'e'd rather do that than come 'ere.

Kelly   So it'll be swingin' then.

Josie   Oh, we can make are own fun, can't we? That's what I said to Bruce. Might as well be all of us in me lovely little palace, it's still the same price. We got ya a lovely cake, Kel. An' there's some cans an' a bottle a bucks fizz in the 'oldall.

Kim *enters from the bedroom.*

Kim   Why do we always come at crap times?

Josie   Stop moanin'. This is a happy day.

Kim   I'm not moanin'. It's me 'ormones.

Josie Kelly's 'ormones are in the same state as yours an' she's not moanin'.

Kim Well she's not sleepin' in the livin'-room, is she?

Josie It is their honeymoon. They deserve a bit a privacy.

Kim So do I. I've got mornin' sickness.

Kelly An' I 'aven't?

Josie Get in with me then.

Kim I'd rather spew in public.

Kim *exits to* **Josie**'s *bedroom.*

Josie (*calling*) Come on, we'll 'ave some cake. It's lovely sponge.

Kelly (*quietly*) I'm tellin' ya, Mum, she's not gonna spoil this week.

Mick (*eating*) Leave it, Kel.

Kelly I won't. I'll tell 'er.

Josie (*quietly*) Now leave it, she's depressed enough as it is.

Kim *enters carrying a four-pack of lager.*

Kim Anyone want a can?

Mick Go 'ead, Kim.

Kim *sits down next to* **Mick**. *They both click open their cans.*

Kelly What 'ave you been told about drinkin'?

Kim It gets ya pissed an' gives ya a red nose. Can I 'ave a drag on that?

Mick Ya can 'ave one if ya want.

Kim Ta.

Kim *takes a cigarette from* **Mick** *and lights up.*

Kelly If ya both gonna smoke ya can sit over there.

Josie *lights a cigarette.*

Kelly (*standing*) 'As nobody got respect for the unborn child? I'll move if ya don't mind.

Kelly *crosses to the table and sits.* **Josie** *passes* **Kim** *a slice of cake.*

Josie D' ya know what? I'd rather cover meself in them expensive plasters an' pretend they were doin' me good than put up with this moanin' for another five months. Pass us that ashtray.

Kelly *does so reluctantly.*

Kim We 'ad a gorgeous gateau at that pub last night.

Josie O, youse missed a lovely choice a puddin's.

Mick I was burstin' after the roast.

Josie I bet ya was.

Kelly Too much stodge is bad for ya anyway.

Josie Is that why ya went 'ome early, Mick? Ya couldn't wait to get it out ya system.

Kelly It's tradition for the couple to go 'ome early from receptions. It is, isn't it, Mick?

Mick I wouldn't know –

Kim It wasn't a reception, anyway. It was a meal in a smelly pub.

Mick I thought we went 'ome cos you felt sick.

Kelly Well it is. It's tradition. (*Pause.*) It's a wonder you never felt sick all the lambrusco you kept downin'.

Kim I can take me ale.

Kelly An' all the shite ya stuff down ya neck.

Josie Now don't start.

Kelly   I'm not startin'. Just that she should 'ave more sense.

Kim   I 'ave got sense. Who'd wanna get married in a poky little room? When it's my turn, I'm gettin' married on a beach.

Kelly   Where? Ainsdale with all the shite? I'm talkin' sense, sense. Sense of responsibility. Sense of well-being. Sense of ya own mind. Sense of – (*She struggles.*)

Kim   Sense a humour? Cos you 'aven't got one.

Kim *laughs.* **Mick** *raises a smile.*

Kelly   Oh, shut ya big fat aarse, you.

Josie   Stop it.

Kim   Shut yours.

Kelly   Just shut ya tits.

Josie   Very nice.

Kim   At least I've got some.

Kelly   Shut ya big fat, saggy, droopy tits.

Kim   Shut ya fishole.

Josie   Now me an' Mick 'ave 'ad enough a this.

Kelly   Shut yours. I can smell it from 'ere, trawler fanny.

Josie   I 'ope youse don't 'ave girls.

Kim *stands and crosses towards the bathroom.*

Kim   I 'ope we do cos mine 'll be better lookin' than 'ers.

Kelly   Cheeky runt.

She opens the door of the bathroom and enters halfway.

(*With venom.*)   Mrs Maguire!

She slams the door and locks it.

Josie (*calling*)   If ya told us who the father was, we might 'ave an idea of what it will look like.

Kim (*off*)   I've told ya.

Josie (*calling*)   You've told me nothin'

Kim (*off*)   'E's fifteen.

Kelly *crosses to sit by* **Mick**.

Kelly   She does my 'ead in.

Josie (*calling*)   Yeh an' I wanna know 'is name.

Kim (*off*)   I've told ya. 'E's fifteen an' ya can't touch 'im.

Josie *goes to the bathroom door.*

Kim   Are you listenin'? I'm tryin' to 'ave a wee. Will ya stop listenin'.

Josie   I'm not bloody listenin'. An' I'm not gonna report 'im, I've told ya that. But I'll see 'is mam an' dad. Why should I 'ave all the worry?

Pause. A toilet flush is heard.

Kelly   Leave 'er. It's 'er own fault.

Mick   She's only a kid.

Kelly   All right for you to say. She'll ruin this week if we let 'er.

Josie (*at the door*)   Come out, babe. Come on, come out.

Silence.

Come on, angel. Come out an' we'll talk.

Kim (*off*)   What d' ya wanna know?

Josie   Come on. We'll 'ave a ciggie an' we'll talk.

Kim (*off*)   I'm not tellin' ya nothin'.

Mick   Shall we get off?

Josie   You stay there. It's best to 'ave a man's opinion an' all.

Kim (*off*)   Is are Kelly there?

Josie   Yeh.

Kim   (*off*)—An' Mick?

Josie   We're all 'ere.

Silence. The bathroom door opens and **Kim** *appears. She stands in a defiant manner, holding onto the bathroom door.*

Kim   What d' ya wanna know?

Josie   I wanna know – (Pause) What's 'e said to ya?

Silence.

Mick (*standing*)   We better go.

Kim (*with haste*)   'E said, 'Ya know when it's born do I 'ave to bring flowers the 'ospital cos I'll feel a cunt.'

Kelly (*in disbelief*)   Bastard.

Josie   An' that was it?

Kim   Yeh.

Josie   Ya better off without 'im.

Silence. **Mick** *still stands.*

Mick   I'm goin' the shop. Anyone want ciggies?

Josie   'Ave some a mine. I've brought plenty.

Mick   I'll get some more.

Kelly   Will it be open?

Josie   I've got loads, Mick. You sit down an' enjoy ya 'oliday.

Mick   I fancy some crisps.

Josie   I've got crisps.

Mick   Or chocolate or somethin'. I'll see ya later.

Mick *exits.*

Josie 'E shouldn't go wastin' 'is money.

Kelly My money.

Josie No luck?

Kelly No jobs.

Kim There is jobs if ya look for them.

Kelly Yeh, with no money.

Kim *stands at the table and starts to pick at the cake.*

Kim Why can't 'e work on the side like normal people?

Kelly There's nothin' goin' in 'is line a work.

Josie What is 'is line a work?

Kelly Dunno. But there's nothin' goin'.

Josie I could see if Bruce can get 'im start on the docks.

Kelly Ya must be jokin'. I wouldn't let Mick be a slave to no one.

Josie What d' ya mean?

Kelly Bruce is at work every hour God sends. Doin' all sorts a jobs, drivin' all sorts a cranes. 'E doesn't even take the weekend off.

Josie Only cos 'e's not allowed.

Kelly Exactly. They're all forced into it.

Josie Sod the long hours, Kel. Think a the money.

Kelly I'd rather 'e signed on. I want Mick to come 'ome at the end a the day.

Josie What are you on about?

Kelly It was Bruce that said it. Long hours are dangerous.

Josie Not on that money they're not.

Kelly Me dad woulda killed you, sayin' that.

Josie Yeh. On 'is bleedin' soapbox. 'Unions this, unions that.' I know about paypackets not unions.

Kim Wish I did.

Kelly I wouldn't know what to do with meself without Mick around.

Josie Well think what ya could do with the money.

Kim I'm gonna get a nanny when I start work. She can 'ave a room in me flat at the docks an' mind it when I go clubbin'.

Josie Think you've already got a soft shite lined up for that.

Kim What?

Josie (*indicating herself*) Granny Grunt. It'll be me left 'oldin' the baby. 'Oldin' two bleedin' babies.

Kelly Yeh. I'll be paintin' the town with me Monday book.

Kim An' me with me maths books. (*laughs.*) Pushin' a pram an' carryin' me lunch box.

Kelly Givin' it 'breast is best' in the middle of English.

Kim Yeh, Mave the Rave. Imagine it. 'Er mouth'd be waterin'.

Kelly At least ya could take it the playscheme with ya in the summer.

Kim Funny.

Josie Eh! You'll bring it 'ere in the summer when –

Kim When I get ya dad's insurance.

Josie Eh! Ya won't be takin' the piss when you've got a proper 'oliday 'ome to come to.

Kelly Kim, we'll teach them Welsh an' everythin'.

Kim (*speaking Welsh*) Yackydar!

Kelly (*joining in*) Cllan – fire – perth – ging – whatever! They'll be multicultured comin' round 'ere.

Josie Ya should count ya selves lucky comin' 'ere any time. All ya'll need is ya spends an' ya petrol money for Mick. (*Pause.*) An' if you want the place to yerselves, I can always stay in Bruce's van.

Kim When?

Josie Whenever.

Kim Who with?

Josie With Bruce.

Kim What for?

Josie I thought you'd be glad of it. Me out the way. You lot can do what ya want then.

Pause.

Kim You make me sick.

Josie What did you say?

Kim You an' 'im.

Josie An' don't ya think it makes me sick?

Kim What?

Josie You. Goin' with the first one that comes along. I thought ya might 'ave been like are Kelly an' saved yerself for someone special.

Kim 'E was special.

Josie 'E's a kid.

Kim An' you're an aald slag.

Kelly Don't you talk to 'er like that.

Kim Why not? It's true. Me dad dies an' she goes with the first aald bastard that comes along. Is Bruce special?

Josie At least 'e talks to me like a person.

Kim   An' me dad never?

Josie   No.

Kim   Ya just a liar.

Kelly   Listen to you.

Kim   I loved me dad an' now 'e's dead youse don't even care.

Kelly   Me mum's got to live 'er life.

Kim   With some dirty docker?

Josie   'E's a very nice man.

Kim   What's that to me?

Josie   Ya should be glad. It's down to me that you'll 'ave a permanent caravan to come to. I could easy spend the insurance on meself, ya know?

Kim   I'm supposed to be grateful for a shed?

Josie   Ya cheeky little bastard. You get out my sight.

Kim   Don't you touch me –

Josie   I wouldn't want to –

Kim   Good. Cos I'm goin'.

Pause.

Kelly   Go on then. Give us all a bit a peace.

Silence. **Kim** *stares. She goes to the door and exits, running.*

Told ya she'd ruin it.

She sits on the back settee, wraps her arms round her waist and leans forward.

Josie   I'm sorry, love. I don't want 'er to ruin the week for ya. (*Pause.*) She'll be back soon, right as rain. We'll all be orright. Then we'll enjoy areselves in me lovely little palace.

Pause.

Kelly   I've got terrible pains.

Josie   Bad?

Kelly   Bad enough.

Josie   Inside?

Kelly   Yeh. (*pause.*) Mum, get Mick.

Josie (*calls*)   Kim! Kim! I won't be long, love.

Josie *exits from the caravan.*

Josie   Kim! Come back, love. We've got to get Mick.

Kelly *lies back on the settee. She curls up, cradles herself and whimpers.*

Scene Four: Garden Party

Music: 'Garden Party' by Rick Nelson.

The caravan. A bright evening in September 1995.

Kim *sits on the steps at the front of the caravan.* **Josie** *stands in the doorway behind her holding a cup of tea, wearing a cowboy hat and smoking a cigarette.* **Bruce**, *wearing a check shirt and western hat, removes the 'For Sale' sign from the ground.*

Country music can be heard being broadcast from a Tannoy system throughout the scene.

Josie   D' ya remember that, Kim?

Kim   No.

Josie   Ya do. When me an' ya dad took the pensioners to Colwyn Bay. Ya must do.

Kim   I don't.

Josie   Anyway, they were all bleedin' paralysed drunk so when we got off the coach we 'ad to walk them 'ome. I took this one fella who lived by us an' when 'is daughter opened the door she goes, 'Dad, what are you doin' 'ere?'

Only turned out 'e shoulda gone back to Llandudno. 'E
was stayin' with 'is wife in the convalescent 'ome. Soft sod.
(*Pause.*) The daughter took 'im back the next day. When
they got there the mother was stiff as a board an' in a
body bag. 'E's never been the same since.

Bruce *lays the sign on the ground near to the caravan.*

Bruce   Funny what a death can do.

Josie   That's right. It affects people in different ways.

Bruce *stands near to the door.* **Josie** *passes him the cup of tea.*

Bruce   An' ya never know when the Lord'll take ya.

Josie   Like Jimmy. Went on the chair-o-planes an' never
come off. Well 'e did come off that was the problem.

Bruce   In 'is prime an' all.

Josie   'E only went on so I could get a photie, didn't 'e,
Kim?

Kim   I wasn't there.

Josie   You weren't there, were ya? Just so everyone'd
know 'e'd been on a Spanish fair. Now no one can forget.
I didn't even manage to take the photo, 'e was flyin'
through the air before I knew what was 'appenin'. I'll never
go abroad again.

Bruce   Enjoy yerself while ya can. That's my motto.

Josie   Well we are.

Bruce   We are.

Josie   We are, aren't we, Kim?

Pause.

Bruce   That's 'ow Linda went an' all. Enjoyin' 'erself.

Josie   The best way, I say.

Bruce   'Aydock. The two forty-five. Just as me 'orse
jumped the last. She grabbed me arm an' whoomph! –

down she went. Powerful thing, strokes. I 'ad a fiver on that 'orse an' all.

Josie Terrible that, isn't, Kim?

Bruce She loved the gee-gees, Linda. I thought I'd never go again meself.

Josie I know nothin' about racin'.

Bruce I'll 'ave to take ya.

From inside the caravan we hear a baby crying.

Josie Ooh, I'd love that. You'd like that, wouldn't ya, Kim?

Kim Is are Kelly comin' or what?

Josie Once she's finished work.

Kim Thank God for that.

Josie That's what I miss about comin' 'ere – the death page in the *Echo*.

Kim Will ya stop bein' morbid.

Bruce Someone's not 'appy.

Kim This is doin' my 'ead in.

Kim *pushes past* **Josie** *and* **Bruce**. *She enters the front bedroom of the caravan. Through the window, we see her nurse a baby without interest.*

Bruce Looks like we're in for a happy weekend.

Josie I shoulda told 'er it was country an' western.

Bruce She'll 'ave me wishin' I was back at work.

'Footsteps' by Daniel O'Donnell is now heard over the Tannoy.

Josie Well let's enjoy areselves while ya not.

Bruce I know. I just keep thinkin' about it.

Josie Will you cheer up an' give us kiss?

Bruce *knocks* **Josie**'s *hat back and kisses her.* **Josie** *breaks away.*

Josie   They played this at the funeral. Right at the end. We 'adn't thought about music. It didn't seem right. The priest's a big fan a Daniel O'Donnell, that's what it is. Plays 'im at weddin's an' all sorts.

Kim *enters from the bedroom.*

Josie   Listen what's playin'.

Kim   Can I get past?

Kim *pushes past and goes down the steps.*

Josie   This was playin' at the funeral, wasn't it?

Kim   No it wasn't.

Josie   It was. At the end.

Kim   It wasn't a funeral.

Josie   Kim.

Kim   It wasn't. It's not like it ever lived. It was already dead. It never died propply. It was dead when it come out an' they just put it in a box.

Josie   Ya don't mean that.

Kim   I do.

The baby cries once again. Pause.

I'm goin' the shop.

She exits.

Josie   Kim! Get back 'ere! (*Pause.*) Come on, Kelly 'll be 'ere soon!

Josie *goes to enter the caravan.* **Bruce** *stands in her way and holds her.*

Bruce   D' ya wanna stay at mine tonight?

Josie   Might do.

Bruce   What's that supposed to mean?

Josie Course I will. Anythin' to get away from all this.

Bruce Cheek!

Josie *enters the caravan and goes into the front bedroom.*

Bruce (*calls*) – We'll go the show after, Jose. Put this strike out me 'ead an' enjoy areselves. What d' ya reckon?

Josie (*off*) – 'Ang on. I can't find 'is dummy.

Bruce (*calls*) – Raymond Froggat an' the Blue Jean Roadshow.

Josie *appears from the bedroom and shuts the door.*

Josie (*whisper*) – Only wanted 'is dum-dum, poor little fella.

Josie *walks down the steps and surveys her surroundings.*

Bruce 'E used to do the same clubs as me, years ago. 'E was a nice fella. Not that good though. Not a good crooner, like me. An' 'e couldn't get the women.

Josie You just wish it was you.

Bruce No I don't. If I was a star, I wouldn't know you.

Josie *kisses him on the cheek.*

Josie It'll be a good night.

Bruce I 'ope so.

Josie They better do some Patsy Cline.

Bruce She's in the finale on Monday afternoon.

Josie Oh aye yeh!

Bruce That girl off *Stars in Their Eyes*.

Josie You'll miss it. You'll be goin' 'ome.

Bruce If there's one thing I 'ate, it's bein' on a picket first thing Monday.

Josie Stay 'ere then an' don't go.

Bruce . I can't.

Josie   Ya can. They won't miss ya but I will.

Bruce   I'll 'ave to see.

Josie   I'll make it worth ya while.

Bruce   I'm sure ya will but people's livelihoods rest on this.

Josie   Just stay 'ere an' 'ave a nice day.

Bruce   Jose –

Josie   Eh! I could get used to this. Days off instead a stupid hours.

Bruce   Don't be sayin' that, sweet'eart.

Josie   Comin' up 'ere when we want. Gettin' work done on the vans. I want tubs like theirs. Two a them. One either side. An' you an' Mick can do a fence all round. I'll do the curtains. I'll do yours. I'll do them matchin'. We can rent them out then. Make a bit a money. I mean, that's what people want. Nice caravans with nice insides.

Bruce   Can do that next year.

Josie   Next weekend.

Bruce   I'd rather I was back at work next weekend.

Josie   Do ya?

Bruce   Jose, we've all got to live. We're on strike, we're not on 'oliday.

Josie   It's a nice idea though.

Bruce   The grass is always greener, Jose.

Josie   Yeh. (*Pause.*) Wish Mick'd get a job.

Bruce   'E'll get one.

Josie   'E's as bad as are Kim. Tele an' tea, that's all they've got.

Bruce   That'll be me before I know it.

Josie   Don't be soft.

Bruce   But this could be it. The bastards could just get rid.

Josie   But there'll always be ships.

Bruce   Yeh. An' no real dockers.

Kelly (*off*)   – Mum!

Josie   Iya, love.

Kelly *rushes on, breathless. She carries an Asda carrier bag.*

Bruce   'Allo, Kelly, darlin'.

Kelly   Iya, Bruce.

Josie   Did ya see are Kim?

Kelly   She's walkin' up with Mick. 'Ow's the baby?

Josie   Ah, 'e's been great.

Kelly   I was dead worried. She said 'e'd been dead nowtty.

Josie   She thinks it an insult if 'e snuffles, Kel.

Kelly (*gesturing the carrier bag*)   – I got 'im a cuddly Power Ranger.

Pause.

Josie   Go on in, e's well away.

Kelly *takes a copy of the* Liverpool Echo *from the bag.*

Kelly   I got the paper as well. (*Pause.*) It's not good news, Bruce.

Bruce   What's 'appened?

Kelly   Looks like they've sacked all of ya. Sacked ya all.

She holds the paper out to **Bruce**.

Bruce   What does it say?

Kelly   Not much. I said to Mick, 'Blink an' ya'd miss it.' Ya'd think it wasn't important. Should I find it?

Bruce   Just tell me what it said.

Kelly *starts to search through the newspaper.*

Kelly   I think they got the P45s this mornin'.

Bruce   Bastards.

Josie   Yours 'll be at 'ome.

Bruce   I know it will.

Kelly   An' I think it says the jobs 'ave already been advertised. I'll find it now.

Bruce   Ya orright, Kel.

Kelly   Well it's there if ya want it.

Kelly *puts the newspaper on top of the gas canister.*

Bruce   Thanks, love.

Kelly   An' if there's anythin' –

Bruce   Thanks, Kel.

Kelly   'As 'e been fed?

Josie   Yes, love. 'E's 'ad plenty.

Kelly *enters the caravan, goes into the bedroom and shuts the door.*

Josie   There's certainly no point goin' back Mondee now.

Bruce   Josie, I've just lost me job. I've just lost everythin'.

Josie   You'll be orright. They're bound to give it ya back. I mean, what will they do? You've worked there years.

Bruce   Jose, when ya don't understand somethin', keep out of it. All right?

Josie   Orright.

Pause.

Bruce   Promise?

He touches **Josie**'s *face.*

Josie   You.

Josie *kisses him. Loud laughter is heard offstage.* **Bruce** *looks in the direction it is coming from.*

Bruce   No peace for the wicked.

Josie   Still, it's good bein' wicked.

She kisses him again. **Mick** *and* **Kim** *enter, still laughing. They carry a large holdall between them.*

Kim   The shame a you.

Mick   Kenny Rogers an' Tammy Wynette.

Kim   It suits ya that, Bruce.

Mick   'Ave to start callin' ya JR.

Josie   I wish 'e 'ad 'is money.

Bruce   I wish I 'ad anyone's money.

Kim   Yeh. We could do with a sugar-daddy, Bruce.

Mick *takes two cans of beer from his holdall and offers one to* **Bruce**.

Bruce   Cheers, son.

Mick   No probs, bud.

Mick *picks up the newspaper, flicks through it and throws it to the floor. He leans against the gas canister, takes off his shirt and takes in the sun.* **Bruce** *picks up the newspaper and sits away from the others on the grass.*

Josie (*to* **Kim**)   – You've perked up.

Kim   Is Kelly seein' to the baby?

Josie   You all right now she's 'ere?

Kim   I was anyway.

Josie   Well you'll 'ave to 'elp out as well.

Kim   Let me enjoy meself first. Can I 'ave a can, Mick?

Josie   'Elp yerself.

Kim *takes a can from his holdall.*

Kim   We all goin' out after?

Mick   Too right.

Bruce   It's all the best a British on tonight, if ya interested.

Mick   None a that line dancin', is it?

Josie   That's on tomorrow in the family bar.

Bruce   Ya can count me out a that.

Mick   Me an' all.

Kim   An' I'm not goin'.

Josie   I don't care if I go by meself.

Kim *removes her T-shirt to reveal a small bikini top.* **Bruce** *opens the paper and looks through it. He pauses on a page and reads. He closes the paper, lies back and puts it behind his head.*

Kim   I'll still be recoverin' from tonight.

Josie   You're not goin' out tonight.

Kim   I am.

Josie   An' who 's gonna mind the baby?

Kim   Are Kelly.

Josie   No she won't. This is 'er chance of a break.

Kim   She likes stayin' in.

Josie   Does she?

Kim   She does, doesn't she, Mick?

Mick   Sometimes, yeh.

Kim   *(calls)* – Kelly!

Josie   Keep ya voice down.

Kim   (*calls*) – Kel!

Josie   They're lookin' out their winda at you.

Kelly   (*off*) – What?

Kim   'Ere a minute.

Kelly *appears at the bedroom door holding the baby.*

Kelly   Keep it down. I'm just gettin' 'im off.

Kim   Don't you like stayin' in?

Kelly   What d' ya mean?

Kim   Rather than goin' out?

Kelly   Dunno –

Kim   Ya do, don't ya?

Kelly   Why?

Josie   Cos she wants you to stay in so she can go out.
I've told 'er no –

Kelly   I'd rather stay in an' watch the baby.

Kim   Told ya.

Kelly   Is that all right then?

Kim   Yeh.

Kelly   All that fuss over you. Ya should see 'is little face.
(*She goes down the steps.*) Smile for ya mum. Go on. Smile for
ya mum, not for Auntie Kelly. 'Ere she is. Ya gonna smile?
Come on, mummy hold ya.

She goes to hand the baby to **Kim**. **Kim** *recoils*.

Kim   I don't want it. Put it back. I don't want it yet.

Kim *sits on the step and begins to sunbathe.*

Kelly   Go to mummy in a minute then, eh? (*She walks
about nursing the baby.*) Ah, look. Look at nanny in 'er funny

hat lookin' all 'yee-hah'. An' there's Uncle Mick. An' Uncle Bruce. Fast asleep like you should be. Ah, poor Uncle Bruce. (*She goes to re-enter the caravan.*) Do you wanna put 'im down, Kim?

Kim   You do it.

Kelly   Ya sure?

Kim   Yeh.

Kelly *takes the baby into the bedroom and shuts the door.*

Josie   You don't know 'ow lucky you are.

Kim   Don't I?

Josie   'E'll start thinkin' she's 'is mother if ya not careful.

Kim   I don't care.

Josie   Ya might one day.

Kim   I don't wanna know.

Josie   No – ya never do.

Josie *lights a cigarette.* **Mick** *and* **Kim** *sunbathe.* **Bruce** *sleeps.*

Act Two

Scene Five: Sisters

Music: 'Sisters' by Annie Lennox and Aretha Franklin.

The caravan. A dull afternoon, March 1996.

Outside the caravan are two white tubs containing flowers, two garden gnomes pulling moonies, and a plastic table and two chairs. The 'For Sale' sign has now been removed completely.

Inside the caravan, the soft furnishings now co-ordinate and the net curtains are whiter than white.

Kelly, *wearing a 'Support the Dockers' T-shirt, sits beside the table studying the racing page of a newspaper. A radio-cassette player stands on a number of betting slips on the table. She turns on the radio – a sports programme is heard. She turns it off. She takes a betting slip from her pocket and looks at it. She kisses the slip.*

Kelly (*slowly, relishing the words*)   Encore un Peu.

She smiles, laughs softly and kisses the slip once more. **Kim** *enters from the bathroom and goes to the door.* **Kelly** *swiftly places the betting slip under the radio.*

Kim   What time does it start?

Kelly   Quarter to.

Kim *goes to the table and sits. She sighs.*

Kim   Wish it'd 'urry up.

Kelly   Wish I was there with them two.

Kim   What one 'ave I got?

Kelly   Young Hustler.

Kim   Is that a good one?

Kelly   Dunno. Gettin' backed though.

Kim   It must be a three-legged donkey.

Kelly   No. It's gone from twenty to one to fourteen to one.

Kim   So do I get more money if it wins?

Kelly   No, ya get less.

Kim   That's not on, that.

Kelly   Might 'ave a good chance though. (*Pause.*) I'd love to see it live.

Kim   Watch it on the tele.

Kelly   I mean the atmosphere – a good day out with Bruce an' Mick, 'avin' a laugh. Instead a bein' stuck 'ere pushin' leaflets.

Kim   That's not like you. You even shout 'Up the dockers' in ya sleep.

Kelly   I'm not gettin' bored of it. It would 'ave been a good day out that's all.

Kim   Listen to you. Never thought you'd be into dockers an' 'orses.

Kelly   It's good.

Kim   What is? Picket lines an' 'orse manure? You've gone weird, Kel.

Kelly   Don't be soft.

Kim   Ya 'ave. I mean, look at today. Ya palm are baby off onto me mum so ya can listen to a 'orse race an' shake a bucket for the dockers in the family bar. Now that's weird.

Kelly   No, it's not. Things change.

Kim   Yeh, they might a bit. But not like you. It's a wonder Mick puts up with ya.

Kelly   Don't worry. 'E doesn't.

Kim   What?

Kelly   E's seein' someone else.

Kim   No.

Kelly   'E is.

Kim   'As 'e told ya?

Kelly   Doesn't 'ave to.

Kim   Well 'ow d' ya know?

Kelly   Cos 'e's been doin' sit-ups.

Kim   Go 'way. Are ya gonna find out who it is an' knock 'er 'ead off?

Kelly *reads the racing pages.*

Kelly   Got more important things to think about.

Kim   So what are ya gonna do?

Kelly   Nothin'.

Kim   'Ow come? D' ya wanna get shut?

Kelly   I only married 'im cos a the baby.

Kim   The photos were nice though. It wasn't a complete waste a time. (*Pause.*) 'Ave ya got any idea who it could be?

Kelly   I thinks it's someone from the job club.

Kim   No.

Kelly   Well 'e's been signin' on for years. All of a sudden 'e goes the job club an' can't get enough of it. What does that say to you?

Kim   Doesn't say anythin'.

Kelly   Course it does. 'E's joined just to get a bit of extra fanny.

Kim   'E might be tryin' to get a job.

Kelly   Mick's 'appy to live on 'andouts an' my Asda ten per cent discount.

Kim   Praps 'e wants to save up. Change 'is life a bit.

Kelly   'E buys scratch cards for that.

Kim   I think you're over-reactin'.

Kelly   Kim, 'e wears Escape For Men whenever 'e goes. Now what does that say?

Kim   That 'e wants to smell nice.

Kelly   Come off it.

Kim   'E might be just tryin'.

Kelly   Tryin' it on. Anyway d' ya think I'm bothered? She can 'ave 'im, the lazy get. I shouldn't 'ave let 'im near me in the first place.

Kim   Will ya kick 'im out me mum's?

Kelly   When I find out who she is.

Kim   I thought ya weren't bothered?

Kelly   I'm not 'avin some scrubber takin' me 'usband just like that. There'll 'ave to be a fight first –

Kim   A proper fight?

Kelly   Then she can 'ave 'im. The sly bastard.

Kim   Kelly, ya don't wanna 'ave loads of upset again. Ya should leave it. Let Mick sort it out 'imself.

Pause.

Kelly   Ya don't think it's someone from the pub, do ya?

Kim   No. Why?

Kelly   It's just that sometimes 'e 'as a smell on 'im. Ya know a smell that ya know but ya don't know why?

Kim   It's probably 'is aftershave.

Kelly   Not that kind a smell. Not a perfume smell, a person smell. The smell a clothes, the smell a skin. A

person smell. A smell that ya know but ya can't think
why –

Kim *turns on the radio. From the commentary, we hear that the race
is in its closing stages. The commentary continues through the rest of
the scene.*

Kim   Kelly, ya missin' ya race.

Kelly   I really know it. (*Slight pause.*) An' don't forget you
owe Bruce for ya bet.

Kim   I know, fifty pence.

Kelly   A pound plus tax. Mine's just got a mention.
That's one pound ten.

Kim   Young Hustler. That's mine.

Kelly   A pound bet an' ten pence for ya tax.

Kim   I don't pay tax.

Kelly   Ya do in the bettin' shop.

Kim   Robbin' bastards.

Kelly   Who was that?

Kim   Lord somethin' an' somethin' else.

Kelly   Not one of ares. (*Pause.*) When I went to Haydock,
Bruce said that whatever wins there – that's us. Imagine if
it's first an' second! I can still smell that –

Kim   Come on, Hustler. Hustle ya bastard.

Kelly   Top weight. Yours 'as 'ad it.

Kim   Ya know that smell, what's it like?

Kelly   Like – like – I can smell it now. Right under me
nose. Like I can never get away from it. Go on, Encore!

Kim   What if it's someone ya know?

Kelly   I'll kill them.

She turns up the radio. The following speeches overlap along with the radio commentary.

Come on, Encore! Don't drop back. Come on for God sake – ya can win this – listen to that – come on, come 'ead. Come on, my son! – Fuck off, Rough Quest – ooh, bloody 'ell – ya lazy get – ya nearly there – Go 'ead, lad – run – run, ya bastard – 'e's in front! It's gonna win! Come on, Encore – come on, Can ya believe that? Can ya believe it?

Kim (*very quietly*) Kel, ya know them, Kel. Ya must do. Ya must know. You must know who it is. Not that I wanna hurt ya, I don't. I don't want ya to be upset. Not after the baby. It 'appened before you. Then it 'appened again. An' now it's like I can't 'elp meself. I've got what I wanted an' that's hard to let go. Rough Quest? Mick's got a fiver on Rough Quest.

The race has come to an end. **Kelly** *turns down the radio.*

Kelly What did ya say?

Kim Mick's won. 'E 'ad a fiver on Rough Quest.

Kelly Typical. 'Im first, me second.

Kim An' I'm third.

Kelly In a photo.

Kim Ya never know.

Kelly Bruce 'ad Superior Finish in the sweep.

Kim I 'ope mine beats 'is.

Kelly Me mum's never even got a mention.

Kim I 'ate losin' to someone who knows it all.

Kelly Ya like Mick. Always 'ave to be the winner.

Kelly *turns off the radio, as the commentary announces there is to be a stewards' inquiry. She reaches inside the caravan door and picks up a sealed bucket, clearly displaying the words 'Support the Dockers'.*

Kim An' 'e is.

Kelly   But not without a fight. I'll 'ave to go an' shake me bucket. See ya.

Kelly *exits. Pause.* **Kim** *takes the betting slips from under the radio, looks at them and puts them back. She turns on the radio as Rough Quest is announced the winner. She takes a betting slip from her pocket and kisses it.*

Kim (*triumphantly*)   Rough bloody Quest!

Scene Six: Stand By Your Man

Music: 'Stand By Your Man' by Tammy Wynette.

The caravan, the following morning.

Josie, *wearing a dressing-gown, sits on the back settee with a large cardboard box at her side.* **Kelly** *sits in front of her on the floor. She stacks leaflets all around her and then counts the contents of each pile.*

Josie   What about these?

Kelly (*as she counts*)   What?

Josie   'Ten things they never wanted you to know about our docks.'

Kelly (*in between counting*)   I'm not takin' them.

Josie   Why not?

Kelly (*she loses count*)   Everyone binned them yesterday. No one's interested.

Josie   I think they're good.

Kelly   Bruce said they're too factual for 'olidaymakers. 'E was right.

Kim *enters from the bathroom. Her hair is wrapped in a towel. She sits at the table and begins to make herself up.*

Josie   I don't think so, d' you, Kim?

Kim   What?

Josie *picks up a handful of leaflets and shows them to* **Kim**.

Josie   These ones.

Kelly   I was countin' them.

Kim   Dunno. Never read it.

Kelly   We're not takin' them anyway.

Josie   We should take whatever we can. Everyone passes through that bar at dinnertime.

Kelly   I would if we were sellin' them.

She hands **Josie** *a pile of leaflets.*

Ee are, take them.

Josie   These new?

Kelly   Yeh.

Josie (*she reads*)   'Stand by our Men.' Who wrote these?

Kim   Tammy Wynette.

Josie (*she reads*)   Ooh, I don't like this. 'We even took the director a birthday cake. It was a sign of good will, a peace offering, an olive branch' – sounds like Jesus – 'Even so we made sure that the cake wasn't a very nice one.' (*She looks up.*) I got that cake. Not very nice? Bleedin' cheek. Who wrote that?

Kelly   Me.

Kim   Ya make them sound like Palestines.

Josie   Ya coulda put it better than that. Like – 'But we 'ad to get a cheap one cos we was skint.'

Kelly   But we didn't want the bastard to 'ave a nice one.

Kim   Yers shoulda got 'im a doughnut.

Kelly   Yeh. Or an ice bun.

Kim (*laughing*)   Imagine an ice bun stickin' through ya letter-box.

Kelly   You'd know there was gonna be trouble.

Josie (*laughing*)   Or you'd think it was your lucky day.

Kelly   Speak for yerself.

Kim   Eh. I'm gonna tell Bruce that ya think 'e's got a thing like a crusty bun –

Josie   But you shouldn't be writing this, Kelly.

Kelly   Why?

Josie   Cos Mick's on the dole not the docks.

Kelly   So?

Jose   It's not your place.

Kelly   It's no one's place. It's support.

She stands and begins to put the leaflets into the box.

I don't see you writin' anythin' for Bruce.

Josie   That's not the point.

Kelly   Yeh it is.

Josie   Some women's 'usbands 'ave worked there thirty-odd years. I've known Bruce five minutes –

Kim   Eighteen months.

Josie   – An' you think ya can go along an' throw yerself in. Writing all sorts, doin' raffles. Ya never at 'ome.

Kelly *checks through the box and closes it.*

Kelly   Is that it? Ya bothered that I'm never at 'ome?

Josie   You'll be treadin' on people's toes.

Kelly   Are ya?

Josie *picks up the last pile of leaflets, 'Ten things . . .', from the floor.*

Josie   What about these?

Kim   Can I lend your 'airdryer?

Kelly I'm not takin' them. Yeh, it's in me mum's room.

Kim It's took me that long to do me nails. It's gonna look crap now.

Kim *exits to* **Josie**'s *bedroom.*

Kelly They're just glad of the 'elp. No matter who it is.

Josie That's what they say.

Kelly *picks up papers from the floor and goes to the table.*

Kelly Ya should do a bit yerself.

Josie I do. I bought the cake.

Kelly You just go to work an' come 'ome again.

Josie Well that's enough. Anyway what d'ya think I'm doin' 'ere?

Kelly You're on 'oliday.

Josie I'm 'elpin' you.

Kelly Sittin' there?

Josie I sit on the stall. I do the raffle.

Kelly An' stay today. No slippin' the bingo.

The sound of a hairdryer in **Josie**'s *room can be heard.*

Josie But Lady Muck gets away with it?

Kelly She's not interested.

Josie Might give 'er somethin' to do.

Kelly Couldn't 'ave the baby there. He's into everythin'.

Josie I'd mind 'im.

Kelly Did I give you that list a raffle prizes?

Josie It's in the box.

Kelly I've got that many lists.

The hairdryer stops.

Josie 'Ope I win that whisky.

Kelly We can't buy tickets.

Josie Why?

Kelly Cos we're runnin' it.

Kim *emerges from the bedroom with partly dried hair.*

Kim Bloody lecky's gone.

Josie You'll 'ave to go the office.

Kim I'm gonna be late now.

Josie An 'urry up cos a the fridge.

Kim The shame a this. I 'ope no one sees me.

Kim *steps out of the front door and looks about. She exits hurriedly.*
Kelly *uses the interruption to revise her lists. She concentrates on her paperwork throughout the following dialogue.* **Josie** *lights a cigarette.*

Silence.

Josie But I could just buy one. It's not like anyone 'd know?

Kelly I would.

Josie I only wanna win it for Bruce.

Kelly Bruce donated it.

Josie 'E what? 'As it got a funny name?

Kelly Somethin' Scottish.

Josie Yeh. I got 'im that. The cheeky bastard. Where is it?

Kelly It's in the back of the car.

Josie *stands.*

Josie I'll 'ave that. Where's ya keys?

Kelly Ya can't take it.

Josie   It's my whisky.

Kelly   It's for the raffle.

Josie   No one 'll know. Just cross it off ya list.

Kelly   It's raisin' money for people to live off.

Josie   A bottle a whisky? Talk sense.

Kelly   The list's typed up now.

Josie   Givin' away bleedin' presents.

Kim *runs on and enters the caravan. She is in a rush.*

Kim   It's freezin' out there. I was gonna wear me satin A-line an' all.

Josie   Ya know that whisky I got for Bruce?

Kim *picks up a mirror from the table and finishes make-up.*

Kim   Off that fella in the Barley Mow?

Josie   'E's only give it in for the raffle.

Kelly   No wonder if some tealeaf's sellin' it in a pub. It's probably rank.

Kim   It is.

Josie   An' 'ow do you know?

Kim   I 'ad some.

Kelly   So the bottle's 'alf empty?

Kim   No. Me an' Mick 'ad a drink in the Barley Mow after we'd been the dole an' Mick bought some off some fella. We 'ad some watchin' *Blossoms in the Dust.* That's a brilliant film. It's black an' white but it's dead good –

Kelly   Mick bought some?

Kim   Yeh but we threw it away.

Kelly   An' 'e moans about money. I could kill 'im. Sittin' on 'is arse. That coulda been another raffle prize, that.

Josie (*to herself*)   Cheeky bastard.

Kim *puts down the mirror and make-up. She makes her way towards* **Josie***'s bedroom.*

Kim   All men are bastards.

Josie   Whoever said that knew what they were on about.

Kim   Course they did. They were probbly a lezzy.

Kim *exits into* **Josie***'s bedroom.*

Pause.

Josie   That's really hurt me, that 'as.

Kelly   Praps 'e doesn't like whisky.

Josie   'E doesn't like somethin', the belchin' bastard. 'E's out every chance 'e gets.

The sound of the hairdryer is heard once more.

Kelly   Only cos a the strike.

Josie   'I'm goin' to HQ, I can't come round.' 'E's out as much as you are.

Kelly   'E 'as to be. 'E's a leadin' man.

Josie   Leadin' someone else, that's for sure.

Kelly *stands and picks up her paperwork.*

Kelly   Are you gonna moan all day?

Josie.   No.

Kelly   Come on, I need ya to 'elp me set up.

Josie (*she snaps*)   Me whole life revolves around this bleedin' strike.

Kelly   'Ow d' ya think I feel?

Josie   That's out a choice. I 'ad somethin' goin' with

Bruce till all this started. Now 'e's out gallivantin' everywhere with God knows who.

Kelly   Don't be stupid.

Josie   Well 'e's gettin' it somewhere cos 'e's not gettin' it from me.

Kelly   Like who?

Josie   Like someone.

Kelly   Like who?

Josie   Someone. Someone at these at conferences.

Pause. The sound of the hairdryer stops.

Like someone at your women's group.

Silence.

Kelly   I don't know where ya get ya ideas from cos they're not from the same place as mine.

Josie   No, yours are from the same place as Bruce's.

Kelly   Praps you should a got involved from the start –

Josie   Imagine me? Thick as two short planks.

Kelly   Instead a bein' pathetic an' twisted. You could a gone on conferences an' weekends –

Josie   Someone 'as to cook the tea.

Kelly   Don't get at me. If I'm not there Mick should do 'is own.

Kim (*off*)   Kel?

Kelly (*quietly, indicating the bedroom*)   An' she should pull 'er weight an' all.

Kelly *picks up the box.* **Kim** *appears from* **Josie***'s room. She is dressed in a short, satin A-line skirt and carries a pair of bright, strappy shoes.*

Kim   When are ya goin', Kel?

Kelly   Now.

Kim   Take us up the nursery. I'm gonna be late.

Kelly   So am I.

Josie   Bleedin' whisky, cheeky get.

Kelly   Are you comin' or what?

Kim *sits at the table and puts on her shoes.*

Josie   I'm gonna 'ave to 'ave the day off today. All that whisky business 'as gone to me 'ead. Ya don't mind do ya, Kel?

Kelly   Ya just not interested. An' that's that.

Kim   I 'ope it doesn't rain on me way back. These'll be ruined.

Josie   Ya don't mind do ya, Kel?

Kelly *(smiling)*   Only if I can raffle ya bingo prizes.

Kim   I looked a meff when I took 'im, I don't wanna look a meff when I pick 'im up.

Josie   Soddin' whisky, cheeky bugger.

Kelly *goes down the caravan steps carrying the box,* **Kim** *follows.*

Kelly   I'll see ya after.

Kim   I mean, ya never know who ya meet pushin' a pram, do ya?

They exit.

Josie *sits with her head in her hands. She sighs and looks up.*

Josie   Fuckin' whisky, bleedin' bastard.

She stands and exits to her bedroom.

(As she goes.) One an' five – fifteen. All the fours – forty-four. Two an' six –

Scene Seven: Promises, Promises

Music: 'Promises, Promises' by Dionne Warwick.

The caravan. A bright summer Tuesday, 1996.

Bruce *sits outside the caravan with his shirt off and his feet on the plastic table. He reads the* Mirror. **Josie** *stands next to the table wearing her dressing-gown and sunglasses. She unpacks a freezer-bag onto the table. Its contents consist of food parcelled in foil and a Thermos flask.*

Josie   So I told 'er. 'Ow was I supposed to know that Thermos flasks explode at thirty thousand feet? It doesn't say nothin' in the brochures. I only took it in case there was nowhere open when we got there. Anyway, she just looked at me. Cheeky bitch. She should've stuck to sellin' Estée fuckin' Lauder.

She takes a baby's dummy from the bag and puts it on the table. She repacks the food and the flask.

So never take a Thermos on a plane. Not full anyway. Ya can take one empty. Or 'alf full. Depends 'ow hot it is. That's 'ow they break, ya see. They get to a point when they get too hot an' that's it. They crack. Well some a them do. There are flasks an' flasks. I've always preferred a Thermos meself.

She picks up the flask and tries to squeeze it into the bag.

You should take one on the line with ya.

Bruce   I'd never get round to makin' it that time a the mornin'.

Josie *(fastening the bag)*   Funny, isn't it? 'Ow do they know to keep hot things hot an' cold things cold.

Bruce *(playing her along)*   Like Japanese radios. It's great 'ow they all talk English.

Josie   Oh yeh. I never thought a that.

She goes to enter the caravan.

When ya think about it, they've got a bleedin' cheek them
air 'ostesses. They think they're somethin' when they're not.
They're no different from me workin' on school dinners. I
mean the only difference is that their canteen flies.

She enters the caravan and goes into her bedroom.

Bruce *opens the bag and takes out a large parcel: He unwraps it
and takes out a cheese sandwich.* **Kim** *enters from the bathroom. She
wears a swimming costume and shorts and carries a cheap women's
magazine. She goes outside.*

Kim   Iya, Bruce.

Bruce   Mornin' love.

She picks up the dummy from the table and wipes the teet.

Kim   What's she like? It'll 'ave all shite on it now.

*She puts the dummy in her mouth and sucks hard. She takes it out
and looks at it.*

Better.

She sits down and starts to read the magazine.

Bruce?

Bruce   Yeh?

Kim   I've just 'ad this terrible dream about you. You
were in it but ya died. Ya were walkin' back to your
caravan right, an' ya just walked into this pane a glass. It
never smashed or nothin'. Ya just walked into it, banged ya
'ead an' died.

Bruce   Thanks for brightenin' me day.

Kim   Me mum was dead upset. An' she invited loadsa
people to the funeral like it was weddin' or somethin'. It
was dead weird.

Bruce   You'll 'ave to find out what it means from one of
them books.

Kim   It wasn't like me dad's funeral. I cried me eyes out at that. In this one I just sat there dead still.

Bruce   It all means somethin'.

Kim   I know yeh. Like when me dad died I used to dream about 'im every night for ages. Suppose that's cos I missed 'im.

Bruce   I still dream about Linda.

Kim   Is that cos ya miss 'er?

Bruce   I think about 'er. But don't tell ya mam.

Kim   I think about me dad. But I miss 'im more than I think about 'im. (*Pause.*) Ya don't mind me sayin' that, do ya?

Bruce   No. Ya dad's ya dad.

Kim   Mm. Jimmy.

Bruce   An' I suppose you're the kid I never 'ad.

Kim   An' Kelly.

Bruce   Well – yeh. Yeh, ya right.

Kim   Just think, Bruce. If you married me mum, we would be.

Bruce   Oh aye yeh.

Kim   But I wouldn't call ya dad. I'd call ya Bruce.

Josie *enters from her bedroom. She wears shorts, a T-shirt and has her sunglasses on her head.*

Bruce   I wouldn't expect ya to.

Josie   To what?

Kim   I was just sayin' that if you got married to Bruce then 'e'd be like are dad an' we'd be 'is kids. But I wouldn't call 'im dad, I'd call 'im Bruce.

Bruce   An' I said I wouldn't expect 'er to.

Kim   But the baby could call ya grandad cos 'e wouldn't know no difference.

Josie   I'm glad to see you've sorted are lives out.

Kim   I just meant if ya did.

Bruce   She sounds keen though, doesn't she, Jose?

Josie (*laughs*)   I woulda bin keen meself if ya 'adn't a started on me butties.

Bruce   Well don't go worryin'. I can't see the support committee givin' us a sub for a weddin' when Seldom Seen's got a repossession order.

Kim   Who?

Bruce   Seldom Seen – 'e was always off sick.

Josie   Don't put the dummy in ya mouth, Kim. It's unhygienic.

Kim   It's my baby.

Josie   Sometimes I wonder.

She takes the dummy from **Kim** *and picks up the bag.* **Kim** *resumes reading.*

An' make sure ya follow me down. Are Kelly was up at the crack a dawn with 'im.

Kim   I will.

Josie   I'll see ya later.

Bruce   D'ya want ya butties?

Josie   No, you 'ave them. Token a my love. Ta-ra.

Josie *exits.*

Bruce   See ya, hon.

Kim   Ta-ra. (*Pause.*) Ya know that Sneldon? Is that 'is real name?

Bruce   Who?

Kim   Sneldon.

Bruce   Seldom. No, it's a nickname.

Kim   Oh.

Bruce   We all 'ave nicknames.

Kim   Do ya? What like?

Bruce   All sorts. Cinderella, Dicky Twice, Enno, Skippy –

Kim   So why's that fella called Seldom Seen?

Bruce   I told ya. Cos 'e's always off.

Kim   An' what's 'is real name?

Bruce   (*laughs*)   Dunno. Never seen 'im to ask.

Kim   Why?

Bruce   Cos 'e was always on the sick.

Kim   No. Why the names?

Bruce   Tradition. You've got to 'ave tradition in a place like the docks otherwise what's the point? Mind you, what is the point? Look at me. I used to be on me break at this time an' now I'm sittin' 'ere doin' nothin'. It's tradition they're takin' away. That an' decent conditions. Not to mention 'undreds of jobs an' a way of life. A city's way of life. A bloody river's way of life. A decent retirement for fellas like me –

Kim   An' what did they call you?

Bruce   Me? 'The man with the mouth.'

Kim   Cos you do all the talkin'.

Bruce   Yeh.

Kim   Well ya know that Cinderella bloke? Was 'e gay?

Bruce   No. 'E just always 'ad to be in for midnight.

Kim   That's good that. What about the others? What were they again?

Bruce   Erm. Right. (*Quickly.*) Cinderella – I've gorra be in

for midnight, Dicky Twice – 'is name was Richard
Richards, Enno – cos 'e was a tight arse, 'Dad, can I 'ave
an ice cream?' N – O, NO – 'Arthur, can I borrow ya
tools?' N – O, NO. Someone wrote them all down once. A
big list. Don't know what 'appened to that.

Kim   They're good them. Like somethin' out the *Viz*.

Bruce   An' soon to be a thing a the past, Kim.

Kim   Yeh. It's gone crap, 'asn't it? I only like the Fat
Slags.

Pause. **Kim** *turns over a page and starts to read.*

Bruce   D' you know who is it we're fightin', Kim?

Kim   Who's fightin'?

Bruce   D'you know what your Kelly's doin' the
campaignin' for?

Kim   For money for the dockers.

Bruce   Yeh. But d'ya know about the principles? D'ya
know what caused it?

Kim   Yeh. Ya all got sacked cos they want young fellas
there who can do more work.

Bruce   They want young fellas so they can pay them a
pittance an' 'ave them workin' like casuals. Kim, we were
the most productive workforce in Europe. Young or not,
they can't do more work than we did.

Kim   They can probbly do it for longer though.

Bruce   At what price?

Kim   Well it'd be more than the dole.

Bruce   I mean safety. I mean lives.

Pause.

Kim   D'ya get paid if ya a scab?

Bruce   Yeh.

Kim   That's all right, isn't it?

Bruce   No. No, it's not.

Kim   But someone's got to do the work.

Kelly *enters. She is out of breath.*

Bruce   Yeh – dockers 'ave. Trained men. Docks are dangerous places, it's a skilled job.

Kelly   They are if ya a scab. Scuse me.

Kelly *runs in to the caravan and enters the bathroom.*

Bruce   Right. The thing is, Kim. It's wrong to take another person's job. Right?

Kim   Yeh.

Bruce   Especially if that person has been doin' that same job for say twenty-odd years? Right?

Kim   Yeh.

Bruce   An' that person 'ad been stopped from doin' his job because they were sacked for bein' on strike. Right?

Kim   Yeh.

Bruce   So that's it. We want are jobs back. We want the same rights as what other people 'ave got. Otherwise we're gonna be back in the dark ages. Now d'ya understand?

Kim   Yeh.

Bruce   Good girl.

Pause. **Kim** reads.

Kim   Ya know what it's all down to, don't ya?

Bruce   What?

Kim   The ozone layer.

Bruce   What is?

A toilet flush is heard.

Kim   The dark ages. Ya wanna read the label on ya deodorant an' use a ice bucket instead of a fridge.

Bruce (*despairing*)   – So that's the reason. I'll 'ave to tell the lads.

Bruce *resumes reading his paper.* **Kelly** *emerges from the bathroom. She hitches up her skirt slightly and goes out of the caravan.*

Kelly   Never thought I'd make it. Them toilets by the beach are rank.

Bruce   Should 'ave gone in the sea.

Kelly   I know –

Kim   Eeh! Would you wee in the sea?

Kelly   No –

Bruce   That's where it goes anyway.

Kelly   But I might if I was desperate.

Kelly *sits on the arm of* **Bruce***'s chair.*

Kim   That's disgustin'.

Kelly   You've done worse.

Kim   I 'aven't.

Kelly   You 'ave. You pissed in the sand in Abersoch.

Kim   I never.

Kelly   Ya did. I remember ya doin' it.

Bruce   It's all comin' out now, Kim.

Kelly   She even said she wanted to do it again.

Kim   No I never.

Bruce   She's goin' red.

Kim   I was about three.

Kelly   Ya were eight.

Kim   At least I wouldn't do it now. Ya should 'ave

respect for nature.

Kelly   So should you. I believe fake tan causes terrible scum in the sea.

Kim   This is my natural colour.

Kelly   What? Orange.

Kim   At least I look attractive.

Kelly   Ya might do to a scally.

Kim   What's wrong with scallies?

Kelly (*laughs*) – In a word? Mick.

Kim   What are ya sayin' that to me for?

Kelly   Cos ya asked.

Kim   You're dead tight on 'im.

Kelly   Tight? 'E's lived off me since I met 'im.

Kim   You don't give 'im a chance.

Kelly   I've give 'im plenty. Just that I'm fed up a livin' with someone who doesn't give a shit about nothin'.

Kim   At least 'e's tryin'.

Kelly   This is the first interview 'e's ever gone to.

Kim   You'll even be moanin' if 'e gets the job, you. What's up, found someone else?

Kelly   No –

Bruce   She deserves better, that's all.

Kelly   I just don't wanna work on a till all me life.

Kim   State a you.

Bruce   Kelly's got ambitions.

Kim   So 'ave I.

Bruce   An' what do you want?

Kim   I want me own business.

Kelly   Doin' what?

Kim   I dunno. Just a business.

Bruce   So ya shouldn't knock Kelly for wantin' to get on in life.

Kim   OK.

Bruce   Cos no one should get knocked for doin' that.

Kim   Orright. I get the message.

Kim *stands and takes some sandwiches from the parcel.*

Kelly   If Mick gets this job we're gonna get a mortgage.

Kim   Can I'ave these? Ya get 'ungry by the sea.

Bruce   Yeh.

Kim   I knew you'd go all snobby.

Kelly   It's not snobby it's sensible. Plannin' for the future.

Kim   Whatever turns ya on. I'll see ya after.

Bruce   See ya, love.

Kim *exits.*

Kelly   She does my 'ead in. I always thinks she knows.

Kelly *sits on the table.*

Bruce   'Ow would she know?

Kelly   Cos she's always gettin' at me.

Bruce   Well ya can't let 'er spoil it.

Pause.

Kelly   Nothin' gets to you, does it?

Bruce   Some things do.

Kelly   Like what?

Pause.

Bruce   Ya not gonna get a house with 'im, are ya?

Kelly   What?

Bruce   A mortgage?

Kelly   I might do.

Bruce   So much for us then.

Kelly   Well you've practically moved into ares.

Bruce   Only so I can see you.

Kelly   Not me mum?

Bruce   Well what can I do? If I lose ya mum, I lose you. You told me that.

Kelly   She is me mum, Bruce.

Bruce   An' I'm doin' me best not to ruin everythin' you've got.

Pause.

Kelly   D' ya sleep with 'er?

Bruce   Kelly.

Kelly   Do ya?

Bruce   When I 'ave to.

Kelly   D' ya enjoy it?

Bruce   No.

Kelly   Does she?

Pause.

Bruce   Yeh.

Kelly   I knew she did. Sometimes I 'ear ya. I never used to 'ear 'er an' me dad.

Bruce   That's cos ya listenin' out for it.

Kelly *stands.*

Kelly   That's cos I can't 'elp 'earin'.

Bruce   Why d' ya think we stay at my van? I do think about ya.

Kelly   While ya doin' it? Thanks.

Kelly *enters the caravan.*

Bruce   I think about ya all the time.

Bruce *follows her inside with the sandwiches. He shuts the door behind him.*

Kelly   Even when ya with 'er?

Bruce   Yeh. Do you?

Pause.

Kelly   Yeh.

Bruce   So ya 'ave sex with 'im?

Kelly   Yeh.

Bruce   Why?

Kelly   I just do.

Bruce   An' ya like it?

Kelly   No. I turn me 'ead away.

Bruce   So why are ya gonna stay with 'im?

Kelly   I'm twenty years of age.

Bruce   You said that made no difference.

Kelly   Between us, it doesn't. It's just everyone else.

Bruce   An' that's it?

Kelly   I don't like it, ya know. I don't like any of it.

Bruce   So what are ya gonna do?

Kelly   I don't know. What are you gonna do? (*Pause.*) Stay at ares with me mum? Stay at your caravan with me mum?

Bruce   It's not what I want.

Kelly   What do ya want?

Bruce   Somethin' different. Why? What do you want?

Kelly   I don't want Mick.

Bruce   So what do we do?

Kelly   (*shrugs*)   I don't know. Life goes on.

Bruce *touches her face. They embrace and kiss. Bruce takes her hand. They exit to* **Josie**'*s bedroom.*

Scene Eight: Sticks and Stones

Music: 'Sticks & Stones' by Donna Fargo.

The caravan, the following evening.

Kelly, *now wearing a light cardigan, is in the kitchen area. She takes cutlery and two plates from a cupboard and places them on the table. She sits on the bench facing forward.*

Mick *enters. He carries two parcels of chips. As he enters the caravan* **Kelly** *stands and approaches him. She takes the parcels from him, unwraps one of them and puts the contents – fishcake and chips – onto a plate.*

Kelly   You were quick.

Mick   I ran.

Kelly   Did ya 'ave enough?

Mick   Just. Yeh.

Kelly   Least they're hot.

Mick   Yeh.

Kelly   I'm bloody starvin'. Never 'ad no dinner.

Mick   'Ow come?

Kelly   Thought I'd wait for you. Me stomach thinks me

throat's bin cut.

Mick   Ya never 'ad to.

Kelly   I'm just sayin' I'm 'ungry.

Mick   Not rubbin' it in that I got 'ere late?

Kelly   No.

Mick   Sounds like it, an' all. I get an interview for the first time in fuckin' years an' you 'ave to start kickin' off cos things run a bit late.

Kelly   I said I was hungry. End a story. Ee are.

She pushes a plate towards **Mick**. *He sits at the table and begins to eat. She begins to unwrap the other parcel.*

But it went all right?

Mick   Not bad. 'Ave ya got any sauce?

Kelly   There's nothin' in. Not even bread.

Mick   Fuckin' disgustin' dry chips.

Kelly   Did they seem to like ya or what?

Mick   Dunno. Doesn't matter, does it, whether they like ya or not? It's a job. They just wanna know if ya can do it.

Kelly   'Ow come ya got me fishcake? Ya know I 'ate it. Bleedin' waste a money.

Mick   I'll eat it, you can 'ave me chips. End a story.

Mick *swaps her fishcake for a small amount of his chips.*

Kelly   (*with irony*)   Easy on the chips, Mick.

He adds a few more chips.

Didn't they 'ave no cod?

Mick   There's cod in these. Just that they're round.

Kelly   Shite a cod, ya mean. It's just mushed-up fish.

Mick   Fish is a rip-off, anyway.

Kelly   I would a give ya money if ya didn't 'ave enough.

She sits next to **Mick** *and starts to eat.*

Ya shoulda said. Ya usually do.

Mick   I 'ad to get ciggies. I forgot.

Kelly   You need nicotine more than I need nutrients? God, just eatin' chips must be so for bad for ya –

Mick   Will you stop moanin'?

Kelly   I've got a right to moan. I sent ya for fish an' chips –

Mick   I've bin tryin' to get a fuckin' job to keep you fuckin' 'appy. I coulda just stayed at 'ome an' not bothered with the fuckin' family 'oliday –

Kelly   I wish ya 'ad.

Mick   I wish I fuckin' 'ad.

Kelly   Ya might as well a done. You don't tell me nothin' anyway. What's it for? The Secret Service?

Mick   Give it a rest.

Kelly   See. Ya can't even 'ave a conversation. I am tryin' ya know? I am interested.

Mick   It was orright.

Kelly   An' 'ow all right's 'orright'? Is it good orright, bad orright, shite orright? What?

Mick   Just orright, really.

Kelly   So ya never got it?

Mick   No.

Kelly   'No' ya never got it?

Mick   No.

Kelly   So ya didn't *not* get it?

Mick   Yeh –

Kelly   So ya got it?

Mick   Yeh –

Kelly   Did ya?

Mick   That's what I said.

Kelly   Why didn't ya say?

Mick   I did.

Kelly   I don't understand you. Ya should be made up. When d' ya start?

Mick   Mondee, I think.

Kelly   And?

Mick   Eight o'clock.

Kelly   An' what are you doin'? What is it? Where is it? 'Ow much?

Mick   It's in town an' there's quite a bit of overtime.

Kelly   A factory or a site or what?

Mick   Labourin'.

Kelly   On a site?

Mick   No.

Kelly   Where?

Mick   On the docks.

Pause.

Kelly   No.

Mick   Not the same docks as where Bruce was. It's a got a different name.

Kelly   Course it's the same docks. I mean ya not talkin' about the Albert Dock, are ya?

Mick   Well ya wouldn't catch me workin' in a art gallery.

Kelly   So you're gonna work on the docks as a docker?

Mick   A dock labourer –

Kelly   You're gonna be a fuckin' scab?

Mick   It's four pound an hour.

Kelly *stands.*

Kelly   I don't believe this –

Mick   It was you who wanted me to get a job.

Kelly   Not like that –

Mick   It's you who wants a house –

Kelly   A house? A scabby 'ouse with a scabby 'usband? With paint on ya door an' bars on ya windas?

Mick   It's a start.

Kelly   I'm on the women's committee, for God's sake. My 'usband can't turn into scab labour.

Mick   That's your trouble. Ya think you're so fuckin' clever with ya women's group an' ya meetin's an' committees. Praps ya should pay attention to what really matters. Like me –

Kelly   Fuck off.

Mick   Don't you fuckin' tell me to fuck off.

He knocks **Kelly**'s *plate to the floor.*

Ya fuckin' moanin' bastard.

Kelly   Don't start, Mick –

He knocks the other plate to the floor.

Mick   I 'aven't started.

Kelly   Pick that up.

Mick   No.

Kelly   Pick it up.

Mick   That's your job.

Kelly   Like providin' for me's yours? Cos ya 'aven't stuck to that part a the bargain, 'ave ya?

Mick   Go on, rub it in me face.

Kelly   An' what's Bruce gonna say?

Mick   It's got nothin' to do with Bruce. This is me an' you.

Kelly   Course it's got somethin' to do with Bruce. 'E's a docker.

Mick   Sometimes I wonder why you're so interested.

Kelly   Don't talk soft. All I care about is stoppin' scum like you from 'elpin' themselves –

Mick   Ya think I'm scum cos I'm 'elpin' meself?

Kelly   To other people's jobs –

Mick   I'm only doin' it for you!

Kelly   Suppose there's always a first time.

Mick   You wanted us to do things propply.

Kelly *begins to pick up the debris from the floor. She does this slowly throughout the dialogue, often stopping completely.*

Kelly   Is that what I said? I must want me 'ead testin' –

Mick   An' now we've got a chance to get somewhere, ya don't wanna know –

Kelly   I don't wanna know –

Mick   D' ya wanna live in ya mam's all ya life, is that?

Kelly   I'd rather that. I'd rather that than be stuck with you for forty years –

Mick   So you'd rather I went?

Kelly   Do what ya want.

Mick   Ya wanna get rid a me?

Kelly   Never wanted ya in the first place.

Mick   I knew this 'd 'appen.

Kelly   I wish I'd just met ya on 'oliday an' left it at that –

Mick   Ya can't do this, Kelly –

Kelly   I mean, it was a waste a time gettin' married –

Mick   Just cos of a job on the docks –

Kelly   I only did it cos a the baby an' look what 'appened to that –

Mick   Ya can't throw it away –

Kelly   I shoulda threw it away long ago.

Mick   But ya can't –

Kelly   Why not?

Mick   Ya can't say that to me now –

Kelly   Mick, I don't want ya. An' I certainly don't want ya now ya messin' up people's lives.

Mick   An' what about mine?

Kelly   Never realised you 'ad one.

Mick   Ya can't just let this go, Kelly.

Kelly   I should 'ave 'ad more sense in the first place.

Mick   You're tellin' me I've been wastin' my life?

Kelly   I've been wastin' mine. Married to scum. What about ya bit a stuff, eh? Can't ya sniff round that?

Mick   What are ya talkin' about?

Kelly   You know quite well. Won't ya get what ya want off 'er? Or won't she bail ya out like I do?

Mick   I don't know what ya on about.

Kelly   Come off it. Ya obviously 'aven't fancied me for ages.

Mick   If I wanted someone else I woulda gone ages ago.

Kelly   What's up? Frightened now you've got no choice? Frightened now I won't be there for ya?

Mick   Ya were 'ardly there anyway.

Kelly   Only cos I can't stand ya.

Mick   An' d' ya think I'm arsed?

Kelly   I think you're a shit. I think –

Mick   Go on.

Kelly   I think you're a worthless scab an' you've got no 'ope a gettin' nowhere unless ya stand on people's shoulders or walk all over them or get them pregnant –

Mick   Well you can't even manage that.

Kelly   Not with you, thank Christ. At least me body's got sense.

Mick   So you've got someone else lined up 'ave ya?

Kelly   I've got me own life to lead first.

Mick   What? On picket-lines?

Kelly   Rather be a picket than a scab.

Mick   Rather be a scally than a snob.

Kelly   I 'ope they treat ya like shit.

Mick   I'm used to it, livin' with you.

Kelly   You'll be glad a the change then.

Mick   Too fuckin' right I will.

Josie and **Bruce** enter, holding hands. **Josie** has a metallic helium balloon with a 'love' message on it tied to her wrist. **Bruce** sits in the plastic chair and fixes his shoes. **Josie** stops beside him for a moment and then enters the caravan.

Kelly   God knows what you'll do without me to sponge off.

Mick   D' ya think I need it? I only took it cos it was there.

Josie   What's goin' on?

Kelly   Ask 'im.

Josie   What's 'appened?

Mick   Nothin'. We 'ad a bit of a row.

Kelly   Bit of a row? You woulda smashed the place up given 'alf the chance.

Josie (*calls*)   Bruce! An' what about the neighbours? They've got little ones. I 'ope they're out.

Bruce *enters the caravan.*

Josie   Ya should be bloody ashamed.

Josie *begins to clear up the remainder of the plates and food.*

Kelly   I am. I'm ashamed of 'im.

Bruce   What's been goin' on?

Josie   Domestic.

Kelly   No it's not. It's 'im. It's cos a what 'e's done.

Bruce   You 'aven't touched 'er, 'ave ya?

Mick   It was just a row.

Kelly   Just a row? Just you wait. Cos ya see 'im, 'e can't even get a job without bein' sly.

Josie   These plates were me Auntie Ada's.

Kelly   I couldn't give a shit while there's a scab sittin' 'ere.

Josie   What?

Kelly   'E's bin took on at the docks, Bruce. 'E's a scab.

Silence.

Bruce   You been there today?

Mick   I start Mondee.

Bruce   Ya can't. Ya can't start. You can't go down to them gates an' walk through. Ya can't take someone else's life – cos that's what you'll be doin'.

Josie   Did the dole push ya into it, son?

Bruce   Doesn't matter if they did. 'E should 'ave the sense not to do it. Bein' a scab when ya own wife goes on the picket-lines –

Kelly   I'm not 'is wife.

Josie   Don't talk wet, Kelly.

Kelly   D'ya think I'm gonna stay married to that? You should 'ave more sense, it could be Bruce's job 'e's takin'.

Josie   At least 'e's tryin'.

Mick   I just thought we could save up an' that.

Josie   See. Ya moan when 'e doesn't work.

Kelly   Well why didn't 'e find a decent job?

Mick   There's nothin' goin' in my line of work.

Bruce   Praps ya should carry on lookin'.

Mick   There's no jobs nowhere.

Kelly   'E's only took this one to get at me.

Bruce   Ya not gonna do it, are ya?

Mick   I've never 'ad a job. I got the job, I'm gonna do it.

Bruce   I'm on the line Monday.

Josie   You'll 'ave to go a bit later so ya won't see 'im.

Bruce   I won't see 'im anyway because as far as I'm concerned he doesn't exist.

Kelly   'E 'asn't existed for ages in my eyes.

Mick   Don't I know it.

Kelly   I've been workin' 'ard, it's you who plays around.

Josie   Staffordshire Crown Pottery.

Mick   You've been workin' 'ard, 'ave ya?

Bruce   She's been fightin' a cause.

Mick   An' won't let anyone forget it.

Bruce   I didn't think you were the type to remember. But sorry, son, I never forget.

Bruce *exits.*

Mick   That strike's ruined what we 'ad.

Kelly   That was already ruined. You were never interested.

Mick   I must a been, I married ya.

Kelly   An' that was it. That was all ya did.

Josie   Kelly, keep ya voice down.

Kelly   I will not. It was you who said marry 'im. Ya only concerned about bein' respectable.

Josie   I am not. What about Kim? I didn't make 'er do anythin' she didn't want to.

Kelly   Well in 'er case, praps ya should.

Josie   She was only a kid but she knew her own mind.

Kelly   Shit. I was supposed to pick 'er up.

Josie   What?

Kelly   She took the baby the doctor's.

Josie   You've left 'er stranded with the baby?

Kelly   She'll 'ave got the bus by now.

Josie   You'd better go, just in case.

Kelly   She'll be back in a minute.

Mick 'E was burnin' up an' all.

Kelly You go an' meet them if ya that concerned.

Josie Poor little bugger.

Kelly Don't make me feel worse than I already do.

Mick 'E's a baby for God's sake.

Kelly I notice 'ow ya capable a talkin' about that baby.

Mick What?

Kelly That baby. That baby a Kim's. Ya can talk about 'im. Why's that? Why's that, eh? I know why. Why don't ya just say? Why don't ya tell us?

Mick What?

Kelly Say it. Go on, say it. Say it, it's obvious.

Mick No.

Kelly I know why. I know why ya talk about it!

Mick 'As she told you? She 'as, 'asn't she? I knew it.

Josie Told 'er what?

Mick I knew she would. I knew she'd ruin it. It 'appened before you. It just 'appened an' then she 'ad the kid. That was that. But she never let it go. It just 'appened an' that was that. But it was 'er – she just wouldn't let it go –

Josie Oh my God.

Kelly (*quietly*) I was only gonna say – Ya can talk about 'im but you've never talked about ares. I knew there was someone – but Kim? It's been Kim all along 'asn't it? Kim an' the baby. Ya wanted 'er but ya ended up with me?

Josie I 'aven't even got a ciggie.

Mick It wasn't like that –

Kelly That's your baby. You must think I'm stupid –

Mick No. I've always wanted you. I wanted ya when I met ya –

Kelly An' so must she. You must a been laughin' at me all the time.

Mick Kelly, no. I just never thought –

Kelly Get out –

Mick I never thought –

Kelly Just get out, get out –

Josie Go, Mick. Go an' meet 'er an' the baby.

Pause.

Mick *exits.*

Kelly 'E ruins everythin'. Everythin' I 'ad. Ruins everythin'. Me whole life –

Josie Come on, love. Sit down.

Kelly 'E does.

Josie Not everythin'. 'E can't ruin everythin'.

Josie *sits down and puts her arm round* **Kelly**.

Kelly 'E already 'as.

Josie No, 'e 'asn't. Not everythin'. (*Pause.*) Me an' Bruce got engaged today. Thought it was about time we made things a bit more permanent. (*Pause.*) No ring, like. The balloon 'ad to do. (*Pause.*) What d' ya think?

Kelly All I can smell is fishcake.

Josie I thought you'd like 'avin' Bruce round permanent?

Kelly Yeh.

Josie So 'e 'asn't ruined it all. There's that to look forward to. One family, one 'ouse, one caravan.

Silence. **Kelly** *continues to cry.*

Scene Nine: Caravans

Music: 'Caravans' by Barbara Dickson.

The caravan. An early evening in late September 1996.

It is raining softly.

Kim *sits on the side settee, she reads a magazine.* **Mick** *sits on the back settee watching the television. There is a 'For Sale' sign displayed outside the caravan.*

Kim (*she reads*)   'Make your own trendy flower pots – just wash your empty food cans, peel off the label and fill them with your favourite plant. The (*She struggles.*) alu-min-i-um will make a lovely contrast to the plant's colours and will brighten your home in no time.' Sad bastards. Imagine 'avin' bean tins all over the flat.

Mick   Yeh.

Kim   Bet are Kelly 'ld do that, given 'alf the chance. At least me mum's got sense. She'd put them straight in the bin.

Mick   Or recycle them.

Kim   Me mum?

Mick   Kelly.

Kim   I was gonna say, what would me mum wanna use a tin again for? But 'er. I could see 'er washin' them out an' puttin' more beans in, couldn't you?

Mick   Not use them, recycle them.

Kim   What d' ya mean?

Mick   Throw them away an' then they get used again.

Kim   So someone takes them out ya bin an' uses them again? That's fuckin' disgustin' that. Ya'd never know whose bin ya tin 'ad been in.

Mick   Yeh.

Mick *laughs.*

Kim   What?

Mick   What?

Kim   What are ya laughin' at?

Mick   Nothin'. Just the tele.

Kim   I 'ate it when ya do that.

Mick   What?

Kim   Laugh at somethin' that's just not funny.

Mick   It was funny, you weren't watchin'.

Kim   I 'eard it. It wasn't funny.

Mick   I don't get much chance to watch the tele. Can't I watch it in peace?

Kim   Thank God ya don't.

Mick   That's nice. Ya'd rather me in work, all day every day, breakin' me back?

Kim   Ya are anyway.

Mick   An' that's why I like I comin' 'ere an' gettin' a bit a peace if I ever get the weekend off.

Kim   I was only sayin'.

Mick   Well don't say.

Pause.

Kim   Ya wouldn't break ya back though, would ya?

Mick   What?

Kim   In work. Like that fella.

Mick   What fella?

Kim   The one who broke 'is back.

Mick   It was a accident. Accidents 'appen.

Pause.

Kim   Me mum said there was no accidents when the real dockers worked there.

Mick   'Ow would she know?

Kim   Bruce said.

Mick   'Ow is it that whatever 'e says ya mum believes?

Kim   Cos she's engaged to 'im.

Mick   You're engaged to me but you don't believe nothin' I say.

Kim   She's got a ring though.

Mick   So will you when me boat comes in.

Kim   Don't you rob one off a ship. I'm not wearin' a knock-off ring.

Mick   When I've got the money.

Kim   An' when will that be? When bettin' shops shut? (*Pause.*) Didn't even know there was jewellery ships.

Pause.

But ya will make sure ya won't 'urt yerself, won't ya?

Mick   No one's 'urt themselves.

Kim   'Ow come that fella's paralysed an' that other fella's got 'is leg in plaster? An' 'ow come your mate broke 'is arm?

Mick   Both 'is arms.

Kim   See. I knew it was true.

Mick   What's she been sayin'?

Kim   That ya should be careful cos there's loads of accidents cos youse aren't real dockers.

Mick   She would say that.

Kim   Why?

Mick If I pack the docks in she can 'ave 'er 'appy family back again.

Kim An' are Kelly 'd really like that?

Mick But, ya mam 'd be gainin' two an' losin' one.

Kim Never thought a that. Praps she was lyin'.

Pause.

Take ya feet off there, Mick.

Mick What?

Kim I'm responsible.

Mick What for?

Kim For keepin' it tidy. We've got to make it seem like we want someone to buy this. You go treatin' it like it's ares an' me mum 'll soon get wind that we want it. Big stains on the couch are a dead giveaway.

Mick Me shoes are clean.

Kim That's not the point. I'm not losin' this caravan cos a your dirty feet. Ya wouldn't do it if me mum was 'ere.

Mick I'm not doin' no 'arm.

Kim Take them down.

Mick No.

Kim Put ya feet on the floor.

Mick What for?

Kim Cos I said. Ya can't go treatin' like it's ares. Not yet. Anyway, you've even started doin' it at 'ome, in case ya 'adn't noticed –

Mick I 'adn't.

Kim – On the new three-piece.

Mick In me socks.

Kim They're still feet.

Josie *enters. She carries two shopping bags filled with groceries.*

Mick Are you sayin' I should be on me best be'aviour in me own 'ome?

Josie *enters the caravan.*

Josie Iya.

Mick *takes his feet off the settee.*

Mick Iya.

Kim You do my 'ead in.

Josie Brought ya some stuff. Ya 'aven't 'ad ya tea 'ave ya? Went the big Co-op, spent a fortune. 'Ope Bruce doesn't notice the hole in me cheque book.

Kim An' where was the baby?

Josie *unpacks the bags.*

Josie Bruce an' Kelly minded 'im. I got the bus. I'm fuckin' knackered. Runnin' round all fuckin' day. An' I brought ya washin' with us. It's in Bruce's. All ironed. I'll bring it after. I'll sneak it out. I 'ad to sneak out with this lot an' that was 'ard enough. I got ya Irish Cheddar instead of red Leicester. That'll make a change on ya butties.

Mick Ta.

Kim An' where is 'e now?

Josie 'E's in Bruce's van. 'E's well away.

Kim *puts some shopping away.*

Kim You've left 'im with them all day?

Josie 'E's fast asleep. They've 'ad 'im on the beach lookin' for shells. The little fella's worn out. Bruce got 'im a bucket. 'E's got all 'is shells an' pebbles an' little dead crabs in it. 'E was made up they said. They were there for hours.

Kim What are ya leavin' 'im with them all day for? They'll 'ave 'im brainwashed.

Josie In case you 'adn't noticed, I've bin runnin' round after you all day. I 'ad to do your ironin' –

Kim I would a done that –

Josie Ya 'aven't got an iron.

Kim I would a done it if I 'ad one.

Josie I 'ad to do ya shoppin'. I can't do that with them around, they'd go ballistic.

Kim Well that's their problem –

Josie It's my problem. I'm the one who's got to sneak about everywhere. D'ya want cheese an' onion, Mick?

Josie *throws* **Mick** *a packet of crisps.*

Mick Ta.

Kim Well we can't go out, Mick's a scab.

Mick I'm a dock worker.

Kim A scab dock worker an' ya can't go out an' neither can I. That's what I meant –

Mick Only where people might know me or durin' the day when we might be seen –

Josie That gives ya plenty a scope –

Kim So it's not my fault that you've got to do me shoppin' even in Wales, is it?

Josie No. It's 'is.

Kim I knew you'd start thinkin' like they do.

Josie Bruce is my fiancé. But that doesn't mean I'd turn me back on you. I wouldn't do that. Not cos of 'im, not cos of any of it.

Kim Are you sayin' 'e's a scab?

Mick You've just said I'm a scab.

Kim That was different.

Josie I'm ya mother. I'll 'elp no matter what. I even got you ya favourite noodles but to get them I 'ad to go to the shops. An' to go the shops I 'ad to leave the baby with Bruce.

Kim I just don't want them fillin' his 'ead with lies an' loadsa shite.

Josie Be thankful they 'aven't been round an' filled Mick's 'ead with a pickaxe. It was three for two on the biscuits. They'll do ya for when ya get 'ome.

Kim *opens a packet of biscuits and takes one.*

Kim (*eating*) I don't want them sayin' that 'is dad's gonna get 'imself killed or worse. Lyin' like they 'ave bin doin'.

Josie Are Kelly loves the bones of that baby.

Kim Wouldn't put it past them.

Josie But there 'ave been accidents, 'aven't there, Mick?
Mick Yeh.

Kim You said there 'adn't.

Mick But there 'ave. I can say it but a picket can't. If a picket says it or a paper says it or the tele says it, it's a lie.

Josie Instead the papers an' the tele say nothin'.

Mick Better than lyin'. What ya don't know won't 'urt ya.

Josie Well Kelly wouldn't say nothin' to the baby.

Kim Just make sure ya bring 'im back after.

Josie I will. An' 'is bucket. Kelly said 'e's made up with it.

Kim She would. All them natural ingredients.

Mick Apart from the plastic.

Kim Ya know what I mean.

Josie At least ya should 'ave a quiet night with 'im,

thanks to them. I'll see ya later.

Kim   D'ya want money for that?

Josie   No.

Kim   Ya sure?

Josie   Don't be soft. Bruce might as well spend all 'is life savin's as 'alf a them.

Kim   Ta.

Josie   They must think I've bin losin' me touch. I told them I was in the bingo. I 'aven't got a thing to show for it. Ta-ra, Mick. Ta-ra, love.

Kim   Ta-ra.

Josie (*as she exits*) — An' don't forget, keep this place spotless cos the office told me there's an interested party. So ya never know – Ta-ra.

Josie *exits.*

Kim   I told ya you'd take ya feet down if me mum was 'ere.

Pause. **Josie** *stands outside the caravan.* **Kim** *sits on the side settee and picks up her magazine.*

Kim   She doesn't know nothin', does she? Did ya 'ear 'er? 'Interested party.' Imagine when she finds out it's us. Ya won't be puttin' ya feet on the seats then, will ya?

Mick   When it's ares I can do what I like.

Kim   Ya better not ruin it cos we'll 'ave it lovely – like a palace. We'll get rid of all this an' 'ave it the way we want it. Do it all out, 'ave it all nice. We can rent it out then. That's what people want – nice caravans with nice insides.

It starts to rain harder.

Mick   As long as we make somethin' out of it.

Kim   We will. She's more or less givin' it away.

Mick   Only cos she's got to.

Kim   An' I wouldn't want all are savin's goin' into their pockets. Imagine it, Mick. Soon we'll 'ave a permanent caravan to come to.

Mick   I've worked 'ard enough for it.

Kim   Ya know what? When we buy this, me dad'll be 'appy. 'E'll look down an' 'e'll be dead 'appy. 'E'll look down an' 'e'll know that I've always wanted this caravan. I'm gonna 'ave it like a palace.

Pause. **Mick** *watches television.* **Kim** *resumes reading.*

(*She reads.*) 'Why not make use of your empty chocolate spread jars. Just clean them out when empty and start collecting them. They make ideal and inexpensive whisky tumblers.' Why can't they just go the Fifty Pence shop an' buy some? Stupid gets.

Pause.

D' ya know what? I can't imagine life without this place.

Mick   What?

Kim   The caravan.

Mick   Why?

Kim   Cos then we wouldn't 'ave nowhere to go.

Kim *reads.*

Mick *watches the television.*

Josie *stares out front.*

Mick *laughs.*

Blackout.

Printed in the United Kingdom
by Lightning Source UK Ltd.
131595UK00001B/48/A

9 780413 713209